GLEN and SHIRE LINES

Malcolm Cooper   Bill Harvey   Bill Laxon

A Ships in Focus Fleet History

Published in the UK in 2005 by Ships in Focus Publications,
18 Franklands, Longton
Preston PR4 5PD

Printed by Amadeus Press Ltd., Cleckheaton, West Yorkshire
ISBN 1-901703-65-7

Front endpaper: *Glenorchy* in the Royal Docks, London on 31st January 1970, not long before her transfer to Blue Funnel
and subsequent sale. *[Roy Kittle].*
Above: *Flintshire. [F. R. Sherlock/Roy Fenton collection]*
Rear endpaper: *Glenogle* makes her way slowly up the New Waterway on 1st May 1976.   *[Paul Boot]*
Back cover top: *Glenearn,* see page 176
Back cover bottom: *Radnorshire,* see page 188.

PUBLISHER'S PREFACE
AND
ACKNOWLEDGEMENTS

This publication originated with a suggestion by Andrew Bell that Ships in Focus might consider publishing Bill Harvey's history of Glen and Shire Lines, the typescript for which Andrew was reviewing. This suggestion we readily accepted but it quickly became apparent that other authors had been at work on these companies. Malcolm Cooper had researched and published on the early history of Glen Line, as Bill Laxon had on Shire Line. Thus, Bill Harvey's work became the seed on which the present book crystallised. Sadly, Bill Laxon did not live to see the work completed.

As published, the Glen Line narrative is Malcolm's, and the Shire Line narrative Bill Laxon's. The Glen Line fleet list results from work by Malcolm and Bill Harvey; the Shire Line fleet list by Bill Harvey, Bill Laxon and Roy Fenton on behalf of the publishers. John Clarkson was responsible for the layout and artwork and, with Paul Boot, sourced the photographs.

Also to be thanked for their valuable input to the text are Andrew Bell, once again, who elaborated on Glen's post-war history and provided his own bit of colour; and Richard Woodman who also recalled his experiences with the company.

As publishers we are especially pleased to publish this history of two historically important and fascinating companies, not least because it continues our published explorations of the British shipowners who pioneered the liner routes to the far east. These publications began with our photographic history of Blue Funnel, continued with Malcolm Cooper's article on Thomas Skinner's Castle Line in Ships in Focus 'Record' 24. We hope to largely complete the story with a new and completely revised edition of Graeme Somner's work on Ben Line.

In researching the fleet lists, use of the facilities of the National Archives, the World Ship Society's Merchant Ship Library and Archive, the Guildhall Library and Lloyd's Register of Shipping are gratefully acknowledged. Particular thanks also to John Bartlett, Clive Guthrie, William Schell and Gordon Wright for information, to Heather Fenton for editorial and indexing work, and to Marion Clarkson for accountancy services.

We thank all who gave permission for their photographs to be used, and for help assembling the photographs we are particularly grateful to the authors themselves, to Andrew Bell, Gerrit J. de Boer, Malcolm Cranfield, Laurence Dunn, Ian Farquhar, Ambrose Greenway, F.W. Hawks, John Hill, Geoffrey Holmes, Peter Newall, Kevin O'Donoghue, Ian Rae, Ivor Rooke, William Schell, George Scott, Ian Shiffman, G.F. Shotter, Theodor Siersdorfer, R. Weeks; to David Whiteside, Jim McFaul and Tony Smith of the World Ship Photo Library; to David Hodge and Bob Todd of the National Maritime Museum; the British Mercantile Marine Collection, the National Museums and Galleries of Wales, the Ulster Folk and Transport Museum, the University of Dundee, the Imperial War Museum, and other museums and institutions listed. In line with our policy, we show the names of both the photographer (where known) and the collection from which it was obtained.

Artwork for flags and funnels was very kindly provided by J.L. Loughran, custodian of the Ships' Liveries section of the World Ship Society's Merchant Ship Library and Archive.

John Clarkson   Roy Fenton

Ships in Focus Publications

Gleniffer at Swansea. *[J. and M. Clarkson collection]*

CONTENTS

Notes on the ships' histories

Unless otherwise stated on the first line, the vessels are steam or motor ships with steel hulls.

On the second line is given the ship's official number (O.N.) in the British Register; then her tonnages at acquisition, gross (g), net (n), and in some cases deadweight (d), followed by dimensions: overall length x breadth x draft in feet or metres. For any substantial rebuild, new dimensions are given on a subsequent line.

On the following line is a description of the engine(s) fitted and the name of their builder. Steam reciprocating engines may be two-cylinder simple (2-cyl.), two-cylinder compound (C. 2-cyl.), three- or four-cylinder triple-expansion (T. 3-cyl. or T. 4-cyl.), or quadruple expansion four cylinder (Q. 4-cyl.). For oil engines are given the type (e.g. Sulzer, Burmeister & Wain), the number of cylinders, whether two stroke (2SC) or four stroke (4SC) cycle, single acting (SA) or double acting (DA). Next come cylinder dimensions where known, for steam engines these are given as the diameter of the cylinders in increasing size of stroke, followed by the horsepower(s) and ship's speed, if known. Any changes of engine are listed, with dates, on subsequent lines.

Subsequent lines give the details of builder and the ship's full career, including dates when and where registered and when the final UK registration was closed. Dates are given to the exact day when known; for sales these are the dates of the bill of sale, for renamings the date when the new name was registered. The port indicated after the title of the owning company is the port in which the owners are domiciled. For ships sold to operators using flags of convenience, efforts have been made to indicate the actual owners and the managers (not always the same body). For these vessels, the flag is that of the state in which the shipowning company is domiciled unless otherwise stated.

Details are taken from the Closed Registers, classes BT107, BT108, BT110 and CUST 130 in the National Archives, Lloyd's Register of Shipping, the Mercantile Navy List and Lloyds Confidential Indexes. Where sources differ, the registration documents have been taken as the final arbiter.

Cardiganshire of 1913. [Ian J. Farquhar collection]

SHIRE LINE
W.A. Laxon

For over a century some of the best-known ships in the trade between British, European and Far Eastern ports were those which bore the names of various Welsh shires in their traditional pre-1974 re-organisation form. Unlike many once famous shipping companies whose story is that of one corporate entity's development through the years, the Shire Line in its final 65 years was a trading name rather than a separate company. Nevertheless throughout that period its naming system was kept alive through no less than four quite diverse ownerships.

Captain David James Jenkins

As with so many commercial undertakings, the Shire Line owes its origins and early success to the efforts and ability of one man. It is also characteristic of a Victorian shipping undertaking that that man should be a qualified master mariner who had come up the hard way, obtaining practical experience of life at sea as an apprentice, deck officer and in command before coming ashore to set up as a shipowner. David James Jenkins was, as his name indicates, of Welsh descent, being the third son of John Jenkins of Haverfordwest, Pembrokeshire, but he was in fact a Westcountryman, having been born in Exeter on 15th April 1824.

His family must have been in reasonable circumstances as, after sending him briefly to Teignmouth Grammar School, they were able to find the quite stiff premium to send him to sea as an apprentice rather than as a ship's boy when he was quite adamant that a career at sea was the only one for him. His first ship was the Bristol-owned *Elizabeth* which he joined in 1837 at the age of only 13. His service in that vessel was brought to an abrupt conclusion when she was lost on the Indian coast near Madras 20 months later, and he finished his apprenticeship with two years in the *Claudine* of London.

Completion of apprenticeship in those unregulated years did not lead immediately to an officer's post, particularly as Jenkins was still only 16, so he then spent nearly three years as an ordinary seaman in two Plymouth-owned ships, the *Refrain* and *John Broomhall*. But he soon became interested in the still somewhat unreliable steamers which were beginning to venture across the world's sealanes. The year 1844 was spent as an able seaman in the London-owned steamer *Queen* trading to the Iberian peninsula.

This experience seems to have convinced him that the age of steam had not yet fully arrived, as at the end of 1844 he began an association with shipowners based in the western Irish port of Limerick which was to last until he came ashore to begin his own business. Still as a seaman, he joined Shaw and Co.'s 179-ton *Souvenir*, built at Bridport in 1837. His ability was soon recognised with promotion to mate. In 1847 he moved to the larger *Undine* in the same position until in 1848 he achieved his first command as master of the 260-ton softwood barque *Heather Bell*. She had been built in Pictou, Nova Scotia, two years previously, and was owned by Sikes and Co. who employed her in the trans-Atlantic trade. Two years in the *Heather Bell* did not end happily for Jenkins as the vessel was wrecked on Anticosti Island at the mouth of the St Lawrence in September 1850.

Then came a turning point in Jenkins' career when he was granted one of the new master's certificates at Greenock in January 1851. In December he took command of the 440-ton steamer *European*, built earlier that year and recently purchased from Glasgow owners by a partnership trading as the London and Limerick Steamship Company. Having demonstrated his ability to handle this type of vessel, in 1853 David Jenkins transferred to his owner's steamer *Holyrood* (533/1852). The Limerick firm was an enterprising one as later that year it ordered from Barclay Curle's Glasgow yard a steamer which was to earn her place in history as the

first to be built with a compound engine newly developed by the firm of Randolph and Elder which had not then moved into shipbuilding as well as engineering. In contrast to all existing simple engines which used the power of their steam only once, even if in more than one cylinder, the compound engine put it to work twice in two cylinders of differing size and, in conjunction with higher boiler pressures, this significantly cut coal consumption. Jenkins was advised that he was to command this revolutionary steamer and, to better fit him for the task, he was issued with a steam endorsement to his master's certificate at Glasgow in May 1854.

The new vessel was launched in March 1854 as the *Brandon*, named after the town and bay in County Kerry. She was of 764 tons and originally intended for the short sea traffic. However, following extensive trials in July/August 1854, she was despatched for New York via Le Havre in the latter month where the economy of her engines on the long trans-Atlantic passage indicated a bright future for her. By the time she returned to England at the beginning of October though, the outbreak of the Crimean War with its enormous demand for transports and supply ships had thrown all plans for available steam tonnage into chaos.

The *Brandon* was chartered to the British Government and later that month sailed for the Crimea with Jenkins still in command. Nearly the whole of 1855 was spent in service in the Mediterranean and Black Seas. She did not return to London for overhaul until December 1855, a lengthy period of service which speaks volumes for the ability of Jenkins in handling his ship and even more so of his engineers and stokehold crew in charge of an entirely new type of machinery. The *Brandon* passed most of 1856 in the same areas apart from a return voyage to Waterford in June 1856. With the conclusion of the war her owners cashed in on the value of the *Brandon* by selling her at Constantinople in March 1857 to Turkish authorities newly conscious of the importance of supply by steamers. Jenkins and his crew were discharged in London in April and he decided that with the experience he had gained in handling of men and stores the time had come to establish himself ashore permanently.

Jenkins the shipowner in sail

In June 1857 Jenkins set himself up at 30 Lime Street in the heart of London's shipping area as a shipping and commission agent under the name of D. Jenkins and Co. For the first few years he confined his attention to these fields, no doubt until sufficient capital had been accumulated, but his goal had always been to become a shipowner, and by 1860 he was ready to take the plunge.

His choice fell on the wood barque *Mary Evans*, then on the Tyneside stocks in the Hutchinson yard at Newcastle. A vessel of 306 tons gross, she was eminently suited to Jenkins' first venture into shipowning for, while quite large enough by the standards of the day, she was not too big to be beyond the reach of his financial resources. Her first voyage took her to the West Indies, and its success encouraged Jenkins to embark on a second venture. At that time the shipbuilders of the Canadian Maritime Provinces were supplying a substantial proportion of the new sailing ships for the British mercantile marine as, with the substantial supplies of softwoods readily to hand, they were able to considerably undercut British shipbuilders. It was common practice for Canadian builders and owners to build a ship on speculation and then sail her across the Atlantic in the sure knowledge that a purchaser could be found, and it was such a ship that provided Jenkins with his second vessel.

The *Eastward Ho* was also a comparatively small vessel with a tonnage of only 386, but her size and price were exactly suited to Jenkins' still limited pocket while the reputation of her birthplace on Prince Edward Island as a home of well-built ships stood high in maritime circles. So in June 1862 the *Eastward Ho* passed into Jenkins' hands and in view of the trade in which her successors were to become so prominent, it would have been hard to find a more appropriate name for her. It may be for this reason that she was never renamed during her time under the Shire flag.

The success of his first two ships emboldened Jenkins to expand his fleet but precaution still prevailed, and the next purchase was made jointly with the established London shipowner and shipbroker, Edward Pembroke, each taking 32 shares. The *Arbutus* was launched in September 1863 from the Shoreham yard of Shuttleworth and Co. and was a wooden ship of 356 tons, originally laid down for the local shipowner, R.H. Penney, whose naming style beginning with Ar- was retained. By the time of her completion Jenkins had placed orders on his sole account for two ships, one of similar size to his first acquisitions and the other much more ambitious at twice the tonnage. Perhaps Jenkins' ancestral blood may have played some part in the selection of the yards where the new ships were to be built, for both were ordered from builders in his father's home shire of Pembroke, the bigger ship from the yard of Allen and Warlow at Pembroke Dock and the smaller one from the Gaddarn yard at Neyland on the opposite side of Milford Haven. In these circumstances it is not surprising that the bigger ship, which was the first to be launched, was christened *Pembrokeshire*, thus setting the pattern for the future, so that although the official name of the firm continued to be D. Jenkins and Co. the fleet and service soon became popularly known as Jenkins' Shire Line.

For those whose geography was a little shaky, no doubt the combination helped them to distinguish the Jenkins ships from those of other well known concerns whose ships later carried the same suffix - Thomas Law's Shire Line and Turnbull Martin and Co., both with Scottish shires, and Bibby's English shires. Despite these Welsh surrounds however, Jenkins turned to the city where he had established himself commercially when it came to providing a house flag for his vessels, and the Shire Line flag was simply that of the City of London - a St George's cross on a white ground with a red dagger in the upper quarter - plus the letters 'J & Co' in the lower left quarter.

The first *Pembrokeshire* was a thoroughly up-to-date vessel, for her hull was built on the then recently developed composite principle, that is iron beams and wooden planking. Metal hulls were still suspect in the China trade because of the believed adverse tainting of temperamental cargoes such as tea, so the composite method was a compromise giving some of the strength of iron without all the objectionable features. Although not nearly extreme enough to be classified as a clipper, the *Pembrokeshire* nevertheless had a reasonable turn of speed, even after her rig was reduced to that of a barque in 1872 when the intensification of competition from steamers following the opening of the Suez Canal necessitated a cut in the manning scale for most sailing ships in the trade.

Between the deliveries of the *Pembrokeshire* and her smaller consort which was named after the adjoining county of Cardiganshire, the Jenkins fleet received an unanticipated addition in the shape of the large American-built ship *Webfoot*, a vessel of over 1,000 tons. She had stranded at Dunkirk in April 1864 and, although got into port, was still severely damaged and so was purchased by Jenkins cheaply. That she was a sound investment is shown by the 20 years' good service that she gave the Shire Line, and in fact she remained the largest sailing vessel that Jenkins ever owned. While she was still under refit, the new *Cardiganshire* was delivered from the Gaddarn yard, a wooden barque of 365 tons which was also to have a long and satisfactory career.

The success of the two new ships plus the steady growth of the Indian and Far East trades encouraged Jenkins to place what was in effect a repeat order for two further improved versions of the *Pembrokeshire* and *Cardiganshire*. Again the larger ship came from Pembroke Dock and the smaller from Neyland, while the success of the composite hull in the *Pembrokeshire* resulted in this method being adopted for both the new ships. Again the larger ship, the

Carmarthenshire, was the first to be completed in the middle of 1865, her smaller consort, the *Carnarvonshire*, following in the spring of 1866. The addition of five ships in two years had in a short space of time transformed the Jenkins organisation from a single ship concern to one of the larger shipowners in the Far Eastern trade, then still largely dominated by the owner/master type of enterprise. Despite this rapid expansion, Jenkins wisely made no attempt to compete with the extreme clippers of the *Ariel*, *Taeping* and *Thermopylae* type but concentrated on building up a reliable fleet with a good carrying capacity. In this task he received no small measure of assistance from his London brokers, Norris and Joyner, and his agents in China and Japan, Adamson, Bell and Co.

Nevertheless all was not fair on the horizon, for the year in which the *Cardiganshire* was delivered also saw Alfred Holt's pioneer Blue Funnel liner *Agamemnon* demonstrate the feasibility of steamers on the long haul round the Cape of Good Hope. So the writing was clearly on the wall for sailing vessels in the Far East trade, whether the long-discussed Suez Canal was completed or not. Jenkins considered though that there would still be an opening for sail for some years and that he would be better to bide his time before taking the highly expensive plunge into steamers.

Accordingly in 1868 when the 790-ton Canadian built barque *Southern Queen* came on the market, he added her to the fleet though, like his other secondhand sail purchases, she was not re-named. It was also a significant time for Jenkins in another direction as in the same year he despatched the *Carmarthenshire* with the first cargo of coal imported into Japan, a country which was to assume ever increasing importance to the Shire fleet. He also returned to the Gaddarn yard with an order for a further of the smaller type of composite barque which was delivered the following year as the *Glamorganshire*. Although of the smaller class, size had crept up appreciably since the *Cardiganshire* as the *Glamorganshire* was of 472 tons.

A sister ship, the *Denbighshire*, the last sailing ship built for Jenkins, was delivered in the summer of 1870, and at the same time his second ship, the *Eastward Ho*, was sold for further trading. One more sailing ship was to hoist the Jenkins flag though, as again in 1874 he acquired rather cheaply and in a damaged condition, the wooden ship *W.W. Smith*, built in Jersey in 1857, and which was already well known in the India and China trades. By then the Suez Canal had been open for over six months and already steamers were starting to pour through the new waterway to India and China, both trades which had hitherto been almost the sole preserve of the contract mail steamer and the sailing ship.

Into steam

The new opportunity presented by the Canal soon brought steamers into the fleets of other companies in the trade, the most important of which so far as the Shire Line was concerned, both at the time and in the future, was McGregor Gow and Co.'s Glen Line. Their first steamer, the *Glengyle*, completed her maiden sailing in 1871, and other owners already well established in sail such as Thomas Skinner and Co.'s Castle Line also made the switch. It was clear that the Shire Line if it hoped to keep a place in the Far Eastern trade must soon adopt the steam engine, but Jenkins proceeded with a caution partly dictated by his financial limitations and partly by a desire to see first how others fared and secondly to get some practical experience of the running of steamers before he committed himself too deeply. For he realised that marine engineering had made vast strides over the past 15 years and the experience he had of small uneconomic vessels of the Crimean War period bore little relation to the large iron-hulled vessels of the 1870s now all powered by the more efficient updated compound engine which he had pioneered in the *Brandon*.

Wales at the time possessed no yards capable of building a steamer of the size required, so Jenkins turned north and in 1871 ordered his first steamer, the *Flintshire*, from the yard of the London and Glasgow Shipbuilding Co. at Govan on the Clyde, a yard which was also building for the rival Glen Line. The *Flintshire* was delivered in the middle of the following year and was a vessel of 1,565 tons gross having a flush-decked iron hull. Her builders also provided the two-cylinder compound engine fed by Scotch boilers which provided a trial speed of 10.5 knots. Like all steamers of the day though, the *Flintshire* was not content to rely on engines alone and square sails could be set on both masts though in later years this was confined to the foremast. A grey hull, white upperworks and a plain black funnel set the pattern for the Shire Line steamers of the future, while under the poop accommodation was provided for some 20 saloon passengers.

The *Flintshire*'s first voyage to the Far East under the command of Captain J. Sturrock was made via the Suez Canal to Colombo, Singapore, Hong Kong, Nagasaki, Kobe and Yokohama. It was very much in the nature of an experiment so far as Jenkins was concerned and it very clearly demonstrated to him two things, first that the new service was unlikely to be successful until he could afford to build up a steam fleet to partner her, and secondly that further experience of modern steamers both for himself and his officers was desirable. The finance he could command limited an early substantial building programme, so the immediate problem was met by the charter of other tonnage. Of the suitability of the new ship herself for the trade there was little doubt, and Jenkins promptly placed a repeat order with the London and Glasgow Co. for a slightly larger and improved sister, which was delivered in 1873 as the *Montgomeryshire*. Two ships were still inadequate for a regular service, so while the *Montgomeryshire* kept the Shire flag flying in steam supported by chartered ships, opportunity was taken to charter the *Flintshire* to the newly formed Eastern and Australian Mail Steam Company which was desperately short of tonnage for its Singapore-Australia service following the loss of its pioneer vessel.

The *Flintshire* herself very nearly followed her to a similar fate as on the return leg of her first Eastern and Australian voyage she ran ashore on Salamander reef in Cleveland Bay when leaving Townsville on 22nd June 1874 with a full complement of European and Chinese passengers including the famous tightrope walker Blondin. Fortunately she was refloated two days later, but extensive repairs were necessary before she could resume service.

While the sailing ships still made some Far East voyages, they went tramping more and more as the 1870s progressed. The backbone of the Jenkins' service was provided by the *Montgomeryshire* and her chartered consorts until rejoined by the *Flintshire* after four round voyages for the Eastern and Australian, and by a third again slightly larger vessel from Govan, the *Radnorshire* of 1876. Up to this time, with the exception of the *Eastward Ho*, Jenkins had retained in his fleet every ship purchased since he first became a shipowner, but 1877 saw the first disposals, beginning with the half share in the *Arbutus*. The second sale was not one of the sailing vessels, but the nearly new steamer *Montgomeryshire*. At this stage the Japanese were making their first tentative steps towards the development of their own shipping companies and wished to buy proven second hand tonnage. Whereas other companies had tended to concentrate on China, the Shire Line from the first had regarded the Japanese trade as of prime importance and in fact their Suez service was advertised as 'the Japan Line of Steamships'. So it was scarcely surprising that an approach to purchase one of his vessels was made to Jenkins by the Mitsubishi Mail Steam Ship Co., a predecessor of N.Y.K. An attractive offer made at a time when trade was somewhat depressed and there was rather a glut of vessels on the run following the post-Canal building boom sealed the bargain and the *Montgomeryshire* hoisted the Japanese flag as the *Akitsushima Maru*.

But Jenkins had lost none of his faith in the long-term development of the Far Eastern trade, and the money realised from the sale enabled him immediately to order not

one but two new vessels from the London and Glasgow yard to bring his fleet of steamers up to four, thus taking a substantial step towards the ultimate goal of a steam service entirely with his own ships. The sisters *Breconshire* and *Merionethshire* were both delivered in 1878 in time to take full advantage of the boom conditions of the early 1880s. Again gross tonnage was up as the new sisters were given a raised forecastle compared to the previous flush deckers, but basically they were again developments of the successful *Flintshire* concept. The *Breconshire* gained some unwelcome publicity early in her career when on 29th October 1880 she collided with and sank the *Braemar Castle* of Thomas Skinner's rival Castle Line when the latter ship was at anchor at Penang. Despite the new deliveries, chartered tonnage still played a prominent part in the Shire service, no fewer than eight vessels running under Jenkins' auspices in 1878. These chartered ships came from many sources, but prominent among them were some of the early Ben steamers of William Thomson and Co. of Leith and vessels of Alexander Carnegie of London and Thomas Sutton of North Shields. An advertisement headed 'The Japan Line of Steamers' appearing on 21st May 1878 lists the following:

Benledi
Benarty
Bengloe
Burmese
Japanese
City of Santiago
City of Valparaiso
Scotland

The same year of 1878 the veteran *W.W. Smith*, the oldest sailing ship in the fleet, was sold for conversion to a coal hulk.

The reliable service for the more valuable cargoes given by the steamers together with the back up for the less important freights provided by the sailing ships over the prosperous four years from 1879 to 1882 completed the laying of the foundations of the Shire Line on a firm basis, enabling it to weather the storms and continue expanding the fleet during the harder times of the later 1880s. Jenkins' policy of building steady earners rather than spectacular speedsters for the tea races also showed its wisdom when, despite or perhaps because of the exploits of their far-famed *Stirling Castle* (4,423/1882), Skinner's Castle Line was forced out of business by the end of the decade.

Yet Jenkin's path was not without its difficulties, his next three ships having only the briefest of careers. The first was a deliberate choice when the *Montgomeryshire* which had been launched at the London and Glasgow yard in January 1880 was sold while fitting out to the Royal Mail Steam Packet Company for which she was completed as the *Humber*. Her replacement of the same name came from a new yard for Jenkins, that of Raylton Dixon at Middlesbrough, but she had the misfortune to be wrecked north of Cape Mondego with the loss of all hands when outward bound on her maiden voyage to the Far East on 28th December 1880. The *Carnarvonshire* which was delivered by the London and Glasgow Company in June 1881 fared a little better, but she too became an early marine loss when she stranded on her way from Yokohama to Kobe on 20th April 1883.

Expansion of interests
As well as supervising his expanding business, Jenkins was also developing his place on the wider national stage. Following an unsuccessful candidature in the Liberal interest for the seaport constituency of Harwich at the 1868 elections, he was returned in February 1874 for the combined boroughs of Falmouth and Penrhyn, a victory that was the more notable as it occurred at an election which saw a general swing to the Conservative candidates across the country. Jenkins continued to sit in the House for twelve years until he retired at the second 'Home Rule' election of 1886. He never progressed beyond the back benches but, as might have been expected,

he took a particular interest in all matters affecting trade and commerce and was a valued member of many committees dealing with those subjects during his period as a member.

More closely linked with his business activities was Jenkins' participation in the early conference system struggling to survive under the direction of John Swire of Butterfield and Swire. On behalf of the Shire Line Jenkins had been a signatory to the original China and Japan Conference in 1879 and the subsequent ones that replaced it, and the Shire Line had been one of the defendants in the long series of litigation by the Mogul Steamship Company in the late 1880s which unsuccessfully sought to have conferences declared illegal. Although the conference yoke irked at times, there can be little doubt that the stability in freight rates which it brought played no small part in the considerable expansion of the Shire fleet during that decade.

The 1880s also saw the complete disappearance of the sailing fleet. First to be disposed of was the *Carnarvonshire* in 1880 and then followed the *Cardiganshire* and the pioneer *Mary Evans* which were both sold in 1882. No less than four of the remaining sailing vessels were sold during 1884/5, and the *Carmarthenshire* was lost off Terschelling in January of the latter year. The veteran *Pembrokeshire*, the first ship built to Jenkins' specifications, was sold in 1887 to a Nova Scotia owner-master, A.B. Troop, only to be lost later the same year. This left only the *Southern Queen* of the sail fleet which had spent her last years tramping the seas until she too was sold in 1888.

Growth of the steam fleet
If the decline of the Shire sail fleet had been swift, the rise of the steam fleet was equally rapid. Until 1881 the steamers had been given the names of Welsh shires not used for the sailing fleet, but from then on the old sailing ship names were to re-appear on steamers. Apparently the authorities were then less concerned with name duplication, for five years before the first *Pembrokeshire* was disposed of a second *Pembrokeshire* appeared in the fleet, while a second *Cardiganshire* followed her in 1883. One would imagine that having two ships of the same name in the one fleet would have led to endless confusion, but perhaps the fact that one was a steamer and the other a sailing ship helped separate the two.

Hitherto all but one of the steamers had come from the London and Glasgow yard at Govan, but with the virtual ship-a-year programme of the 1880s, a pattern was set of alternate orders from that yard and from the Tyne yard of Swan and Hunter at Wallsend. The ships of this decade represented a substantial increase in size over their predecessors, working steadily up from 2,500 to nearly 3,000 tons at its close. The first five were all of three-island hull form with very much reduced provision for sail, the transition point being marked by the *Monmouthshire* of 1886 which could be regarded as the first of the modern Shire liners, for she introduced not only a steel hull in place of the heavier iron of the earlier vessels, but also triple-expansion engines with their greatly increased economy over the previous compounds. London and Glasgow was an early builder for Glen Line, so at times vessels for these rival fleets must have been under construction alongside each other. The Clyde-built vessels were mostly larger and faster with greater passenger accommodation than those from the Tyne. An expanding fleet also required extended office facilities and in 1886 Jenkins and Co. moved to 1 Whittington Avenue from 17 Lime Street where it had been established since moving from its original office on the other side of Lime Street in 1874.

It was as well for the continuity of the service that this steady shipbuilding programme had been followed, for two steamers were soon to be lost in quick succession. The first casualty was the *Radnorshire* of 1876 which was wrecked off Malta while outward bound from Hamburg to Nagasaki on 19th June 1885, while the following February the *Breconshire* was wrecked on the Chinese coast as she approached Swatow. To fill the gaps, the three-year-old steamer *Numida*, the only secondhand steamer acquired by Jenkins, was purchased from London owners and became the second *Breconshire*, the urgency of the purchase being due to the boom conditions that were again dominating the Far East trades during the closing years of the 1880s.

To meet the demands on its services, the Shire Line took delivery in 1887/8 of their biggest vessels yet, the 2,929-ton *Carmarthenshire* from Wallsend in 1887 and the 2,879-ton *Flintshire* from Govan in 1888. The delivery of the latter marked the end of Jenkins' pioneer steamer, the first *Flintshire*, which was sold in that year to Singapore owners

Glamorganshire of 1884 transiting the Suez Canal. *[Ambrose Greenway collection]*

Carmarthenshire of 1887 in Swan Hunter's yard. *[Ian Rae collection]*

and soon after passed into the fleet of Alfred Holt and Co. In case it should be wondered what Holts were doing in acquiring a former cast-off from one of their then major competitors, it should be explained that Holts wanted the *Flintshire* for their feeder services in the East Indies archipelago based on Singapore. The *Flintshire* continued to serve in Far Eastern waters under the British, Dutch and Japanese flags until she was finally lost in collision at Nagasaki in 1898. Another disposal was the *Merionethshire* which went to the Quebec Steam Ship Co. in 1890 for service between the St. Lawrence and the West Indies, her place in the Shire fleet being taken by the second *Radnorshire* from Swan and Hunter in the autumn of 1890.

At this stage the nine Shire Line steamers were maintaining a regular fortnightly service from Hamburg, Antwerp and London to Singapore, Hong Kong, Hiogo and Yokohama with calls at Penang, Manila, Nagasaki and China coast ports as required. The latest ships of the fleet accommodated both first- and second-class passengers for whom a doctor and a stewardess were provided. The Line's regular berth in London was in the Royal Albert Docks, and freight arrangements continued to be in the hands of its regular brokers, Norris and Joyner.

A new generation

The *Radnorshire*'s entry into service marked the end of the good trading years and also the end of the Shire Line building programme as a general retrenchment followed. But the depressed trading conditions were only partly responsible for this; personal factors played a large part in the Shire Line story at this stage. For David Jenkins' health was failing. Following his retirement from the House of Commons, he had left more and more of the day-today management of the business to his son, Noble, and in March 1891 David Jenkins died. From an obscure position as a merchant navy apprentice he had, virtually unaided, built up one of the leading liner companies in the Far East trade and set a high standard for his son to follow. Despite his commercial success, David

Jenkins never forgot his ancestral land and not only were his ships named after the Welsh shires, but during his era practically every master in his service was a Welshman. In fact it would seem that an officer with an Anglo-Saxon name had small chance of reaching a Shire command compared with the prospects of those with names like Davies, Evans, Griffiths, Owens, Thomas and Williams who were among the masters in the fleet during the 1870s and 1880s.

Naturally for his first four years as managing partner, Noble Jenkins was to some extent feeling his way. There was less cargo on offer in the depressed trading conditions of the early 1890s, and some weeding out of the older units of the fleet took place. First to go in 1893 were the stop-gap second *Breconshire* to Newcastle owners and the second *Pembrokeshire* which joined the *Merionethshire* in the fleet of the Quebec Steamship Co. as the *Fontabelle*. In the following year the *Cardiganshire* and *Denbighshire* were sold to Japanese owners, the latter continuing in service for over 30 years before she was wrecked on the Japanese coast. Her bell was salved from the wreck, however, and sailed the seas for many more years on the training barque *Nippon Maru*.

But if there was retrenchment in some directions, there was also expansion in the way of new routes, for it was during the 1890s that the Shire Line first began to continue its Far Eastern voyages across the Pacific to the west coast of Canada and the United States before beginning the long trek home via Cape Horn, for there was no Panama Canal in those days. This development was to a large extent due to the influence of the Line's Far Eastern agents, Dodwell, Carlill and Co. (the successors to Adamson, Bell and Co.) who had considerable interests in the trans-Pacific trade. Sometimes a call would be made at east coast American ports on the homeward voyage also, but in any event the vessel had been away from home for some six to eight months and had encircled the globe. Trans-Pacific sailings continued into the early years of the twentieth century, but ceased after the First World War.

It was during the 1890s also that the Shire Line had in its service an officer who was probably its most famous graduate. He was Ernest Shackleton, later to win world renown as an Antarctic explorer, who joined the *Monmouthshire* as third mate in November 1894. He had actually been appointed as fourth mate, but in typical forthright Shackleton fashion told Noble Jenkins that he did not like the quarters provided for that rank but would take the third mate's berth. Later asked why he had not fired him on the spot, Noble Jenkins replied, 'But I rather liked the chap', a feeling to be shared by many others who were later to come in contact with Shackleton's Irish persuasiveness. Promotion to second mate of the *Flintshire* followed in 1896, but by 1898 Shackleton had fallen in love and found the lengthy Shire Line voyages somewhat hampering to his suit. So at the beginning of 1899 he resigned to join the Castle Line with its shorter voyages to South Africa. An echo of his old associations came almost at the end of his life when, by this time the famous explorer Sir Ernest Shackleton, he called at Lisbon in October 1921 while outward bound in the *Quest* and was there visited by his old shipmate C.G. Morris, then in command with the Royal Mail Steam Packet Co. He was among the last to see Shackleton who died at South Georgia only three months later.

Formation of the company
The sale of the *Cardiganshire* and *Denbighshire* marked the end of the retrenchment period for the Shire Line as already the first of the new ships had been ordered. For this and all the remaining ships built under the Jenkins regime, the Shire Line went to a new builder, the Sunderland Shipbuilding Co., and the first delivery in January 1895 was the 3,012-ton *Merionethshire*, a three-island steel-hulled vessel not greatly larger than the existing fleet. Her commissioning led to the sale of the *Flintshire* of 1888 to N.Y.K. later the same year, but already a considerably bigger third *Flintshire* was on the stocks at Sunderland.

Before she was delivered, however, the business itself has undergone a major change by being registered as a limited liability company on 27th May 1896 under the title of Jenkins and Company Ltd. The partners in the existing business, who were David Jenkins' widow, sons and daughter, sold their interests to the new company in return for the allotment of shares in it, an arrangement which was obviously much more suited to the operation of the business than the previous arrangement of a number of non-working partners. So far as the day-to-day management was concerned, however, the change made little difference to the fleet which was augmented the following month by the third *Flintshire*. Her gross tonnage of 3,815 foreshadowed the considerable increase in size that was to mark the next few years, though she featured the graceful, if by then somewhat archaic, ornament of a clipper bow complete with female figurehead under the bowsprit.

A temporary setback befell the new concern in March 1897 when the *Glamorganshire* of 1884, by then the oldest steamer in the fleet, was lost near Cape James on her way home from Hong Kong. She was though, with the exception of vessels sunk through enemy action, the last Shire Line vessel to become a marine loss. The company's building programme was resumed in 1899 with the launch in January of the 4,129 ton *Cardiganshire*, followed at the end of the year by the slightly smaller *Denbighshire*. The *Cardiganshire* never entered Jenkins' service as she was purchased on completion by the Mitsui Steamship Co. and became their *Tsurugisan Maru*. It was a pattern that was to become familiar during the next few years.

The first of 1901 ships to be named *Pembrokeshire* had been sold while fitting out to Glasgow owners who had second thoughts and resold her as the *Allanton* to W.R. Rea of Belfast. Both the *Glamorganshire* of 1900 and the second *Pembrokeshire* of 1901 were sold to Japanese owners within two years of their delivery, the former to the N.Y.K. as the *Bombay Maru* and the latter joining the *Cardiganshire* in the Mitsui fleet as the *Mandasan Maru*. All three ships were to give lengthy service under the Japanese flag, and it would seem that it was only the high prices which the Japanese were prepared to pay as they looked towards the coming struggle with Russia and the need to build up their merchant fleet that persuaded Jenkins to part with such quality tonnage. In the case of the *Pembrokeshire* the decision was probably precipitated by a severe stranding on Saddle Island in the Chusan archipelago in 1903. Despite the hazardous journey south, the extensive repairs were carried out by the Hong Kong and Whampoa Dockyard in eight weeks compared with an estimate of five months from the closer Shanghai yards.

Monmouthshire of 1902 in the buff funnel adopted in 1907. *[W. A. Laxon collection]*

Of the six ships ordered for the fleet between 1899 and 1902, only the *Denbighshire* and the second *Monmouthshire*, completed in the last year, remained for any length of time. The *Monmouthshire* at 5,092 tons was both the last and easily the largest of the Jenkins' Shires, and was a typical example of the cargo liner of her day with a three-island hull, the hatchways being divided by largely rakeless masts and derrick posts. The last remaining ships of the 1880s, the *Monmouthshire* and *Carmarthenshire*, followed some of their consorts into the Caribbean trade on their sale to other British owners in 1901/02, so that by the end of 1902 the Shire fleet was again one of five ships, still maintaining the customary service from British and Continental ports to the Far East and particularly to Japanese ports, though now reduced to four-weekly intervals. Conditions were sufficiently encouraging for the company in that year to increase its capital to provide funds for future development, but as events turned out, this was not to be.

The joint services

The longer term outlook was not bright and, with its main interests concentrated in Japan, Jenkins and Co. found the problems which the outbreak of the Russo-Japanese war of 1904 brought in its train a considerable burden. As well as the risks of interception at sea by units of the Russian fleets, there was a considerable incursion of outside tonnage into the trade, all anxious to share in the inflated freight rates. Among these concerns which looked on with interest was the Liverpool shipping company of Thos. and Jno. Brocklebank which traced its origins back to 1770 and was one of the oldest shipping companies in the world. Latterly Brocklebanks had concentrated on the Calcutta trade, but some recent orders had left them with prospective surplus tonnage for which they were anxious to find employment. They therefore began a new service from Antwerp to Singapore, Shanghai, Kobe and Yokohama which immediately brought them into direct competition with the Shire Line. Combined with the uncertain circumstances following the end of the Russo-Japanese war and the return to normal service of the Japanese merchant fleet, the presence of this further competition was most unpalatable to Jenkins, so negotiations were soon opened and in May 1906 it was announced that agreement had been reached for the purchase by Brocklebanks of a half interest in the Shire Line goodwill (but not in Jenkins and Co.), a condition being that Brocklebanks should transfer five ships from their own Eastern service to enable the four-weekly Shire service to be increased to a two-weekly one.

As an indication of the new ownership, the Shire Line flag was changed very ingeniously by incorporating the Jenkins pattern into the white half of the blue and white Brocklebank emblem. The five ships which now joined the Shire fleet from Brocklebanks were a somewhat mixed bag, comprising the four-masted steamers *Ameer* and *Gaekwar* of 1889/90 and the slightly larger similarly rigged *Pindari* of 1891. All three were products of the Harland and Wolff yard at Belfast, and they were named respectively *Cardiganshire*, *Carnarvonshire* and *Breconshire*. The remaining ships were much more modern, though of similar size and rig to the *Pindari*. They were the sisters *Marwarri* and *Bengali*, built by Gourlay Brothers at Dundee in 1900 and 1901, and they became the *Glamorganshire* and *Montgomeryshire*. All five ships retained their Brocklebank officers and crews and, although the

service was operated as one, each division continued to run its ships in much the same way as before. The Brocklebank brokers, Alex. Howden and Co., now became linked with Norris and Joyner as brokers to the service, but the ports of call remained as before, that is Hamburg and Antwerp for Continental cargoes, Middlesbrough for heavy steel goods, London general cargo from the Royal Albert Docks berth and thence via the Suez Canal to Penang, Singapore, Hong Kong, Shanghai, Nagasaki, Kobe and Yokohama.

Although the new arrangement was effective from the 1st June, the Brocklebank ships were at that stage naturally scattered along the shipping lanes to the Far East and so were taken over progressively as they returned to U.K. waters, the last of the five steamers not assuming her Shire name until nearly the end of the year. The infusion of the new tonnage from Liverpool was a shot in the arm for the ailing Shire service, but even more fundamental changes in the organisation of the Line were only just round the corner.

It would seem that the Jenkins family was still somewhat disenchanted with their enterprise and with the continuing strenuous competition in the trade. Nevertheless it was something of a bombshell that was dropped into the shipping world when it became known in April 1907 that the Royal Mail Steam Packet Company had purchased an interest in line to became an equal third partner with Jenkins and Brocklebanks. The Royal Mail was one of the most venerable and best known of all British shipping companies, having been incorporated by Royal Charter in 1839. With the exception of one or two excursions into other fields in the 1850s, it had hitherto confined its interest to the West Indies and South American trades and at the turn of the twentieth century its fortunes were at a very low ebb. Certainly there could have been no thoughts at that stage of an expansion into the Far East.

Yet in the space of a few short years the whole aspect of the Royal Mail had changed from one of decay to one of aggressive expansion. The reason for this dramatic change was to be found in the person of a dynamic Welshman, Owen Philipps, who had become Chairman of the Royal Mail Court of Directors in March 1903 only three months after becoming

Pindari of 1891, renamed *Breconshire* when transferred along with four other Brocklebank steamers to the Shire Line. [*J. and M. Clarkson collection*]

MESSRS JENKINS & CO'S AFFAIRS

We regret to announce that another firm of shipowners is in difficulties, namely, Messrs, Jekins & Co. Limited (Shire Line). At a recent meeting of shareholders a resolution in favour of voluntary liquidation was unanimously adopted. The gross liabilities are estimated at £214,264. At July 15 the company's affairs stood as follows:

LIABILITIES

		Expected to rank:
Unsecured creditors		£35,395.07.01
Creditors fully secured	£148,412.18.01	
Estimated value of securities	£179,232.17.11	
Surplus per contra	£30,819.19.10	
Creditors partly secured	£27,026.00.10	
Less estimated value of securities	£21,133.17.05	£5,892.03.05
Other liabilities	£3,345.18.00	Nil
Preferential creditors:-		
For Salary	£60.16.11	
For Rent	£23.05.06	
Deducted per contra	£84.02.05	£41,287.10.06
Issued capital:-		
6,309 ordinary shares of £10 each		£63,090.00.00
3,531 preference shares of £10 each		£35,310.00.00
		£98,400.00.00

ASSETS

		Estimated to produce
Property - stock of stores		£200.00.00
Office furniture - say		£50.00.00
Debts due to the company		
Good	£5,392.08.05	
Doubtful - as claims are expected to be made which will have the right to set off	£1,098.04.01	
Bad	£1,420.10.02	
	£7,911.02.08	
Estimated to produce		£5,392.08.05
Surplus from securities in the hands of creditors fully secured (per contra)		£30,819.19.10
		£36,462.08.03
Deduct - preferential creditors		£84.02.05
		£36,378.05.10

The following steamers are owned by the company;-

DENBIGHSHIRE	3,844 tons gross	built 1899
FLINTSHIRE	3,815 tons gross	built 1896
MONMOUTHSHIRE	5,092 tons gross	built 1902
RADNORSHIRE	2,898 tons gross	built 1890
Total	15,649 tons gross	

a director. Already a successful shipowner in his own right, having founded the King Line in 1889, he immediately set about putting the Royal Mail back on its feet with an extensive building programme of large modern ships to replace the ageing and outdated tonnage which still figured largely in the fleet, and having got this well under way was eager for new worlds to conquer. His first move in this direction had been the purchase from the Pacific Steam Navigation Company of its half interest in the Orient Line trading to Australia. Why his choice next fell on the Shire Line we shall now never know as its services lay right outside both his own experience and that of the Royal Mail, but perhaps the real reason was his half-formed ambition to head a shipping combine serving all parts of the world, plus the fact that the Jenkins family was a willing seller.

Nevertheless it was a peculiar arrangement that was come to, for only three of the existing ships were involved in the deal, nor were any Royal Mail ships to be transferred to the Shire fleet, though this is scarcely surprising as few of them would have been suitable. The vehicle for the new partnership was a newly formed company known as the Shire Line of Steamers Ltd., but its function was a purely management one, the vessels themselves remaining owned by the three partners.

It was scarcely to be expected though that such an arrangement could suit a person of Philipps' calibre for long, and in fact the new partnership lasted for only three months until July 1907 when the Royal Mail bought out the Jenkins interest entirely and became joint owners of the service with Brocklebanks. The Far Eastern trade was still in a period of decline and the new partners considered that a less frequent service requiring only seven ships would suffice until trade picked up again. The *Breconshire* was therefore diverted to other Brocklebank trades, leaving four of their ships on the service while the Royal Mail retained the three ships it had purhased from Jenkins the previous April, the *Flintshire*, *Denbighshire* and *Monmouthshire*, as its contribution to the service. The remaining two Jenkins ships were sold out of the trade and Jenkins and Co. Ltd. went into voluntary liquidation, to be finally dissolved by court order in 1914. So in July 1907 the last of the Jenkins family retired from active connection with the Shire Line which subsequently became entirely part of a public rather than a private concern. As symbolic of the new order, the Jenkins' St. George's cross and dagger were removed from the hoist half of the Shire flag and replaced by the Royal Mail saltire and crown while the funnels were changed from Jenkins black to Royal Mail buff, the hulls now becoming black with a white riband.

Another 18 months were to pass before a gradually returning prosperity enabled the previous fortnightly service to be restored, each of the partners contributing five ships. Brocklebanks returned the *Breconshire* from their Indian trades, but the Royal Mail had to find fresh tonnage which they did by transferring in June 1909 the *Sabor* and *Segura* from their West Indian service. The newcomers were sisters, having been built in 1893 by Harland and Wolff as the *Gaul* and *Greek* for the Union Line's intermediate service to South African ports, and they now became the *Carmarthenshire* and *Pembrokeshire*. Both vessels had comfortable accommodation amidships for 60 saloon passengers and represented a return by the Shire Line to the passenger trade which had been abandoned in the 1890s. They could also if required carry several hundred coolie or pilgrim passengers in the 'tween decks when business of these classes was offering, but they were not particularly high powered, their sea speed of 12 knots comparing rather unfavourably with tonnage that other companies were building for the same route.

In fact the *Carmarthenshire* and *Pembrokeshire* were more in the nature of stop-gaps than ships particularly suited for the Far Eastern trade, and perhaps the reason for this lay in the fact that the new ownership of the Shire Line was proving a somewhat uneasy partnership. Owen Philipps was very much a lone hand who ran the Royal Mail rather as a one-man enterprise, and was therefore not easy to associate

with as an equal. Anderson, Anderson and Co. and F. Green an Co. had already found this with their Orient Line after the Royal Mail took over the Pacific Steam Navigation's half interest in 1906, with the result that by 1908 they had been forced to buy him out themselves. After four years of uneasy running in tandem, Harold and Aubrey Brocklebank were presented with the same choice, buy out or be bought out, but with opposite results. For unlike the Andersons and the Greens who were full of vigour and determination and had not other interests, the Brocklebanks were themselves going through a period of change, having merged their business with that of the Bates family earlier that year. Both concerns were primarily interested in the Calcutta trade, so it was natural that they should elect to concentrate on it.

When *Pembrokeshire* (5), with her accommodation for 60 passengers, entered the fleet in 1909, Shire Line re-entered the passenger trade abandoned in the 1890s. *[J. and M. Clarkson collection]*

Philipps and Royal Mail in charge

So it was that in July 1911 the shipping world learnt that henceforth the Royal Mail Steam Packet Company would become the sole proprietor of the Shire Line and that the Brocklebanks were withdrawing their interest. Outwardly there was little sign of the change except that the white riband was now dropped from the hull and the ships abandoned the composite flag in favour of the ordinary Royal Mail one. The three oldest ex-Brocklebank ships were handed back and immediately sold foreign, the *Cardiganshire* and *Breconshire* to Japanese owners and the *Carnarvonshire* to Norwegians for whaling purposes. It proved mutually convenient to both parties to retain the newer *Glamorganshire* and *Montgomeryshire* in the Shire service for some time on charter, and it was not until May 1912 that the former completed her last Shire voyage and returned to Brocklebank service. Even then both ships retained their Shire names on Brocklebank's Calcutta run until into 1913.

The popular expectation when the Royal Mail purchase was announced was that the Shire service would immediately be combined with that of the Glen Line. The reason for this belief lay in the fact that in 1910 Philipps had begun the first of his many take-over bids for established shipping companies by a share exchange with the Elder Dempster group, bereft of its leading personality since the death of Sir Alfred Jones the previous year. Philipps then became Chairman of Elder Dempster as well as Royal Mail, and early in 1911 the former concern had purchased the Glen Line. Glen remained a company in its own right, albeit a subsidiary of Royal Mail. Shire disappeared as a company as a result of the Royal Mail takeover and its vessels were owned directly by the parent company, although they retained their names. Despite common ownership, there were difficulties in the way of fusing the Glen and Shire interests.

The management of the Glen Line was largely in the hands of its brokers, McGregor, Gow and Co. which had been purchased by Elder Dempster at the same time whereas the Shire Line's brokers continued, as they always had been, to be Norris and Joyner. No merger of the two services was a practical proposition while each had different brokers, so on 1st February 1912 Philipps resolved the problem in his usual direct way by purchasing the business of Norris and Joyner and promptly merging it with McGregor, Gow's under the new style of McGregor, Gow, Norris and Joyner Ltd. This was subsequently changed in 1917 to McGregor, Gow and Holland Ltd. on the appointment of Charles Holland as Managing Director, and it continued under that title for the remaining life of the Glen and Shire service.

Having finally obtained complete control of the Shire Line under the banner of Royal Mail, Sir Owen Philipps (as he had then become) was not long in bringing the dominant force of his personality to bear on the Line's future. He was convinced that a great period of prosperity lay ahead for shipping services to the Far East and that the prize for success in it would go to the owners whose ships best answered its expanding needs. His conception of this answer was a series of ships larger, faster, and with a far wider range of cargo handling gear than anything previously attempted, and the same year an order for five such ships was placed with Belfast yards, four with Workman Clark and Co. and one from Harland and Wolff, on account of the Shire Line section of the Royal Mail, with two similar ships ordered from Hawthorn Leslie for the Glen Line. It might have been expected that now the two concerns were so closely connected that there would be a fusion of names, but Shire names were retained for the Belfast ships while the Newcastle vessels kept the Glen names. The reason was probably the very practical one of maintaining Shire Line's rights in the Far Eastern Conference.

The building of such large and relatively complicated ships inevitably took some time, and a much earlier solution was required to replace the two ships which had been on charter from Brocklebanks. So at the beginning of 1913 Philipps purchased for the Shire service a pair of sisters then in course of construction in the Sunderland yard of Bartram and Sons for John Mathias and Sons' Cambrian Steam Navigation Co. Ltd. These vessels had already been launched as the *Salopian* and *Reptonian* but before completion they were respectively renamed *Radnorshire* and *Merionethshire*. Neither of the two ships met Philipp's requirements for the new service as they were of only 4,300 tons, or much the same size as the existing fleet, but they were well able to hold the fort until the new tonnage arrived at which time they could provide a slower secondary service complementary to the faster main one. Alterations to the ships to suit them for Shire Line requirements delayed their completion until June 1913 in the case of the *Radnorshire* and the following October for the *Merionethshire*. A third ship on order for Mathias at Bartrams was subsequently taken over to become Glen Line's *Glenearn*.

By that time the first of the specially designed ships were well under way, the *Cardiganshire* going into the water at Belfast on 30th September 1913 and running successful trials at the end of November. Her sister, the *Carnarvonshire*, was completed in March 1914, and they were among the finest cargo liners of their day. Hitherto the Shire fleet had not been particularly marked out from other cargo vessels, but at one bound it leapt to the forefront of cargo liner design, with emphasis on the word 'liner', for the two ships were larger and faster than many passenger liners of the period. It is some measure of their advance over previous Shire ships that their tonnage was half as big again while their deadweight capacity of 13,500 tons placed them among the world's largest cargo ships. Continuing the interest in the passenger trade, accommodation was provided for 12 first class passengers in the bridge deck, plus temporary berths in the 'tween decks for over 1,000 coolies or pilgrims as required. They were powerful-looking ships, distinguished by a lengthy forecastle, centrecastle and poop, a heavy lift derrick on the foremast

Radnorshire of 1913, purchased along with her sistership *Merionethshire* whilst both were under construction at Sunderland for the Cambrian Steam Navigation Co. Ltd. [*The Mariners Museum, Newport News, Virginia/Peter Newall collection*]

Cardiganshire of 1914, first of the large new 14-knot ships which Kylsant had built for Shire Line. *[B. and A. Feilden/J. and M. Clarkson]*

and no less than six pairs of kingposts serving the seven hatches. They were equally well equipped down below where four coal-fired boilers fed twin triple-expansion steam engines to provide a comfortable 14 knots in service.

The delivery during 1913 of the first of the new fleet plus the two purchased ships enabled some weeding out of the remaining Shires. The last of the clipper bowed ships, the *Flintshire* of 1896, was sold to the Ellerman Line, while the *Carmarthenshire* and *Pembrokeshire* were transferred within the parent company to open a new service better suited to their capabilities from Canada to the West Indies under the new names of *Chaleur* and *Chignecto*. The year 1914 dawned fair for the Shire Line as its largest building programme to date swung into full gear. By the end of the year it was hoped to have all seven of the new fast ships in commission maintaining the main Glen and Shire service while the older units provided the secondary service. The outbreak of war was to shatter this vision as was the similar tragedy to shatter its successor 25 years later.

The Shire fleet at war
The declaration of war found the Shire fleet scattered along to the sea lanes to the east on their lawful occasions, but the conflict was soon to sweep them up in its path. The brand new *Carnarvonshire* was taken up in the Far East and hastily fitted out as a transport to convey troops back from Chinwangtao to Southampton in September 1914, while her sister, the *Cardiganshire*, which was in home waters took many of the original British Expeditionary Force across the Channel. The *Cardiganshire* was also at the Dardanelles campaign later the same year, and both ships were subsequently engaged in transporting American troops across the Atlantic during the last year of the war.

Meanwhile the second pair of sisters in the new programme had been completed, the *Carmarthenshire* in February 1915 and the *Pembrokeshire* two months later. Externally they were very similar to the initial ships, but were some 30 feet shorter, their tonnage was some 1,500 tons less and they were single screw rather than twin screw ships with an imposing quadruple-expansion engine providing the motive power. Due to war conditions, both ships made their maiden voyages in the Royal Mail service to South America before going to the Far East, and were subsequently liable to diversion far and wide under the Liner Requisition Scheme which came into effect in 1917.

The last of the new ships was even longer in entering service. Although laid down in February 1914, urgent war work in Harland and Wolff's yard prevented her launch until 12th September 1916 and she was not finally completed until the following January. She was named *Brecknockshire*, the

only unit of the fleet to bear this alternative name for the Shire of Brecon, and her tragically short career certainly did not encourage any repetition. Although of the same hull form as the second Workman Clark pair, the *Brecknockshire* was quite different in outward appearance as she was rigged with four masts, two forward and two aft of the midships structure, as well as three sets of derrick posts. She was destined never to see the Far East, for on her maiden voyage she loaded coal in Liverpool for Rio de Janeiro and after passing through a severe storm which caused some damage on deck was nearing her destination when she was intercepted in the South Atlantic by the German commerce raider *Moewe*. The

Pembrokeshire of 1915, the last of four ships delivered to the company in 1914/1915. *[Nautical Photo Agency/Peter Newall]*

Brecknockshire's single stern gun was no match for the long range artillery of the raider, and after the crew had abandoned ship the vessel was sunk by time bombs placed in the holds by the raider's crew.

The loss was the second depredation of the Shire Line fleet by the *Moewe* in as many months, for on the previous 7th January she had intercepted the *Radnorshire* homeward bound in the South Atlantic on Royal Mail service and had similarly despatched her with bombs. The *Radnorshire*'s crew were fortunate in being transferred to the *Hudson Maru* and taken back to Pernambuco soon afterwards, but the *Brecknockshire*'s complement was less favoured as they were taken back to Germany in the raider and held prisoner for the rest of the conflict. The only other Shire Line loss during the war was that of the *Merionethshire* which was torpedoed and sunk 150 miles north of the Azores on 27th May 1918, the whole complement getting safely away in the boats to be picked up the following day. In fact although three fine vessels were destroyed not one life was lost in the Shire Line through enemy action during the entire war.

Not that this meant that the Shire Line had an easy war. Although it was true that once its vessels had passed through the Suez Canal they were in waters relatively free from enemy action apart from the occasional raider, and that cargo working in eastern ports was comparatively unhindered, they were often diverted both to other Royal Mail services and by the Government to routes where every peril could be encountered. In May 1917 the *Monmouthshire* fought off a submarine in the Atlantic with her stern gun, while the *Cardiganshire* had already used her speed to escape a similar fate in the Mediterranean the previous January. In April of the same year the *Carmarthenshire* faced an even more dangerous encounter when she had a running gun duel with a submarine in the Western Approaches which lasted for two hours before the submarine broke off the action. The Shire Line's final encounter with the enemy came on 30th May 1918 when the veteran *Denbighshire* was narrowly missed by a torpedo as she made her way through the Mediterranean.

Reconstruction

The close of hostilities found the Shire Line with its fleet reduced to six ships, four of the new cargo liner type and two veterans from the Jenkins era. The latter had no place in the post-war Far Eastern trade and in 1919 were transferred to the West Indian cargo services of the Royal Mail Lines which badly required tonnage of this size, the *Denbighshire* becoming the *Tamar* and the *Monmouthshire* the *Tyne*.

But if the Shire Line did not need additions to its main line fleet, it was certainly bereft of secondary vessels, a situation which was remedied by the allocation to it of three standard cargo vessels from the British Government's huge wartime shipbuilding programme. The Government had no desire to continue their shipping activities after the war and, in common with other major shipowners, the Royal Mail Group took over a large number of the existing ships and shipbuilding contracts which were distributed through the fleets of the various members. The Shire Line's allocation was a somewhat mixed bag. By far the nearest to a cargo liner was the 8,192-ton *Glamorganshire* which had been built in Japan in 1917 as the *War Armour*, and managed by Shire for the Shipping Controller from the time of her completion. She was a twin-screw vessel, originally coal fired, but well capable of a sea speed of 12.5 knots when her boilers were converted to oil firing before she entered the Shire service.

Also delivered in 1919 was the *Radnorshire* which had been taken over on the stocks in Thompsons' yard at Sunderland and completed to Shire specifications. She too was somewhat better than the average standard ship, being of the F type cargo design which, with their deadweight tonnage of 10,800, were among the largest of the standard types. The last of the three, the *Montgomeryshire*, was not delivered until 1921, and was originally ordered as one of the large N class prefabricated cargo vessels with no sheer or rake and extremely utilitarian. The fact that her construction in Armstrong Whitworth's yard at Newcastle had not even begun when the Shire Line took over the contract enabled several improvements such as a full poop and extra samson posts to be fitted, but her most important departure from previous Shire practice was her propelling machinery consisting of two double-reduction geared turbines fed from three water tube boilers. Although of similar size to the *Radnorshire*, she was thus a ship of very different type and appearance.

All three of the standard ships were intended to serve on any of the Royal Mail routes as required as well as the Shire Line's own, and in fact, particularly in their later years, spent most of their time on charter to various other Group companies. Both the *Radnorshire* and the *Montgomeryshire* made several voyages under Royal Mail auspices with cotton from Galveston soon after their delivery, while the latter was taken up under Government charter for Eastern Mediterranean service during the Chanak crisis of 1922/23.

Naturally their strenuous service during the war had taken its toll on the surviving large Shire ships, and all four were sent back to their builders' yard at Belfast for a thorough refit as soon as circumstances permitted. At the same time their boilers were converted to burn oil fuel to enable them to keep up comparable running performances to the new Glen Line motor ships.

Integration and retrenchment

As post war trade settled down again, Philipps decided that the time had come to take a further step towards integration of the Glen and Shire services. In 1920 therefore the sailings of the two firms were completely amalgamated under the title of Glen and Shire Lines and the management of McGregor, Gow and Holland. The Shire ships still retained their Royal Mail houseflag and yellow/buff funnel. One further change at this time was the final abandonment of the old Jenkins extension from China and Japan across the Pacific to West Coast North American ports. The opening of the Panama Canal during the war had completely transformed the accessibility of Pacific North West ports from Europe and the Royal Mail itself now inaugurated a direct service under its own name, a venture which was subsequently to be carried on by the well known Loch class vessels. Henceforth the Shire Line's interests were to be confined to the Europe-Far East service.

The 1920s were to prove the quietest decade in the whole of the Shire Line's history. After 1921 no new ships were built, the fleet suffered no mishaps of any note, and it was not until the very end of the period that any ships were disposed of. Although trade fluctuated, it was the calm before the coming storm that was to shake the Shire Line to its very foundations. Just before the economic deluge burst, two of the Workman Clark quartet were sold, but in spite of the fact that they went to the same purchasers it was not exact sisters that were disposed of but the 9,426-ton *Cardiganshire* and her smaller consort, the 7,823-ton *Carmarthenshire*. Their purchasers were Christian Salvesen's South Georgia Co. which renamed them *Salvestria* and *Sourabaya* and converted them to whale factory ships. The rebuilding operation completely destroyed their handsome lines as it included the construction of a stern ramp for hauling the whales into the ships for processing and an almost continuous deckhouse from bow to stern. However, both ships gave good service in their new guise until both were lost during the Second World War.

Not long in following them out of the fleet were the standard ships which had recently had little more than their names to associate them with Shire activities. The *Radnorshire* was the first to go, passing to H.M. Thomson of London for tramping as the *Sithonia* in 1930, while the *Montgomeryshire* was sold to Yugoslav buyers as the *Riv* the following year. Of the three, only the *Glamorganshire* reached the breakers' yard on her sale to Dutch scrappers in 1933.

The Royal Mail debacle and final integration

In the meantime, however, the Royal Mail empire had crashed about the ears of its creator, Lord Kylsant (as Philipps had

How the great are fallen ! The South Georgia Company bought the *Carmarthenshire* of 1915, converted her into a whale factory ship and renamed her *Sourabaya*. As such she gave a further 13 years' service under the flags of the Falkland Islands, Ireland and Jersey before being torpedoed and sunk with a heavy loss of life in October 1942. *[Ships in Focus]*

become in 1923). This story is not the place to trace the intricate financial manoeuvrings which led to the Royal Mail collapse in 1930. Suffice it to say that in effect the company had been trading at a loss for most of the 1920s, but the position had not been readily apparent as dividends continued to be paid from the large profits made during the immediate post-war years. The depression of the early 1930s brought matters to a head, and the Government was forced to intervene to protect the advances made to the Group under the Trade Facilities Act for the construction of new tonnage. Kylsant was obliged to resign his directorships of all the Group companies and the two parent concerns, Royal Mail and Elder Dempster, were placed in receivership while an attempt was made to sort out the complicated interlocking financing.

The departure of Kylsant under a cloud should not obscure his real achievement insofar as the Shire Line was concerned. He had raised it from its doldrums at the close of the Jenkins era to one of the foremost liner concerns in the

Eastern trade, and his policy of building the finest cargo liners possible for the service had set the pattern for the future. With David Jenkins of the early years and Sir Herbert McDavid of later Glen Line years he remains one of the three dominant personalities in this story.

The position of the Shire Line at the Kylsant collapse was not easy to resolve as it was merely a name describing part of the Royal Mail trade and fleet. Even those had dwindled considerably for only the *Carnarvonshire* and *Pembrokeshire* remained in active commission. The position was resolved in 1933 by Glen Line Ltd. purchasing both ships from the Royal Mail receivers so that the whole of the Glen and Shire operation came under the legal ownership of Glen Line Ltd. for the first time. This completed the full merger which had been spoken of over the previous twenty years. The joint service could now present a united front in all its ports of call, a facility which was to become of increasing importance with the need to present an image to customers.

Montgomeryshire, the last ship to which Royal Mail gave a Shire name. *[Ships in Focus]*

Fleet list

S1. MARY EVANS 1861-1882 Wooden barque
O.N. 29767 306g 114.3 x 26.8 x 16.3 feet.
11.4.1861: Completed by Hutchinson, Newcastle-upon-Tyne.
27.4.1861: Registered in the ownership of David J. Jenkins, London.
9.1.1882: Sold to Bruce B. Nicoll, Dundee.
5.6.1882: Registered at Sydney, New South Wales.
1883: Sold to Joseph E. Mitchell, Newton, near Sydney, New South Wales.
1886: Sold to James Gulland, Brisbane.
24.7.1886: Registered at Brisbane.
1893: Sold to J. Moncrieff, Brisbane.
1893: Demolished at Brisbane

S2. EASTWARD HO 1862-1870 Wooden barque
O.N. 42900 386g 117.3 x 28.3 x 17.0 feet.
10.1861: Launched by Bollen, Egmont Bay, Prince Edward Island.
2.12.1861: Completed.
17.12.1861: Registered in the ownership of Edward Heard, Charlottetown, Prince Edward Island.
23.6.1862: Acquired by David J. Jenkins, London.
13.8.1870: Sold to Henry Cliff, Quentin Aisne, France, retaining British registry.
9.9.1872: Sold to buyers at Yokohama.
9.9.1885: Register closed.

S3. ARBUTUS 1863-1877 Wooden barque
O.N. 48508 336g 125.1 x 26.7 x 16.3 feet.
15.9.1863: Launched by Shuttleworth and Company, Southwick, Shoreham.
26.9.1863: Registered at London in the ownership of David J. Jenkins (32/64) and Edward Pembroke (32/64), London.
8.4.1877: Sold to Henry Field, Shoreham.
4.5.1877: Registered at Shoreham.
1879: Sold to Robert H. Penney, Shoreham.
1881: Sold to Francis Gauntlett, Southsea.
25.10.1882: Ashore at Stensssa, Oland in the Gulf of Bothnia whilst on a voyage from Grangemouth to Stockholm with a cargo of coal.
26.10.1882: Refloated by the salvage steamer POSEIDON and taken to Kalmar, where her cargo was unloaded prior to repairs.
1883: Sold by auction when owners refused payment for the repairs.
10.1883: Wrecked.

S4. PEMBROKESHIRE (1) 1864-1887 Wooden ship with iron beams
O.N. 48695 721g 157.4 x 31.6 x 20.0 feet.
26.1.1864: Launched by Allen and Wharton, Pembroke Dock for David J. Jenkins, London.
27.2.1864: Completed.
1872: Reduced to a barque.
5.4.1887: Sold to Abraham B. Troop, Annapolis, Nova Scotia, retaining London registry.
29.7.1887: Wrecked off the Abrolhos Islands, Brazil whilst on a voyage from London to Rio de Janiero.
12.10.1887: Register closed.

S5. WEBFOOT 1864-1885 Wooden ship
O.N. 50041 1,061g 180.8 x 37.6 x 22.1 feet.
1856: Launched by Shiverick Brothers, East Dennis, Massachusetts for P.S. Crowell, Boston.
8.4.1864: Stranded at Dunkirk.
26.7.1864: Registered at London in the ownership of David J. Jenkins, London who purchased the damaged ship from underwriters.
9.1885: Sold to William J. Woodside, Belfast.
23.9.1885: Registered at Belfast.
12.11.1886: Destroyed by fire at Cape Flattery whilst on a voyage from Port Townshend, Washington Territory, USA to Callao with a cargo of timber.
15.12.1886: Register closed.

S6. CARDIGANSHIRE (1) 1864-1882 Wooden barque
O.N. 50109 365g 124.0 x 26.4 x 17.0 feet.
30.9.1864: Completed by Gaddarn Brothers, Neyland, Pembroke for David J. Jenkins, London.
6.10.1864: Registered at London.
9.1882: Sold to Robert Jones, Criccieth, Caernarvonshire.
17.2.1892: Abandoned in mid Atlantic whilst on a voyage from Monte Christi to Havre.
12.3.1892: Register closed.

S7. CARMARTHENSHIRE (1) 1865-1885 Wooden ship with iron beams
O.N. 52734 812g 174.6 x 32.7 x 20.5 feet.
6.1865: Launched by Allen and Varlow, Pembroke Dock for David J. Jenkins, London.
16.7.1885: Registered at London.
9.1.1885: Wrecked off Terschelling, Netherlands whilst on a voyage from Bangkok to Bremen with a cargo of rice.
12.2.1885: Register closed.

S8. CARNARVONSHIRE (1) 1866-1880 Wooden barque with iron beams
O.N. 54647 388g 132.2 x 26.2 x 16.5 feet.
3.1866: Launched by Gaddarn Brothers, Neyland, Pembroke for David J. Jenkins, London.
28.3.1866: Registered at London.
9.3.1880: Sold to Rees D. Richards and Griffith Williams, Barmouth.
20.7.1886: Sold to Gregory B. Wadsworth junior, Goole.
15.3.1887: Registered at Goole.
2.1.1893: Wrecked off Atalia Point, Rover Amazon, Brazil whilst inward bound from Cardiff.
24.2.1893: Register closed.

S9. SOUTHERN QUEEN 1868-1888 Wooden ship
O.N. 55058 790g 157.2 x 33.2 x 21.8 feet.
5.1866: Launched as a speculation by Ruddock and Company, New Brunswick as BLONDE.
1866: Completed for George Campbell, Liverpool as SOUTHERN QUEEN.
8.2.1867: Registered at Liverpool in the ownership of William J. Lamport and George Holt, Liverpool.
10.11.1868: Purchased by David J. Jenkins, London.

24.12.1888: Sold to Henry and George Curwen, Preston.
31.12.1888: Register closed.
31.12.1888: Register closed on sale to Olaf Lohne, Mandal, Norway.

S10. GLAMORGANSHIRE (1) 1869-1885 Wooden barque with iron beams
O.N. 60923 472g 148.0 x 27.5 x 17.5 feet.
16.3.1869: Launched by Gaddarn Brothers, Neyland, Pembroke for David J. Jenkins, London
6.4.1869: Registered at London.
3.1.1885: Sold to Joseph M. Kirby, London.
1885: Sold to S. Otto, Christiansand, Norway and renamed SOLA.
12.11.1885: Register closed.
1898: Sold to J. Chr. Nilssen, Christiansand.
6.12.1900: Wrecked off the Maranham Bar whilst inward bound from Cardiff.

S11. DENBIGHSHIRE (1) 1870-1885 Wooden barque with iron beams
O.N. 63632 483g 156.5 x 28.2 x 17.5 feet.
6.1870: Launched by Gaddarn Brothers, Neyland, Pembroke for David J. Jenkins, London.
8.8.1870: Registered at London.
1885: Sold to C.N. Pappalos, Syra, Greece and renamed OMONIA.
12.11.1885: Register closed.
6.1.1893: Wrecked near Eupatoria, Crimea whilst outward bound from Azov.

S12. W.W. SMITH 1871-1876 Wooden ship
O.N. 14685 661n 175.9 x 31.4 x 20.9 feet.
25.4.1857: Launched by Frederick C. Clarke, Havre des Pas, Jersey
28.5.1857: Registered in the ownership of John J. Melhuish (16/64), Philip A. Holzberg, Liverpool (16/64), William Melhuish, Liverpool, Frederick C. Clarke, Jersey (8/64), John Hartley, Lancaster (8/64), William W. Smith, Liverpool (8/64) and others.
1865: Sold to C.F. Trepplin, Liverpool.
1866: Sold to Philip A. Holzberg, Liverpool.
1867: Sold to J.H. Hind, Liverpool.
29.7.1867: Register closed on sale to Hong Kong.
12.11.1869: Sold to Noble C. Richardson, Willington-on-Tyne.
15.7.1871: Sold to William E. Hawkesley, London.
2.8.1871: 32/64 shares acquired by David J. Jenkins, London.
8.2.1872: David J. Jenkins, London now owns 62/64 shares.
1875: Reduced to a barque.
28.2.1876: Sold to Isaac Henderson and Thomas Cuthbertson, Singapore.
11.2.1878: Sold to William H. Smith, Gibraltar and converted into a coal hulk at Gibraltar.

S13. FLINTSHIRE (1) 1872-1888 Iron
O.N. 65736 1,548g 1,243n 270.7 x 32.8 x 23.8 feet.
C.2-cyl. by the London and Glasgow Engineering and Iron Shipbuilding Co. Ltd., Glasgow (31" and 54½" x 33"); 150 NHP.
3.7.1872: Launched by the London and Glasgow Engineering and Iron Shipbuilding Co. Ltd., Glasgow (Yard No. 162) for David J. Jenkins, London.
9.9.1872: Registered at London.

9.5.1888: Sold to William McKerrow, Singapore.
20.6.1888: Registered at Singapore in the ownership of Lim Tiang Hee, Singapore.
8.2.1890: Registered in the ownership of the Ocean Steam Ship Co. Ltd., Liverpool.
1891: Owners became the East India Ocean Steam Ship Co. Ltd., Liverpool.
1892: Owners became the Nederlandsche Stoomvaart Maatschappij Oceaan, Amsterdam, Holland.
13.7.1892: Register closed.
16.9.1895: Registered at Liverpool in the ownership of the East Indian Ocean Steam Ship Co. Ltd., Liverpool.
1896: Sold to Okazaki Tokichi, Kobe, Japan and renamed YAYEYAMA MARU.
9.12.1896: Register closed.
13.12.1898: Sank following a collision off Moji with the steamers BRINDISI (3,688/1880)and TOKOMARU.
1896: Broken up.

S14. MONTGOMERYSHIRE (1) 1873-1877 Iron
O.N. 68520 1,751g 1,146n 308.0 x 32.9 x 24.0 feet.
C.2-cyl. by the London and Glasgow Engineering and Iron Shipbuilding Co. Ltd., Glasgow (35" and 62" x 42"); 200 NHP.
20.12.1873: Launched by the London and Glasgow Engineering and Iron Shipbuilding Co. Ltd., Glasgow (Yard No. 172) for David J. Jenkins, London.
27.2.1874: Registered at London.
1877: Sold to the Mitsubishi Mail Steamship Company, Yokohama, Japan and renamed AKITSUSHIMA MARU.
3.8.1877: Register closed.
10.10.1883: Wrecked ten miles off Odanozawa Aomori Prefecture, Hokkaido, Japan.

S15. RADNORSHIRE (1) 1876-1885 Iron
O.N. 73739 1,838g 1,201n 301.0 x 34.2 x 24.0 feet.
C.2-cyl. by the London and Glasgow Engineering and Iron Shipbuilding Co. Ltd., Glasgow (36" and 66" x 42"); 250 NHP.
17.11.1876: Launched by the London and Glasgow Engineering and Iron Shipbuilding Co. Ltd., Glasgow (Yard No. 194) for David J. Jenkins, London.
20.12.1876: Registered at London.
20.6.1885: Wrecked on Sorelle Rocks, Tunis whilst on a voyage from Hamburg and London to Nagasaki.
3.7.1885: Register closed.

S16. MERIONETHSHIRE (1) 1878-1890 Iron
O.N. 77095 1,907g 1,245n 301.5 x 34.2 x 24.0 feet.
C.2-cyl. by the London and Glasgow Engineering and Iron Shipbuilding Co. Ltd., Glasgow (36" and 66" x 42"); 250 NHP.
5.4.1878: Launched by the London and Glasgow Engineering and Iron Shipbuilding Co. Ltd., Glasgow (Yard No. 205) for David J. Jenkins, London.
8.5.1878: Registered at London.
14.7.1890: Sold to the Quebec Steamship Company, Montreal, Quebec.
7.10.1890: Renamed CARIBBEE.
30.9.1901: Owners became the Quebec Steamship Co. Ltd., Montreal.
8.4.1907: Sold to William H.A. Walker, New York, USA retaining London registry.

8.6.1908: Foundered in the Atlantic during a voyage from Matanzas to New York with a cargo of molasses.
27.7.1908: Register closed.

S17. BRECONSHIRE (1) 1879-1886 Iron
O.N. 79674 1,902g 1,241n 299.7 x 34.4 x 24.0 feet.
C.2-cyl. by the London and Glasgow Engineering and Iron Shipbuilding Co. Ltd., Glasgow (36" and 66" x 42"); 250 NHP.
12.12.1878: Launched by the London and Glasgow Engineering and Iron Shipbuilding Co. Ltd., Glasgow (Yard No. 209) for David J. Jenkins, London.
12.2.1879: Registered at London.
17.3.1886: Wrecked on White Rocks, Lamock Islands, China, whilst on a voyage from Nagasaki to Hamburg.
30.4.1886: Register closed.

S18. (MONTGOMERYSHIRE) (2) 1880 Iron
O.N. 81618 2,371g 1,528n 330.0 x 35.8 x 25.6 feet.
C.2-cyl. by the London and Glasgow Engineering and Iron Shipbuilding Co. Ltd., Glasgow (38" and 71" x 48"); 350 NHP.
13.1.1880: Launched by the London and Glasgow Engineering and Iron Shipbuilding Co. Ltd., Glasgow (Yard No. 213) for David J. Jenkins, London as MONTGOMERYSHIRE.
3.3.1880: Registered at London in the ownership of the Royal Mail Steam Packet Company, London as HUMBER.
15.2.1885: Left New York for London and disappeared, with the loss of 56 lives.
3.6.1885: Register closed.

S19. MONTGOMERYSHIRE (3) 1880-1881 Iron
O.N. 82827 1,929g 1,257n 270.2 x 35.4 x 24.3 feet.
C.2-cyl. by Thomas Richardson and Sons, Hartlepool (36" and 67" x 36"); 250 NHP.
4.11.1880: Launched by Raylton Dixon and Co., Middlesbrough (Yard No. 174) for David J. Jenkins, London.
13.12.1880: Completed and ran trials.
14.12.1880: Registered at London.

28.12.1880: Wrecked nine miles north of Cape Mondego, Portugal whilst on her maiden voyage from Cardiff to Singapore with a cargo of coal with the loss of all her crew.
23.3.1881: Register closed.

S20. CARNARVONSHIRE (2) 1881-1883 Iron
O.N. 82886 2,362g 1,531n 330.0 x 35.8 x 25.6 feet.
C-2-cyl. by the London and Glasgow Engineering and Iron Shipbuilding Co. Ltd., Glasgow (38" and 71" x 48"); 350 NHP.
30.4.1881: Launched by the London and Glasgow Engineering and Iron Shipbuilding Co. Ltd., Glasgow (Yard No. 218) for David J. Jenkins, London.
13.6.1881: Registered at London.
20.4.1883: Wrecked at Mitari Saki, Shingu Bay, Japan whilst on a voyage from London to Kobe with general cargo.
8.5.1883: Register closed.

S21. PEMBROKESHIRE (2) 1882-1893 Iron
O.N. 85171 2,632g 1,717n 330.0 x 38.8 x 25.6 feet.
C.2-cyl. by the London and Glasgow Engineering and Iron Shipbuilding Co. Ltd., Glasgow (42" and 74" x 48"); 400 NHP.
3.6.1882: Launched by the London and Glasgow Engineering and Iron Shipbuilding Co. Ltd., Glasgow (Yard No. 226) for David J. Jenkins, London.
29.6.1882: Registered at London.
24.10.1893: Sold to William Briggs, Sunderland.
16.11.1893: Sold to the Quebec Steamship Co. Ltd., Montreal, Quebec; still registered in London.
25.11.1893: Renamed FONTABELLE.
25.4.1906: Sold to John J. King and Sons Ltd., Garston, probably for breaking up, but resold to Companhia Commercio e Navegação, Rio de Janeiro, Brazil and renamed CANOE.
6.10.1906: Register closed.
1913: Converted into a storage hulk at Rio de Janeiro.

Pembrokeshire of 1882. *[Peter Newall collection]*

S22. CARDIGANSHIRE (2) 1883-1894 Iron
O.N. 87133 2,486g 1,623n 317.3 x 38.1 x 24.5 feet.
C.2-cyl. by R. and W. Hawthorn, Newcastle-upon-Tyne (38" and 70" x 45"); 275 NHP.
24.5.1883: Launched by C.S. Swan and Hunter, Wallsend-on-Tyne (Yard No. 71) for David J. Jenkins, London.
11.7.1883: Registered at London.
17.7.1883: Completed.
1894: Sold to Hokaido Tanko Tetsudo K.K., Hokaido, Japan and renamed IBURI MARU.
27.9.1894: Register closed.
1907: Owners became Hokaido Tanko Kisen K.K., Hokaido.
23.1.1909: Sank following a collision with the French steamer SYDNEY (4,232/1883) in Tokyo Bay whilst on a voyage from Uraga to Yokohama in ballast.

S23. GLAMORGANSHIRE (2) 1885-1897 Iron
O.N. 89651 2,835g 1,843n 340.2 x 40.2 x 26.5 feet.
C.2-cyl. by the London and Glasgow Engineering and Iron Shipbuilding Co. Ltd., Glasgow (43" and 78" x 54"); 450 NHP.
19.11.1884: Launched by the London and Glasgow Engineering and Iron Shipbuilding Co. Ltd., Glasgow (Yard No. 244) for David J. Jenkins, London.
9.1.1885: Registered at London.
5.6.1896: Owners became Jenkins and Co. Ltd.
7.3.1897: Wrecked on Rosslyn Reef, 80 miles off Cape James, Cochin, China whilst on a voyage from Hong Kong to Saigon in ballast.
12.7.1897: Register closed.

S24. DENBIGHSHIRE (2) 1885-1894 Iron
O.N. 89669 2,538g 1,663n 317.0 x 38.0 x 24.5 feet.
C.2-cyl. by R. and W. Hawthorn, Newcastle-upon-Tyne (38" and 72" x 48"); 300 NHP.
15.1.1885: Launched by C. S. Swan and Hunter, Wallsend, Newcastle-upon-Tyne (Yard No. 88) for David J. Jenkins, London
26.2.1885: Registered at London.
27.2.1885: Completed.
1894: Sold to Osaka Shosen Kaisha, Osaka, Japan, and renamed FUKUOKA MARU.
8.11.1894: Register closed.
1912: Sold to Akita Shokwai Goshi Kaisha, Nishinomiya, Japan.
1920: Sold to Yamasaki Kisen K.K., Hakodate, Japan.
23.1.1927: Wrecked at Kawajiri Bay, north east coast of Noto Peninsula, whilst on a voyage from Fushiki to Tsuruga.

S25. MONMOUTHSHIRE (1) 1886-1902
O.N. 91901 2,874g 1,871n 344.0 x 40.2 x 26.5 feet.
T.3-cyl. by the London and Glasgow Engineering and Iron Shipbuilding Co. Ltd., Glasgow (30", 47"and 70"x 51"); 600 NHP.
21.1.1886: Launched by the London and

Glamorganshire in the Suez Canal. *[W. A. Laxon collection]*

Denbighshire. [Ian Rae collection]

Fukuoka Maru, the former *Denbighshire. [Ambrose Greenway collection]*

Glasgow Engineering and Iron Shipbuilding Co. Ltd., Glasgow (Yard No. 248) for David J. Jenkins, London.
25.2.1886: Registered at London.
27.2.1886: Completed.
5.6.1896: Owner became Jenkins and Co. Ltd.
23.7.1901: Sold to the Quebec Steamship Co. Ltd., Montreal, Quebec.
14.10.1901: Renamed KORONA.
20.4.1916: Sold to Canada Steamship Lines Ltd., Montreal.
15.2.1917: Registered at Montreal.
1.1.1920: Sold to Furness, Withy and Co. Ltd., London.
29.11.1920: Sold to the Quebec Steamship Company, Montreal.
15.2.1922: Sold to George W. Barkley, New York, USA.
3.1922: Sold to the Korona Steamship Corporation (Globe Line, managers), Callao, Peru.
8.1924: Towed from Cadiz to Bilbao for breaking up.

S26. BRECONSHIRE (2) 1886-1893
Iron
O.N. 89511 2,544g 1,648n 299.7 x 37.3 x 24.3 feet.
C.2-cyl. by Blair and Co., Stockton-on-Tees (36½" and 68" x 42"); 250 NHP.
13.11.1883: Launched by the Sunderland Shipbuilding Co. Ltd., Sunderland (Yard No. 120) for William H. Senier and Gilbert Porteous, London as NUMIDA.
14.1.1884: Registered at London.
2.6.1886: Acquired by David J. Jenkins, London.
24.6.1886: Renamed BRECONSHIRE.
5.10.1893: Sold to Northern Trust Ltd., Newcastle-upon-Tyne.
18.10.1893: Sold to the Breconshire Steamship Co. Ltd. (John W. Thompson and John R. Elliot and Co., managers), Newcastle-upon-Tyne.
30.4.1894: Wrecked at Bethel Creek, east coast of Florida, whilst on a voyage from New York to Tampa, Florida in ballast.
31.5.1894: Register closed.

S27. CARMARTHENSHIRE (2) 1887-1901
O.N. 91991 2,726g 1,176n 329.5 x 40.0 x 25.1 feet.
T.3-cyl. by R. and W. Hawthorn, Newcastle-upon-Tyne (27", 43" and 70" x 45"); 340 NHP.
25.1.1887: Launched by C. S. Swan and Hunter, Wallsend, Newcastle-upon-Tyne (Yard No. 100) for David J. Jenkins, London.
7.3.1887: Registered at London.
8.3.1887: Completed.
5.6.1896: Owner became Jenkins and Co. Ltd.
1.7.1901: Sold to the Trinidad Shipping and Trading Co. Ltd. (George Christall, manager), Glasgow.
3.8.1901: Renamed MARACAS.
27.10.1914: Sold to James F. Butler, New York, USA.
1914: Sold to New York Transatlantic Steamship Corporation, New York.
23.12.1914: Register closed.
22.2.1915: Left New York for Rotterdam and Copenhagen.
18.3.1915: Arrived at Hull to discharge after being seized by the British and sent to

Kirkwall for inspection.
9.11.1915: Sold as a prize to Akties. Solgran (Andreas Meling Junior, manager), Stavanger, Norway, and renamed MAJOREN.
3.9.1917: Captured and shelled by the German submarine U 95 25 miles west of Tory Island in position 55.14 north by 08.56 west whilst on a voyage from Philadelphia to Glasgow with a cargo of lubricating oil.

S28. FLINTSHIRE (2) 1888-1894
O.N. 95500 2,879g 1,871n 344.0 x 40.1 x 26.5 feet.
T.3-cyl. by the London and Glasgow Engineering and Iron Shipbuilding Co. Ltd., Glasgow (30", 48"and 75" x 51"); 650 NHP.
3.11.1888: Launched by the London and Glasgow Engineering and Iron Shipbuilding Co. Ltd., Glasgow (Yard No. 254) for David J. Jenkins, London.

3.12.1888: Registered at London.
20.12.1888: Completed.
5.9.1894: Sold to George S. Thomson, Yokohama (with power to resell for not less than £36,000).
1894: Sold to Nippon Yusen K.K., Tokyo, Japan, on behalf of the Imperial Japanese Navy, and renamed TOYOHASHI MARU.
3.12.1894: Register closed.
1894: Transferred to the Imperial Japanese Navy as the torpedo depot ship TOYOHASHI.
1914: Decommissioned.
About 1918: Sold to Nihon Kaiun Yekisaikai, Yokohama (Japan Seaman's Relief Association) for use as a training ship and renamed TOYOHASHI MARU.
1923: Renamed WING FAT (YEIHATSU).
1924: Sold to Shinyei Shokai Goshi Kaisha, Dairen, Manchuria and renamed SHINYEI MARU.

Carmarthenshire of 1887, from a painting of her entering Hong Kong on 23rd April 1897. [National Museums and Galleries of Wales, Department of Industry, P92.416]

Carmarthenshire.   [Peter Newall collection]

Flintshire of 1888 in the Thames with the Tilbury Hotel in the background. *[Ambrose Greenway collection]*

1926: Sold to Yeitoku Shokai Goshi Kaisha, Dairen, Manchuria and renamed YEITOKU MARU.
1928: Sold to Nomura Naoji, Yokohama, Japan.
1933: Sold to Nippon Godo Kosen K.K., Fuchu, Japan
27.10.1935: Foundered after springing a leak off Ishikawa Prefecture whilst on a voyage from Hokkaido to Konan, Korea with a cargo of iron ore.

S29. RADNORSHIRE (2) 1890-1907
O.N. 98155 2,898g 1,889n 312.0 x 41.0 x 20.5 feet.
T.3-cyl. Wallsend Slipway and Engineering Co. Ltd., Newcastle-upon-Tyne (23", 38" and 61" x 39"); 350 NHP, 1,500 IHP, 9 3/4 knots.
9.7.1890: Launched by C.S. Swan and Hunter, Wallsend, Newcastle-upon-Tyne (Yard No. 157) for David J. Jenkins, London.
3.9.1890: Registered at London.
5.6.1896: Owners became Jenkins and Co. Ltd.
1907: Sold to the Bank of Athens (M.D. Assimacos, manager), Athens, Greece and renamed ASSIMACOS.
14.9.1907: Register closed.
1912: Owner became M.D. Assimacos, Andros, Greece.
1912: Sold to A. Diapoulos and L. Voulgaris, Andros, Greece.
1915: Sold to M. Embiricos, London but remained registered in Andros, Greece.
11.9.1916: Captured and sunk with explosive charges by the German submarine UB 18 45 miles south of the Seven Stones in position 49.15 north by 06.06 west whilst on a voyage from Glasgow to Genoa.

S30. MERIONETHSHIRE (2) 1895-1907
O.N. 104830 3,012g 1,950n 343.0 x 41.1 x 26.0 feet.
T.3-cyl. by North Eastern Marine Engineering Co. Ltd., Sunderland (25", 41 1/2" and 69" x 45"); 500 NHP, 2,900 IHP, 11 knots.

27.11.1894: Launched by the Sunderland Shipbuilding Co. Ltd., Sunderland (Yard No. 174) for Noble F. Jenkins, trading in the name of David J. Jenkins and Company, London.
1.1.1895: Registered at London.
5.6.1896: Owner became Jenkins and Co. Ltd., London.

23.11.1907: Sold to Ellerman Lines Ltd. (Frederick Swift, manager), London.
15.2.1908: Renamed BAVARIAN.
8.1928: Sold to Cohen and Company for £6,000 for demolition.
28.8.1928: Arrived at Briton Ferry.
31.7.1929: Register closed.

Above: *Merionethshire.* *[Peter Newall collection]*
Below: *Merionethshire* as *Bavarian* after her sale to Ellerman Lines. *[World Ship Photo Library]*

Flintshire, in Royal Mail colours, the ship on which the explorer Ernest Shackleton served as second mate. *[Peter Newall collection]*

S31. FLINTSHIRE (3) 1896-1913

O.N. 105833 3,815g 2,476n 364.0 x 45.2 x 27.7 feet.
T.3-cyl. by the North Eastern Marine Engineering Co. Ltd., Sunderland (25", 41½" and 69" x 45"); 400 NHP, 2,000 IHP, 11 knots.
29.4.1896: Launched by the Sunderland Shipbuilding Co. Ltd., Sunderland (Yard No. 183) for Jenkins and Co. Ltd., London.
1.6.1896: Completed.
4.6.1896: Registered at London.
20.9.1907: Transferred to the Royal Mail Steam Packet Company, London.
24.10.1913: Sold to Ellerman Lines Ltd., London (Hall Lines Ltd., Liverpool, managers).
22.11.1913: Registered at Liverpool as ALGERIAN.
12.1.1916: Sank after hitting a mine laid by the German submarine UC 5 one and a half miles south west of the Bridge Buoy off the Needles, Isle of Wight whilst on a voyage from Cowes to Avonmouth, light.
8.2.1916: Register closed.

S32. (CARDIGANSHIRE) (3) 1899

O.N. 110072 4,129g 2,560n 356.0 x 45.2 x 18.7 feet.
T.3-cyl. by the North Eastern Marine Engineering Co. Ltd., Sunderland (24", 40" and 64" x 42"); 292 NHP.
27.1.1899: Launched by the Sunderland Shipbuilding Co. Ltd., Sunderland (Yard No. 198) for Jenkins and Co. Ltd., London as CARDIGANSHIRE but sold whilst fitting out.
2.1899: Completed for Mitsui Bussan Gomei Kaisha, Mihara, Japan as TSURUGISAN MARU.
1923: Sold to Dairen Kisen K.K., Dairen, Manchuria and renamed OYAMA MARU.
1928: Sold to Fuji Shosen K.K., Dairen, Manchuria.

Flintshire in service as a United States Army transport at the time of the Spanish-American War. *[Peter Newall collection]*

1938: Sold to Sugaya K.K., Kobe, Japan and renamed MIHARU MARU.
14.12.1941: Foundered south of Hokkaido in position 41.55 north by 145.15 east.

S33. DENBIGHSHIRE (3) 1899-1919

O.N. 112630 3,844g 2,489n 356.0 x 45.2 x 18.7 feet.
T.3-cyl. by the North Eastern Marine Engineering Co. Ltd., Sunderland (24", 40" and 64" x 42"); 400 NHP, 1,450 IHP, 10 knots.
5.10.1899: Launched by the Sunderland Shipbuilding Co. Ltd., Sunderland (Yard No. 200) for Jenkins and Co. Ltd., London.
16.11.1899: Completed.
20.11.1899: Registered at London.
22.8.1907: Owners became the Royal Mail Steam Packet Company, London.

22.9.1919: Renamed TAMAR.
19.12.1922: Sold to Amelia Steamship Co. Ltd. (Logothettis and Rogers, managers), Newcastle-upon-Tyne.
24.5.1923: Renamed JOYCE NANCY.
25.9.1924: Sold to the Melissa Steamship Co. Ltd. (Demetrios and Stavros Antonaropulos, managers), London and Newcastle-upon-Tyne.
19.1.1925: Renamed SASSA.
15.10.1925: Sold by order of the Admiralty Marshall to George Vergottis, Argostoli, Greece and renamed ARGOSTOLI.
25.11.1925: Register closed.
1928: Sold to N. D. and J. D. Rossolymos and R. Harrisson, London and renamed AVGY, retaining the Greek flag.
8.1929: Gutted by fire.
24.11.1930: Arrived Danzig to be broken up.

Above: Denbighshire completed in November 1899 and photographed at Amsterdam on 10th June 1900 by W. M. Holtzapffel *[Gerrit J. de Boer]* Below: *Monmouthshire* in Shire colours when new. *[Peter Newall collection]*

S34. GLAMORGANSHIRE (3) 1900-1902
O.N. 112745 4,353g 2,830n 377.2 x 47.1 x 28.3 feet.
T.3-cyl. by the North Eastern Marine Engineering Co. Ltd., Sunderland. (25", 42" and 70" x 45"); 354 NHP, 1,800 IHP, 11 knots.
14.6.1900: Launched by the Sunderland Shipbuilding Co. Ltd., Sunderland (Yard No. 204) for Jenkins and Co. Ltd., London.
10.8.1900: Registered at London.
11.8.1900: Ran trials.
15.8.1900: Completed.
18.11.1902: Sold to Nippon Yusen K.K., Tokyo, Japan and renamed BOMBAY MARU.
2.12.1902: Register closed.
1923: Sold to Dai-Nippon Yengyo K.K., Tokyo, Japan.
1927: Sold to Shimizu Kitaro, Kobe, Japan.
1931: Sold to Tsutsui Seimatsu, Hyogo-ken, Japan.
1933: Sold to Iino Shoji, Tokyo for demolition and broken up during the fourth quarter of 1933.

S35. PEMBROKESHIRE (3) 1901
O.N. 113977 4,253g 2,775n 360.0 x 48.1 x 28.4 feet.
T.3-cyl. by the North Eastern Marine Engineering Co. Ltd., Sunderland (26", 42$^{1}/_{2}$" and 69$^{1}/_{2}$" x 45"); 353 HP, 1,760 IHP, 10 knots.
18.5.1901: Launched by the Sunderland Shipbuilding Co. Ltd., Sunderland (Yard No. 210) for Jenkins and Co. Ltd., London as PEMBROKESHIRE but subsequently sold.

15.6.1901: Ran trials for McLaren and McLaren, Glasgow as ALLANTON, but not accepted.
26.9.1901: Registered at Glasgow in the ownership of William R. Rea, Belfast.
13.1.1909: Clark and Service appointed managers by mortgagees.
10.8.1909: Sold to the Arecuna Steam Ship Co. Ltd. (Robert and Claud Allen, managers), Glasgow.
23.11.1911: Sold to John E. Wellwood, Belfast.
25.11.1911: Sold to Thomas Dixon and Sons, Belfast.
3.1.1918: Torpedoed and sunk by the German submarine UB 50 twenty miles north of Cape Bon whilst on a voyage from Hull to Malta with a cargo of coal.
1.2.1918: Register closed.

S36. PEMBROKESHIRE (4) 1901-1903
O.N. 114724 4,294g 2,767n 360.0 x 48.1 x 28.3 feet.
T.3-cyl. by the North Eastern Marine Engineering Co. Ltd., Sunderland (26",

42$^{1}/_{2}$" and 69$^{1}/_{2}$" x 45"); 353 NHP, 1,900 IHP, 11 knots.
4.7.1901: Launched by the Sunderland Shipbuilding Co. Ltd., Sunderland (Yard No. 209) for Jenkins and Co. Ltd., London.
31.7.1901: Registered at Liverpool.
1.8.1901: Ran trials.
1903: Sold to Mitsui Bussan Kaisha, Tokio, Japan and renamed MANDASAN MARU.
26.10.1903: Register closed.
1933: Broken up in Japan.

S37. MONMOUTHSHIRE (2) 1902-1919
O.N. 115893 5,092g 3,297n 400.0 x 52.0 x 28.1 feet.
T.3-cyl. by the North Eastern Marine Engineering Co. Ltd., Sunderland (28", 46" and 77" x 48"); 800 NHP, 3,000 IHP, 12 knots.
7.7.1902: Launched by the Sunderland Shipbuilding Co. Ltd., Sunderland (Yard No. 214) for Jenkins and Co. Ltd., London.

9.9.1902: Completed.
13.9.1902: Registered at London.
15.8.1907: Transferred to the Royal Mail Steam Packet Company, London.
10.4.1919: Renamed TYNE.
1922: Sold to Tokai Kisen K.K., Dairen, Manchuria (Nisshin Kaiun Shokai, Kobe, Japan, managers) and renamed TOKU MARU.
13.10.1922: Register closed.
12.1933: Sold to Japanese shipbreakers and demolished in 1934.

S38. CARDIGANSHIRE (4) 1906 - 1911
O.N. 96370. 4,014g. 2,696n. 400.6 x 45.2 x 28.1 feet.
T.3-cyl. by Harland and Wolff Ltd., Belfast (22½", 37" and 64" x 48"); 338 NHP.
24.8.1889: Launched by Harland and Wolff Ltd., Belfast (Yard No. 218) for T. and J. Brocklebank Ltd., Liverpool as AMEER.
7.10.1889: Registered at Liverpool.
9.8.1906: Renamed CARDIGANSHIRE.
1911: Sold to Tatsuma Kisen Goshi Kaisha, Nishinomiya, Japan and renamed HAKUSHIKA MARU.
28.7.1911: Register closed.
1916: Sold to Ginjiro Katsuda, Kobe, Japan and renamed IDE MARU.
1919: Sold to Figueras Steamship Co. Ltd., Hong Kong.
14.11.1919: Registered at Hong Kong as CARDIGANSHIRE.
14.5.1920: Renamed PACO FIGUERAS.
29.1.1921: Register closed on transfer to US flag, registered in Manila.
1923: Broken up at Hong Kong.

S39. CARNARVONSHIRE (3) 1906-1911
O.N. 97758 4,202g 2,710n 400.6 x 45.2 x 28.1 feet.
T.3-cyl. by Harland and Wolff Ltd., Belfast (22½", 37" and 64" x 48"); 320 NHP, 1,600 IHP, 9½ knots.
24.12.1889: Launched by Harland and Wolff Ltd., Belfast (Yard No. 219) for Sir Thomas, Thomas and Harold Brocklebank, Liverpool as GAEKWAR.
11.3.1890: Registered at Liverpool.
15.3.1890: Completed.
2.11.1895: Owners became Thomas and Harold Brocklebank, Liverpool.

Top: *Monmouthshire* of 1902, in Royal Mail colours, on 8th October 1912. *[F. W. Hawks]*
Middle: *Ameer* of 1899, later the *Cardiganshire*. *[J. and M. Clarkson collection]*
Bottom: *Carnarvonshire*, the former *Gaekwar* of 1890. *[W. A. Laxon collection]*

Pindari of 1891 at Amsterdam. Renamed *Breconshire* in 1906 and sold to Japanese buyers in 1911 she lasted until 1925. *[W.M. Holtzapffel/Gerrit J de Boer]*

28.9.1898: Owners became T. and J. Brocklebank Ltd., Liverpool.
6.10.1906: Renamed CARNARVONSHIRE.
1911: Sold to A/S Rethval (N. Fredriksen, manager), Christiania, Norway, converted to a whale factory ship and renamed FALKLAND.
16.8.1911: Register closed.
1914: Sold to Aktieselskapet Ørnen (Soren L. Christensen, manager), Sandefjord, Norway and renamed ORN 2.
1930: Sold to Hvalfangerselskapet Pontos A/S (Bruun and Von der Lippe, managers), Tønsberg, Norway and renamed PONTOS.
1934: Broken up by Jarlsø Verft, Tønsberg during the second quarter .

S40. BRECONSHIRE (3) 1906-1911
O.N. 99338 5,713g 3,696n 446.0 x 49.2 x 30.0 feet.

Two T.3-cyl. by Harland and Wolff Ltd., Belfast (19", 31" and 52" x 42") driving twin screws; 375 NHP, 10½ knots.
17.10.1891: Launched by Harland and Wolff Ltd., Belfast (Yard No. 245) for Sir Thomas, Thomas and Harold Brocklebank, Liverpool as PINDARI.
27.11.1891: Registered at Liverpool.
5.12.1891: Completed.
2.11.1895: Owners became Thomas and Harold Brocklebank, Liverpool.
28.9.1898: Owners became T. and J. Brocklebank Ltd., Liverpool.
14.12.1906: Renamed BRECONSHIRE (PEMBROKESHIRE also reported as having been proposed).
1911: Sold to Kishimoto Kisen K. K., Osaka, Japan, and renamed SHINYO MARU.
16.6.1911: Register closed.
1925: Broken up in Japan.

S41. GLAMORGANSHIRE (4) 1906-1913
O.N. 110637 5,659g 3,622n 445.0 x 50.2 x 30.1 feet.
T.3-cyl. by Gourlay Brothers and Company, Dundee (26½", 46" and 76" x 51"); 287 NHP, 3,000 IHP, 11½ knots.
16.12.1899: Launched by Gourlay Brothers and Company, Dundee (Yard No. 190) for T. and J. Brocklebank Ltd., Liverpool as MARWARRI.
16.2.1900: Registered at Liverpool.
25.10.1906: Renamed GLAMORGANSHIRE.
26.9.1913: Renamed MARWARRI.
1920: Sold to Ravano and Corrado, Genoa, Italy and renamed SANT'ANDREA.
6.2.1920: Register closed.
30.11.1924: Arrived at Genoa to be broken up.

Glamorganshire, the former *Marwarri*. *[Ships in Focus]*

S42. MONTGOMERYSHIRE (4) 1906-1913

O.N. 113454 5,665g 3,620n 445.0 x 50.2 x 30.1 feet.
T.3-cyl. by Gourlay Brothers and Company, Dundee (27", 46" and 76" x 51"); 286 NHP, 3,200 IHP, 12 knots.
20.12.1900: Launched by Gourlay Brothers and Company, Dundee (Yard No. 196) for T. and J. Brocklebank Ltd., Liverpool as BENGALI.
15.2.1901: Registered at London.
17.9.1906: Renamed MONTGOMERYSHIRE.
16.10.1913: Renamed BENGALI.
13.9.1917: Torpedoed by the German submarine UC 34 in the Mediterranean, in a position 115 miles north of Derna whilst on voyage from Tobruk to Alexandria and Calcutta in ballast.
17.9.1917: Beached at Derna, subsequently repaired and refloated.
8.4.1918: Sunk by a torpedo from the German submarine UC 34, 14 miles north of Alexandria whilst en route there for permanent repairs.
13.6.1918: Register closed.

S43. CARMARTHENSHIRE (3) 1909-1913

O.N. 98863 4,745g 3,047n 400.5 x 47.2 x 26.7 feet.
Two T.3-cyl. by Harland and Wolff Ltd., Belfast (18½", 30" and 50" x 42") driving twin screws; 418 NHP, 2,200 IHP, 11 knots.
16.2.1893: Launched by Harland and Wolff Ltd., Belfast (Yard No. 261) for the Union Steam Ship Co. Ltd., London as GAUL.
5.5.1893: Registered at London.
6.5.1893: Completed.
14.5.1900: Transferred to the Union-Castle Mail Steamship Co. Ltd., London.
6.7.1906: Sold to the Royal Mail Steam Packet Company, London.
13.8.1906: Renamed SABOR.
6.1909: Renamed CARMARTHENSHIRE.
4.11.1913: Renamed CHALEUR.
7.1927: Sold to N.V. Frank Rijsdijk's Industrieele Ondernemingen, Holland for demolition.
6.8.1927: Register closed.
15.8.1927: Delivered at Rotterdam. Subsequently broken up at Hendrik-Ido-Ambacht.

S44. PEMBROKESHIRE (5) 1909-1913

O.N. 98870 4,745g 2,999n 400.5 x 47.2 x 26.9 feet.
Two T.3-cyl. by Harland and Wolff Ltd., Belfast (18½", 30" and 50" x 42") driving twin screws; 418 NHP, 2,200 IHP, 11 knots.
18.5.1893: Launched by Harland and Wolff Ltd., Belfast (Yard No. 268) for the Union Steam Ship Co. Ltd., London as GREEK.
23.8.1893: Registered at London.
26.8.1893: Completed.
14.5.1900: Owners became the Union-Castle Mail Steamship Co. Ltd., London.
2.3.1906: Sold to Royal Mail Steam Packet Company, London.
16.6.1906: Renamed SEGURA.
27.9.1909: Renamed PEMBROKESHIRE.
4.11.1913: Renamed CHIGNECTO.
7.1927: Sold to N.V. Frank Rijsdijk's Industrieele Ondernemingen, Holland, for demolition.
20.7.1927: Register closed.
2.8.1927: Arrived at Rotterdam under tow from London. Subsequently broken up at Hendrik-Ido-Ambacht.

Above: *Bengali* later *Montgomeryshire*. *[J. and M. Clarkson collection]*
Below: *Carmarthenshire* at Charlton, River Thames, 3rd May 1913. *[F. W. Hawks]*

Above: *Pembrokeshire* on the River Thames 25th September 1912. *[F. W. Hawks]*
Below: *Chignecto*, ex *Pembrokeshire*. *[Nautical Photo Agency/World Ship Photo Library]*

Radnorshire launched as *Salopian* at Sunderland in 1913. *[Peter Newall collection]*

Merionethshire, launched in August 1913 as *Reptonian* for the Cambrian Steam Navigation Co. Ltd. *[W. A. Laxon collection]*

S45. RADNORSHIRE (3) 1913-1917
O.N. 135237 4,302g 2,694n 385.0 x 52.0 x 25.1 feet.
T.3-cyl. by John Dickinson and Sons Ltd., Sunderland (26", 43" and 71" x 48"); 401 NHP, 1,960 IHP, 11½ knots.
22.5.1913: Launched by Bartram and Sons Ltd., Sunderland (Yard No. 228) for the Cambrian Steam Navigation Co. Ltd. (John Mathias and Sons managers), Aberystwyth as SALOPIAN but sold whilst fitting out.
28.6.1913: Registered in the ownership of the Royal Mail Steam Packet Company, London as RADNORSHIRE.
2.7.1913: Completed and ran trials.

7.1.1917: Captured and sunk by explosives by the German raider MOEWE in the South Atlantic 110 miles east of Pernambuco in approximate position 08.00 south by 33.00 west whilst on a voyage from Santos to London with a cargo of coffee.
22.3.1917: Register closed.

S46. MERIONETHSHIRE (3) 1913-1918
O.N. 135277 4,308g 2,686n 385.0 x 52.0 x 25.1 feet.
T.3-cyl. by John Dickinson and Sons Ltd., Sunderland (26", 43" and 71" x 48"); 401 NHP; 1,960 IHP, 11½ knots.
20.8.1913: Launched by Bartram and Sons

Ltd., Sunderland (Yard No. 229) for the Cambrian Steam Navigation Co. Ltd. (John Mathias and Sons, managers), Aberystwyth as REPTONIAN but sold whilst fitting out.
11.10.1913: Registered in the ownership of the Royal Mail Steam Packet Company, London as MERIONETHSHIRE.
15.10.1913: Completed and ran trials.
27.5.1918: Sunk by a torpedo from the German submarine U 62 in a position 120 miles north by half east (true) from Flores, Azores whilst on a voyage from London to Rio de Janiero with general cargo.
22.8.1918: Register closed.

Cardiganshire. [World Ship Photo Library]

S47. CARDIGANSHIRE (5) 1913-1929
O.N. 132045 9,426g 5,993n 500.3 x 62.4 x
34.6 feet.
Two T.3-cyl. by Workman, Clark and Co.
Ltd., Belfast (24", 40½" and 68" x 48")
driving twin screws; 977 NHP; 12½ knots.
30.9.1913: Launch attempted by
Workman, Clark and Co. Ltd., Belfast
(Yard No. 324) but failed to enter the water
fully.
2.10.1913: Successfully launched for the
Royal Mail Steam Packet Company, London.
21.11.1913: Registered at Belfast.
25.11.1913: Ran trials and completed.
13.5.1929: Sold to the South Georgia Co.
Ltd. (Christian Salvesen and Co., managers),
Leith for £75,000 for conversion to a whale
factory ship.
29.7.1929: Renamed SALVESTRIA;
tonnages now 11,938g 8,597n.
7.4.1930: Registered at Port Stanley,
Falkland Islands.

17.8.1935: Registered at Dublin.
8.8.1939: Registered at Jersey.
27.7.1940: Mined and sunk 2.8 miles north
east of Inchkeith, Firth of Forth in position
56.04 north by 03.05 west whilst on a voyage
from Aruba to Grangemouth with a cargo of
9,201 tons of fuel oil. Ten of her crew of 57
were lost.
5.9.1945: Register closed.

S48. CARNARVONSHIRE (4) 1914-1935
O.N. 132049 9,406g 5,955n 500.3 x 62.4 x
34.6 feet.
Two T.3-cyl. by Workman, Clark and Co.
Ltd., Belfast (24", 40½" and 68" x 48")
driving twin screws; 978 NHP, 5,000 IHP,
12½ knots.
13.12.1913: Launched by Workman, Clark
and Co. Ltd., Belfast (Yard No. 325) for
Royal Mail Steam Packet Company, London.

5.3.1914: Registered at Belfast.
7.3.1914: Completed at a cost of £170,095.
12.10.1932: Owners became Royal Mail
Lines Ltd., London.
8.4.1933: Owners became Glen Line Ltd.,
London.
1.10.1935: Sold to The Red 'R' Steamship
Co. Ltd. and the Whalton Shipping Co. Ltd.
(Stephens, Sutton Ltd., managers),
Newcastle-upon-Tyne for £20,000 in order
to be traded in under the Government's
'Scrap and Build' scheme.
14.10.1935: Sold to Pedder and Mylchreest
Ltd., London.
10.1935: Sold to Italian shipbreakers for
£17,500, but contract cancelled.
1936: Resold to Amakasa Sangyo Kisen
K.K., Osaka, Japan for £20,000.
26.2.1936: Arrived at Osaka.
29.10.1936: Register closed.

Carnarvonshire. [Ships in Focus]

Carmarthenshire. [Martin Lindenborn]

S49. CARMARTHENSHIRE (4)
1915-1929
O.N. 136347 7,823g 4,969n 470.2 x 58.4 x 32.2 feet.
Q.4-cyl. by Workman, Clark and Co. Ltd., Belfast (27½", 39½", 57" and 82" x 54"); 735 NHP, 3,750 IHP, 12 knots.
5.11.1914: Launched by Workman, Clark and Co. Ltd., Belfast (Yard No. 336) for the Royal Mail Steam Packet Company, London.
3.2.1915: Registered at Belfast.
8.4.1917: Pursued by the German submarine U 55 south west of Lands End.
1924: Placed on Glen-Shire service to the Far East.
5.4.1929: Sold to South Georgia Co. Ltd. (Christian Salvesen and Co., managers), Leith for £66,500 in order to be converted to a whale factory ship.
29.7.1929: Renamed SOURABAYA (10,107g 7,194n).

15.6.1931: Registered at Port Stanley, Falkland Islands.
17.5.1935: Registered at Dublin.
8.8.1939: Registered at Jersey.
27.10.1942: Torpedoed and sunk by the German submarine U 436 in the North Atlantic in position 54.32 north by 31.02 west whilst on a voyage from New York to Liverpool in Convoy HX.212 with a cargo of 7,800 tons of fuel oil and 200 tons of war stores with heavy loss of life. Twenty-six crew, four gunners, 16 distressed British seamen and 31 passengers were lost from her crew of 63, 8 gunners, 32 D.B.S. and 55 passengers.
5.9.1945: Register closed.

S50. PEMBROKESHIRE (6) 1915-1933
O.N. 136349 7,821g 4,968n 470.2 x 58.3 x 32.2 feet.
Q.4-cyl. by Workman, Clark and Co. Ltd.,

Belfast (27½", 39½", 57" and 82" x 54"); 735 NHP, 3,750 IHP, 12 knots.
17.12.1914: Launched by Workman, Clark and Co. Ltd., Belfast (Yard No. 337) for the Royal Mail Steam Packet Company, London.
13.4.1915: Registered at Belfast.
13.4.1915: Completed at a cost of £155,689.
12.10.1932: Owners became Royal Mail Lines Ltd.
8.4.1933: Owners became Glen Line Ltd., London.
24.1.1936: Sold to Queen Line Ltd. (Thomas Dunlop and Sons, managers), Glasgow for £19,750 in order to be traded in under the Government's 'Scrap and Build' scheme.
1936: Sold to Danzig breakers for £14,700.
4.4.1936: Arrived at Danzig.
23.4.1936: Register closed.

Pembrokeshire on 14th July 1934. *[F. W. Hawks/Roy Fenton collection]*

S51. BRECKNOCKSHIRE 1917
O.N. 136359 8,422g 5,351n 470.2 x 60.3 x 32.3 feet.
Q.4-cyl. by Harland and Wolff Ltd., Belfast (27$\frac{1}{2}$", 39$\frac{1}{2}$", 57" and 82$\frac{1}{2}$" x 54"); 778 NHP, 3,500 IHP, 11$\frac{1}{2}$ knots.
12.9.1916: Launched by Harland and Wolff Ltd., Belfast (Yard No. 453) for the Royal Mail Steam Packet Company, London
10.1.1917: Registered at Belfast.
11.1.1917: Completed.
15.2.1917: Captured and sunk by gunfire by the German raider MOEWE in the South Atlantic 490 miles east by north (true) of Cape Frio whilst outward bound on her maiden voyage from Liverpool to Rio de Janeiro with a cargo of coal.
25.4.1917: Register closed.

S52. GLAMORGANSHIRE (5) 1919-1933
O.N. 142426 8,192g 5045n 445.0 x 58.0 x 40.0 feet.
Two T.3-cyl. by Ishikawajima Shipbuilding Co., Tokyo* (22", 36$\frac{1}{2}$" and 61" x 48") driving twin screws; 703 NHP, 5,600 IHP.
12.1917: Completed by Asano Shipbuilding Company, Tsurumi, Japan (Yard No. 6) for the ownership of the Shipping Controller (Royal Mail Steam Packet Company, managers), London as WAR ARMOUR
21.5.1918: Registered at London.
23.10.1919: Acquired by the Royal Mail Steam Packet Company, London.
28.10.1919: Renamed GLAMORGANSHIRE.
12.10.1932: Owners became Royal Mail Lines Ltd. London.
4.2.1933: Register closed.
5.1933: Broken up by N. V. Frank Rijsdijk's Industrieele Ondernemingen at Hendrik Ido Ambacht, Holland.

* According to Lloyd's Register Kobe Steel Works Ltd., Kobe built the engines.

Above: The only photographs known of *Brecknockshire* were taken at her launch on 12th September 1916. There are no views of her trials in the builder's archives, and with a wartime life of just over a month there was little chance of others taking her. [Ulster Folk and Transport Museum H2282]
Below: *Glamorganshire* - a Japanese built First World War standard type steamer. [J. and M. Clarkson collection]

S53. RADNORSHIRE (4) 1919-1930

O.N. 143441 6,723g 4,133n 412.5 x 55.5 x 34.4 feet.

T.3-cyl. by John Dickinson and Sons Ltd., Sunderland (27", 44" and 73" x 48"); 597 NHP, 2,800 IHP, $10^{3/4}$ knots.

1919: Laid down by J.L. Thompson and Sons, Sunderland (Yard No. 538) for the Shipping Controller, London as WAR DIAMOND.

12.6.1919: Launched for the Royal Mail Steam Packet Company, London as RADNORSHIRE.

2.10.1919: Registered at London.

12.1919: Completed.

1922: Placed on Glen-Shire service to the Far East.

1924: Returned to Royal Mail.

1929: Placed on Glen-Shire service to the Far East.

27.3.1930: Sold to Henry M. Thomson, Edinburgh for £36,000.

4.10.1930: Renamed SITHONIA.

13.7.1942: Torpedoed and sunk by the German submarine U 201 north west of the Canary Islands in approximate position 29 north by 25 west whilst on a voyage from Barry and Belfast Lough to Montevideo with a cargo of 8,026 tons of coal in convoy OS.33. Seven of her crew of 53 were lost.

21.4.1943: Register closed.

S54. MONTGOMERYSHIRE (5) 1920-1931

O.N. 145246 6,650g 4,097n 412.3 x 55.8 x 34.7 feet.

Two steam turbines by C.A. Parsons and Co. Ltd., Newcastle-upon-Tyne double-reduction geared to a single shaft; 676 NHP, 2,300 SHP, $10^{1/4}$ knots.

1932: Oil engine 4-cyl. 2SCSA by Societa Anonima 'Fiat' S.G., Turin, Italy (760 mm x 1,200 mm); 610 NHP, 3,050 BHP.

1919: Laid down by Sir W.G. Armstrong, Whitworth and Co. Ltd., Newcastle-upon-Tyne (Yard No. 961) for the Shipping Controller, London as WAR VALOUR.

27.10.1920: Launched as MONTGOMERYSHIRE.

4.1921: Completed.

21.6.1921: Registered in the ownership of the Royal Mail Steam Packet Company, London.

Above: A policeman watches as *Radnorshire* waits in the locks. *[Nautical Photo Agency/J. and M. Clarkson collection]*
Below: *Radnorshire* as *Sithonia* *[Ships in Focus]*

1922: Chartered for government service in the eastern Mediterranean during the Greek-Turkish crisis.

8.1923: Returned to commercial service.

1928: Placed on Glen-Shire service to the Far East.

1929: Returned to Royal Mail.

1931: Sold to Societa Commerciale di Navigazione, Genoa, Italy for £18,000 and renamed RIV.

13.10.1931: Register closed.

1932: Re-engined.

6.4.1941: Bombed and damaged by British aircraft in the Mediterranean. Reached Tripoli.

29-30.8.1941: Again bombed and sunk by British aircraft in Tripoli harbour whilst awaiting repairs. Later refloated by British salvors and broken up.

Montgomeryshire in Royal Mail colours. *[W. A. Laxon collection]*

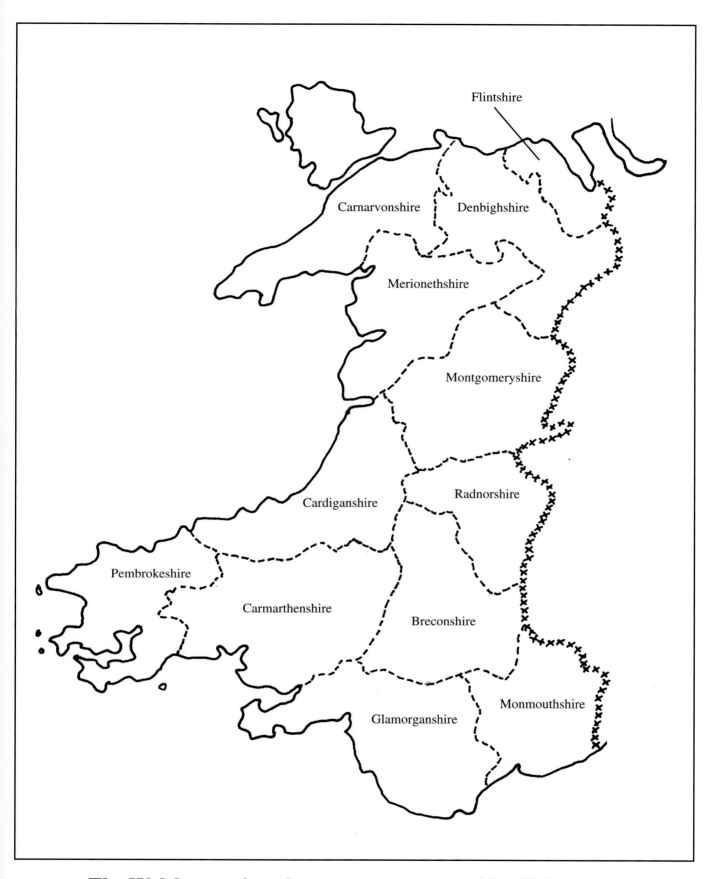

The Welsh counties whose names were used by Shire Line.

The short-lived *Brecknockshire* of 1917 used an old name for Breconshire.
The names of the counties shown disappeared in the local government reorganisation of 1974.

Glenorchy is secured in the entrance lock to the King George V Dock. Pierhead staff handle the ship's ropes with the Dockmaster watching. *[Peter Newall collection]*

GLEN LINE
Malcolm Cooper

The road to the glens

Two of the most important nineteenth century events in the history of maritime commerce happened within a few years of each other in the 1860s. In the middle years of the decade, the development of a reliable and fuel-efficient compound steam engine opened up the possibility of using steamships on long ocean routes where hitherto only subsidised mail lines had been able to operate at a profit. In 1869 the Suez Canal opened, eliminating the need to make the long voyage around Africa to reach the rapidly growing markets of India and the Far East, and thus cutting the voyage east by a staggering 8,000 miles. These two events together spawned some of the most famous companies ever to operate fleets under the red ensign. The most notable (and durable) was the Liverpool-based Blue Funnel fleet of Alfred Holt and Co., which had actually begun to build up its fleet before the Canal opened, but rapidly capitalised upon it to become the pre-eminent non-mail line on the service to the Far East. A number of other new concerns soon began to compete with Holts, particularly for the lucrative carriage of China tea back to home markets, a business in which compound-engined steamships gained one of their earliest victories over the sailing ships which still made up the huge majority of the world's ocean-going vessels. Notable among the early entries to the trade were Thomas Skinner's Castle Line, David Jenkins' Shire Line, and the Glen Line of A.C. Gow and Co. It was the third of these which was to prove the most successful of Blue Funnel's rivals.

Like many of the new British steamship companies which began life in the second half of the nineteenth century, the Glen Line had its origins in a rather modest shipbroking business. Allan Carsewell Gow had been born in Glasgow in 1823, the son of an Arbroath merchant. When he came of age, he found employment in the shipbroking office of Galbreath and Carsewell, a firm set up by some of his mother's relatives. While still in his twenties, Allan C. Gow entered business on his account as a ship and insurance agent under the name A.C. Gow and Co., soon persuading his younger brother Leonard away from a career in the church to join him. The elder brother appears to have made only one venture into shipowning, registering the Miramichi-built barque *Fleetwood* (543/1851) at Glasgow on 24th September 1858. Gow died of typhus at Kilcreggan in January 1859 and the *Fleetwood* was wrecked two months later. By this time, however, the Gows had obtained a new partner, a man who was to become more closely associated with the success of A.C. Gow and Co.'s most famous venture than either of the brothers.

James McGregor had been born three years after Allan Gow, in the small Banffshire village of Tomintoul. Although it has since become associated with a notable malt whisky distillery, even this distinction was far in the future in the early nineteenth century. As late as the 1880s, it was described as 'the dirtiest, poorest village in the whole of the Highlands.' It was hardly surprising that McGregor moved from it as a young man to seek his fortune in Glasgow, finding employment as a clerk with A.C. Gow and Co. and rising to be a partner soon before the founder's premature death.

The first moves of Leonard Gow and James McGregor into shipowning came in 1867 on two separate fronts. They purchased a 13-year old wooden sailing ship, *Jane Leech*, from a Liverpool owner. Almost simultaneously they took a majority share in a new iron barque building at the Port Glasgow yard of Laurence Hill and Co. The vessel, to be managed by A.C. Gow and Co., was called *Estrella de Chile*, and as her name suggests, she was intended for the trade with the west coast of South America. There may have

been an element of speculation in these first investments, and *Jane Leech* would last only four years before being lost, but they were quickly followed by others which, both by nomenclature and intended trade, have more claim to be the forerunners of later and greater endeavours.

In 1868-69, A.C. Gow and Co. ordered a series of three quite different iron sailing vessels, all from the Dumbarton yard of Archibald McMillan and Son. The first, *Glenavon*, was a medium-sized ship intended for the Far East trade. She was followed by the much larger *Glenorchy*, a fully-fledged clipper ship of 1,286 tons register. *Glenorchy* was wrecked in the Irish Sea, outward bound for India on her first voyage, and perhaps because of this, the third vessel, *Glenaray*, was a much more modest 661-ton barque. The choice of names for the last three vessels is almost certainly evidence that James McGregor was taking more and more of a leading role in the firm. All three ships were named not only after Highland glens, but also after glens with a strong personal or Clan McGregor connection. *Glenaray* would be sold after only four years trading, while *Glenavon* was also finally sold in 1880. *Estrella de Chile* remained under A.C. Gow colours for her entire life, eventually being wrecked in the Solway Firth in 1888. By this time, however, a much larger steam enterprise had eclipsed the sail interests of the founders, and in this context another new building was perhaps more significant. Six months after *Glenaray* took to the water, McMillan launched a small composite screw brig, *Eastern Isles*, for the partnership. She would be sold within five years, but she was very much a harbinger of greater things to come.

With the firm already involved in the trade to the east, it was perhaps not surprising that it decided to move decisively into steam when the Suez Canal opened. The first iron steam ship was ordered from the Govan yard of the London and Glasgow Engineering and Iron Ship Building Co. Ltd. Launched on 27th August 1870, *Glengyle* marked a fairly conservative debut in iron steamship ownership. At just over 1,600 tons gross register, she was significantly smaller than the trio of vessels with which Alfred Holt and Co. inaugurated their Far East service. Holts, however, had already built up significant experience in steam, while Gow and McGregor were new to the concept. In addition, *Glengyle*, costing £25,700, represented a fairly conservative capital investment, an important consideration given that the partners must still have had limited resources themselves, and did not yet have a big enough reputation to attract a large number of outside shareholders.

Glengyle left the Clyde of her maiden voyage on 11th October 1870, calling at Liverpool to complete her cargo before finally departing for the east on 2nd November. She was destined not for China, but for Madras and Calcutta in India. It is not clear whether Gow and McGregor at this stage were already intent on entering the China route or whether the object was still simply to trade to the Far East in general. It is probable that the venture was still an experimental one, and that the choice of initial destination was driven by the fact that it was one of which the partners already had experience. In any event, *Glengyle's* maiden voyage proved a success, with a profit of just under £5,000 being declared after her arrival in London in May 1871. By this stage, Gow and McGregor had definitely moved their attention to China. *Glengyle* was despatched on her second voyage to Shanghai. More importantly, the partners had already ordered a new vessel for the same service.

The second Glen steamer also came from the London and Glasgow yard, which was to build all but four of the company's nineteenth century ships. Such close connections between builders and owners were not uncommon in the early decades of steam, and were often reinforced by significant cross shareholdings between the two parties. The new vessel represented a significant step forward in size, speed and cost over her predecessor. *Glenroy*, launched on 14th October 1871, was more than 50 feet longer than *Glengyle* and was powered by a compound steam engine rated at 250 nominal horse power compared to the smaller vessel's 185. At £36,800 she was also almost fifty percent more expensive. *Glenroy* represented the real start of the Gow and McGregor challenge to the established players in the China trade. James McGregor, already the driving force in the business, had decided that size and, more importantly speed, were the key ingredients to success in a business where the fast carriage of teas from China still brought the greatest rewards.

The best working plant in the trade
The early sailings of the fleet were extremely profitable. Of nine round trips completed by the end of 1873, only one, the fifth voyage of *Glengyle*, did not earn a satisfactory return. More than half the voyages earned a profit of over £5,000, with *Glenroy* getting off to a particularly felicitous start. Although not to be as famous as some of her later sisters, she was actually one of the more profitable ships in the fleet. She had more than covered her cost by the end of her eleventh voyage in early 1878, and the proceeds of her sale in 1889

Voyage Results, 1871-1873				
Year	Closing date	Vessel	Voyage No.	Profit
1871	21st April	*Glengyle*	1	£4,893
	12th September	*Glengyle*	2	£3,331
1872	14th February	*Glengyle*	3	£5,961
	4th September	*Glenroy*	1	£8,127
	18th October	*Glengyle*	4	£7,624
	26th December	*Glenroy*	2	£6,283
1873	9th June	*Glengyle*	5	£351
	2nd October	*Glenlyon*	1	£8,077
	31st December	*Glenroy*	3	£6,656

brought the total earned in excess of her building costs (£36,800) and an 1880 engine and boiler refit (£8,290) to just over £57,000. Over her life, she thus returned to investors both their original capital and an additional 155%.

The successful *Glenroy* was used as a model for a series of five sisters, all delivered by London and Glasgow between 1872 and 1874. Hull dimensions and deck fittings were broadly similar in all six ships, but engine size was progressively increased as owner and builder pushed for higher speeds to meet the demands of the tea trade. The first arrival was *Glenlyon*, delivered in November 1872 at a cost of £41,310. She was followed in June 1873 by *Glenfalloch*, and then by *Glenartney* and *Glenearn* in October and December of the same year. The sextet was completed in May 1874 by *Glenfinlas*. *Glenfalloch* cost £49,900, and the last three an average of £55,500 each. Most of the increment in cost was due to larger engine size. Nominal horsepower went up from 250 in *Glenroy* to 275 in the next two vessels, and 320 in the last three.

The new vessels and the increasing investment in speed paid good dividends for the Glen ships. The most important feature of the business year was the annual race to deliver the first China teas of the season to home markets. There were two reasons why owners like Gow and McGregor were prepared to spend more in search of success in this race. The first was the immediate financial reward, in the form of premium freight rates for making the fastest passage. This remained just as critical with the steamships of the 1870s and 1880s as it had with the famous clipper ships of the 1860s. Equally important to steamship owners, however, was the need to build a reputation for a fast and efficient service. Such a reputation could be used as a foundation to build good relations with both outward and homeward customers, and allow a firm to command a steady flow of cargo at attractive rates on a year-round basis.

Of the six sisters delivered between 1871 and 1874, the fourth *Glenartney* was to prove the fastest. She actually won the homeward tea race for three years in a row between 1874 and 1876, reducing her passage time on each occasion. Although all of the steamship companies joined in the competition for early season tea cargoes, Glen's most persistent rival in the race itself was the Castle fleet of Thomas Skinner. Until the early 1880s, each successive step forward

A painting of *Glenartney* of 1873, the most successful tea steamer of her time, breaking the record for the fastest homeward passage in three successive years, 1874, 1875 and 1876. *[Peter Newall collection]*

A painting by a Chinese artist depicts *Glencoe*, Glen's last record breaker from the age of tea races, winning in 1880 and 1881. *[Peter Newall collection]*

in engine capacity by one company was quickly matched or exceeded by the other. Skinner would eventually build the fastest ship to enter the trade during the tea race era, and would win two consecutive races with her in the early 1880s at ruinous expense to his firm. For most of the rest of the period in question, it was the Glen ships which triumphed, thus establishing the groundwork for a highly successful and expanding business.

The Glen-Castle rivalry intensified as the decade wore on, but in the early years, with neither company having sufficient tonnage to offer a regular service, there was actually a degree of cooperation. Although A.C. Gow was the first to enter steam, Skinner was the better established shipowner, managing a medium-sized fleet of sailing clippers before he added his first steamer in 1872. Both businesses had started in Glasgow, but both soon moved to London, which was the focal point of both outward and homeward business with the Far East. Skinner arrived first, and in 1873 was actually advertising the first sailings of the new Gow ships *Glenfalloch* and *Glenartney* as part of his Castle Line service. The Glen steam business soon moved its headquarters to London as well, establishing a new firm, called McGregor, Gow and Co. to reflect James McGregor's leading role, to act as London agents for the China service. The formal notice of opening for the London business was dated 10th November 1873, but correspondence makes clear that the branch was actually in operation by October.

The London-based service was initially advertised simply as the 'India, China and Japan Line of Steamers', but by mid-decade all sailings were being advertised under the Glen Line banner. Formal management of the ships themselves stayed with A.C. Gow and Co. until 1880 when it was finally transferred to McGregor, Gow and Co. A.C. Gow and Co. remained in existence, running the remaining sailing ships, acting as Glen Line's agents for occasional sailings from Glasgow, and running some tramp steamers on its own account, beginning with *Waterloo* in 1879. The Glasgow firm also acted as managers of an Atlantic passenger business, the State Line, from 1875 and of the newly incorporated Scotia Shipping Co. Ltd., whose sailing ships flew the Gow flag, from 1877.

With the steam fleet having reached a strength of seven in four and a half years, there was a pause in fleet expansion at mid-decade. There was a sharp dip in the trade cycle in these years, and while the Glen ships made reasonable profits, their owners were given sufficient cause to be cautious. A new vessel, to be called *Gleneagles*, was actually advertised in the company's advertisements at the beginning of 1874,

but the ship was not actually to be built until 1877. In these mid-decade years, Glen made some use of chartered tonnage to extend its number of sailings, as did other London-based fleets such as Skinner's Castles and Jenkins' Shires. A.C. Gow and Co.'s newly acquired management of the State Line proved of assistance in acquiring chartered tonnage. The State Line had suffered severely from the drop in emigrant traffic caused by the trade depression, and was forced to move most of its ships temporarily off its Atlantic passenger service. Two of them, *State of Louisiana* and *State of Alabama*, spent brief periods on the Glen service in 1876-77. Neither appears to have done particularly well, and both were soon returned to the Atlantic, the first ship after making two round trips and the second after only one (including two chartered voyages between Calcutta and Macao). Initially it had been hoped to make larger and more permanent use of State tonnage to build the Glen service up into a 'continuous line', but trade conditions simply would not support such a move.

The next permanent addition to the fleet did not appear until almost two years after *Glenfinlas*, coming not from the builders but from the second-hand market. *Glenorchy* had been built on the Clyde at John Elder's Govan yard in 1871 as *Willem III* for a Dutch company. She had been seriously damaged by fire in the Channel on her maiden voyage and abandoned to the underwriters at Plymouth. Repaired, she entered the British merchant marine as *Quang-Se* and had served several owners in quick succession before McGregor bought her for £45,000 in January 1876. Although slightly shorter than the *Glenroy-Glenfinlas* sisters, she was more than 10% broader in beam, and with a gross tonnage just short of 2,800 tons became the largest vessel in the fleet. Designed for the Far East trade, with sufficient speed to keep pace with the London and Glasgow ships, she was to prove a reasonable purchase. Even though she was never one of the highest earners, she would outlive all but one of her predecessors in Glen colours.

1870s expansion was completed by the arrival of three more vessels in 1877-78. None of these were sisters. *Gleneagles*, finally delivered in February 1877, and *Glencoe*, completed in December 1878, were both built by London and Glasgow. Each represented a jump forward in size and engine capacity, driven by the desire to maintain the company's reputation for speed in the annual tea race. Not surprisingly, building costs continued to escalate, *Gleneagles* costing £60,220 and *Glencoe* £63,319. Each vessel therefore cost more than twice as much as the pioneer *Glengyle*. This expense did buy significant larger and faster ships. *Glencoe* was more than 100 feet longer than *Glengyle* and was powered by engines of almost three times the nominal horsepower. It also bought continued success in the annual race to bring new season teas back to London. *Gleneagles* was narrowly beaten by Skinner's new *Loudoun Castle* (2,472/1876) in her inaugural year, but reversed the verdict in the following year. *Glencoe* made the fastest homewards sailing twice in 1880-1881. Nonetheless, capital calls on the managing partners and what was still a fairly small circle of private investors had increased significantly over the decade.

The other new addition to the fleet might well have been the result of a search for cheaper tonnage. At the end of 1877, McGregor purchased the steamship *Ladybird*, building at Sunderland for a London owner, while the ship was still on the stocks. Completed as *Gleniffer*, the vessel cost only £30,647, half the price of the London and Glasgow ships being built at the same time. Writing to his agents in China a few months after the purchase, McGregor explained: 'We fear fast boats are not sufficiently appreciated, as we find slow going vessels with small consumption get the same rates of freight as our fast going vessels and are of course very much more profitable.' While this may well have been the recipe on which the rival Blue Funnel service was built, it was not to prove successful for Glen. *Gleniffer* was actually to be the only non-Clyde-built vessel to join the fleet until 1889. She was also, however, destined to be sold after the shortest service life of any nineteenth century vessel not lost to marine hazard. An old-fashioned looking vessel compared to her fleet mates, *Gleniffer* was significantly smaller and slower than every other ship except *Glengyle* and would not prove able to earn a high enough return to justify her retention when more new ships could be built. Despite McGregor's apparently temporary misgivings, speed and size were to remain better guarantors of profits for the Glen fleet.

Early financial performance

After the arrival of *Glencoe*, there was to be another pause of more than two years in fleet development. This allows an opportunity to look back at the financial performance of the Glen Line during its first decade of existence. As the fleet itself did not have a single corporate entity, there were no consolidated financial statements, but a good overview can be gained from aggregating voyage results, for which a complete set exist up until 1881. Total voyage profits doubled between 1872 and 1877, and doubled again between 1877 and 1881. While there was some fluctuation due to varying trade conditions, average voyage profits remained satisfactorily high throughout, with the last years bringing returns similar to those of the first, after something of a trough at mid-decade. If we assume an average capital cost per vessel of £55,000, then a ship could be expected to pay for itself in a perfectly satisfactory 12-14 years if earnings could be maintained at the average of the years covered.

Voyage profits, 1871-1881				
Year	Ships at year end	Voyages completed	Total profits £	Voyage average £
1871	2	2	8,224	4,112
1872	3	4	27,994	6,999
1873	6	3	15,082	5,027
1874	7	10	28,972	2,897
1875	7	13	38,490	2,961
1876	8	13	37,710	2,901
1877	10	16	65,377	4,086
1878	11	16	60,790	3,799
1879	11	20	54,038	2,702
1880	11	22	108,568	4,935
1881	13	24	134,399	5,600
			Average per voyage	4,184

The dramatic increase in both total profits and average voyage profits was not the product of an improvement in trading conditions as much as it was a dramatic change in the organization of the trade itself. Increasing competition had been driving rates down throughout the late 1870s, and in August 1879, the Far East Freight Conference came into being (almost entirely through the efforts of John Swire) in an effort to protect the participating shipowners from potentially ruinous rate-cutting. The mechanism of shipping conferences, and the often stormy history of the pioneering Far East example have been well documented and will not be covered in depth here. From the Glen point of view, there can be no doubt that the conference itself was a very positive innovation. A smaller firm with a less extensive capital base than either P&O's subsidized mail service or the Holt's well-established Blue Funnel fleet, it had everything to gain from an arrangement which helped protect the market position it had won. With the largest and best equipped of the smaller fleets, Glen also tended to receive good rates from the conference system, normally on par with those of Blue Funnel, and at a premium to those of either Castle or Shire.

One of the principles of the arrangement was agreement on exclusivity of homeward berths. This meant that Glen would become and remain very much an east coast firm and Blue Funnel a west coast one. Although Glen ships would occasionally call at Liverpool on homeward voyages, and Blue Funnel ships would make sporadic appearances on Glen's London berth, this was normally done on an agreed short-term basis. In some senses the division of the UK berths along geographical lines actually cemented Holt's existing advantage, as Liverpool was the more natural outlet for the Midlands textiles and industrial goods which made up the largest part of Britain's growing Far East exports in the late 1870s and throughout the 1880s. This notwithstanding, there can be little doubt that the protection of its London berth did benefit Glen in the early years. It would, however, leave it far more exposed than Blue Funnel when competition from foreign companies intensified towards the end of the century.

The complete set of voyage results for Glen's first decade also allows an interesting analysis of comparative performance between vessels. Six of the first seven vessels in the fleet were near sisters, with increased engine power being the only significant difference across the class. Each was clearly more profitable than the smaller and slower *Glengyle*, which was also troubled by leaky boilers from early in her career and eventually required expensive repairs. Although all the larger ships were successful, there was considerable variation in financial performance between them. This cannot be explained entirely in terms of engine power. Indeed, given the far higher freights that could be earned by catching the first tea cargoes, timing and luck must have been at least as important, and from the very beginnings of the service there had been considerable juggling with short-term coastal charters in the Far East in an attempt both to extract extra revenues from vessels and to have as many as possible available for the peak season tea sailings.

The faster, larger vessels introduced towards the end of the decade were also very profitable in their early years. *Gleneagles* had covered her building costs by the end of her tenth voyage and *Glencoe* had covered hers by the end of her eighth voyage. *Glencoe*, in fact, was to prove the most successful vessel to enter the nineteenth century fleet, earning twice as much per voyage as the mid-1870s record setter *Glenartney*. A comparison of the voyage results of *Glencoe* and *Gleniffer* provides clear confirmation that size and speed were still a better recipe for success than inexpensive construction.

Reorganisation and re-equipment

1881-82 saw some reorganisation of the fleet, following on from the formal transfer of management to McGregor, Gow and Co. In 1881, the pioneering *Glengyle* was sold to British owners. She was followed out of the service a year later by *Gleniffer*, which hoisted the French flag after only seven round trips to the Far East. Both vessels had performed respectably, but

Comparative vessel performance, 1871-1881							
	Glengyle	*Glenroy*	*Glenlyon*	*Glenfalloch*	*Glenartney*	*Glenearn*	*Glenfinlas*
Completed	1870	1871	1872	1873	1873	1873	1874
Cost	£25,700	£36,800	£41,310	£49,900	£55,136	£55,324	£56,156
Voyages	19	17	15	15	15	16	14
Total earnings	£37,128	£65,691	£43,404	£57,134	£71,575	£69,467	£48,536
Average per voyage	£1,954	£3,864	£2,894	£3,809	£4,768	£4,341	£3,467
Boiler account	(£7,117)	(£8,290)	-	-	-	-	-
Credit balance 12.1881	£4,311	£20,601	£2,094	£7,234	£16,379	£14,137	(£7,620)
Voyages to cover cost*	10/18	11/13	15	14	12	14	17

*For vessels undergoing boiler/engine refits, first figure shows voyage when initial building cost covered, second figure voyage when all cost covered. *Glenfinlas* did not cover her cost until 1883.

Gleniffer vs *Glencoe*, 1879-1882

	Gleniffer				*Glencoe*			
Tonnage	2,165g				2,913g			
Dimensions	291.0 x 34.7 x 24.6 feet.				387.2 x 38.2 x 26.5 feet.			
Engine	C.2-cyl. 26 inches/58 inches x 45 inches, 250 NHP				C.2-cyl. 48 inches/88 inches x 60 inches, 550 NHP			
Cost	£30,647				£63,319			
	Date	**Voyage**	**Result**	**Balance**	**Date**	**Voyage**	**Result**	**Balance**
1879	16 January	1	£4,035	(£26,612)	6 August	1	£9,002	(£54,317)
	14 October	2	£1,419	(£25,193)				
1880	12 May	3	£3,438	(£21,755)	13 February	2	£7,132	(£47,195)
	30 November	4	£5,029	(£16,725)	29 July	3	£12,036	(£35,159)
1881	July	5	£2,073	(£14,652)	12 January	4	£13,101	(£22,058)
	12 December	6	£4,958	(£9,694)	July	5	£10,269	(£11,790)
					15 December	6	£8,324	(£3,466)
1882	4 July	7	£1,204	(£8,491)	23 September	7 and 8	£5,496	£2,030
Total			£22,156				£65,349	
Average			£3,165				£8,169	

neither was really up to the demands of the trade. John Swire made the thinking behind the sale clear in a letter to Alfred Holt, many of whose ships Swire believed suffered from similar shortcomings.

'McGregor has sold *Gleniffer* to a French Company. Two years ago he told me that she was too slow, and the *Glengyle* too small and too slow to pay in the China trade – and that he should sell both. He has done so.'

The sales did not signal any contraction in the fleet. After a break of two years from the delivery of *Glencoe*, London and Glasgow delivered a pair of shorter, but broader sisters of roughly the same gross tonnage, *Glenfruin* in January 1881 and *Glenavon* two months later. The change in dimensions and a slight decrease in engine power might have indicated that Glen was moving away from its emphasis on speed, but this was not in fact the case. The next vessel to enter the fleet after the 1881 pair to represent the firm's most exaggerated, and expensive, attempt to build a fast record-breaker for a trade which still revolved to a considerable extent around the annual race to bring back the first tea cargoes from China.

Glenogle, launched by London and Glasgow in February 1882, was 60 feet longer and 25% larger by gross tonnage measure than her immediate predecessor *Glenavon*, and her engines had a 32% higher nominal horsepower rating. This was the largest single leap forward in size and power in the 1870/1880s evolution of Glen Line vessels. Costing almost fifty percent more (£90,123) than the most expensive previous vessel, Glen's only two-funnel ship represented an expensive gamble on the theory that higher speed would earn higher freights. Simultaneously, Glen's greatest rival in the

tea races, Thomas Skinner, was building an even faster and more expensive vessel, *Stirling Castle* (4,423/1882), at the neighbouring Govan yard of John Elder.

Neither ship would fulfil her promise. *Stirling Castle*, whose engine rated an astounding 1,500 nominal horsepower, comfortably beat *Glenogle* in the tea races of 1882 and 1883. Despite winning the higher freights that went to the victor, *Stirling Castle* was a commercial disaster. Far too expensive to run, her construction stretched Skinner too far, and he was forced to sell her out of the Far East service to meet his financial obligations. While she was on the Far East route, she completely overshadowed *Glenogle*. In 1883, for example, she made the passage from off Woosung to London in only 29 days, arriving four days before *Glenogle*, which had actually left 36 hours before her. The extra money McGregor, Gow had invested in *Glenogle* was only sufficient to shave a couple of days off the record set before by *Glencoe*. The ship actually recouped some of the investment in her during a lucrative charter to the Admiralty at the end of 1885, when she was taken briefly into service as an Armed Merchant Cruiser during the Russian crisis of that year. This charter paid a total hire of just over £25,300, on which the company made a profit of £21,857. Even with this, however, she proved a poor investment. She was actually to last in the fleet until the early twentieth century, her economic worth being supported by conversion to more economic triple expansion in 1890 (a conversion that cost her the distinctive second funnel). A comparison of her results with those of her two immediate predecessors, *Glenfruin* and *Glenavon*, makes it clear that she simply extended the size and speed formula further than the compound steam technology of her day could support.

Glenfruin/Glenavon vs *Glenogle*, 1881/2 - 1897			
	Glenfruin	*Glenavon*	*Glenogle*
Built	1881	1881	1882
Cost	£56,114	£55,945	£90,123
Voyage profits to 1897	£77,831	£81,973	£108,695
New engines and surveys	£12,369	£14,368	£16,039
Net voyage profits	£65,462	£67,605	£92,656
Net surplus over cost	£9,348	£11,660	£2,533
Net return on investment	16.7%	20.8%	2.8%

While *Glenogle* might just have paid her way, and was never the expensive disaster that her faster rival *Stirling Castle* became, there was no question of anything like her being repeated. The next two additions to the fleet, *Glengarry* and *Glenelg*, both delivered by London and Glasgow in 1883, were in fact near copies of the *Glenfruin/Glenavon* pair built two years before. Their arrival brought the McGregor, Gow steam fleet up to a strength of 14 vessels, with an average age of only six years. The fleet was broadly homogeneous in composition, with only the flawed thoroughbred *Glenogle* and the second-hand *Glenorchy* not being from the same design concept. Even the smaller and older ships were still well capable of meeting the demands of the trade, and there would not, in fact, be any further sales out of the fleet until the end of the decade. The fleet was now large enough to allow in principle for fairly regular sailings twice a month outwards from London. In practice this was a theoretical rather than a practical norm, and there was some deviation from it. Occasional outward sailings were still being made from Glasgow, and the steady availability of ships on UK berths was disrupted by homeward sailings being bunched around the tea season, with some tea cargoes being destined for New York rather than London.

Above left: The two-funnelled *Glenogle* of 1882 was the company's last attempt to build a record breaker, but was overshadowed by Skinner's *Stirling Castle*.
Above right: The fees earned during *Glenogle's* brief commission as an armed merchant cruiser helped support what would otherwise have been a loss-making career.
Below: *Glenavon* at Hong Kong in 1898, immediately before her loss. She is no longer carrying yards. *[all Peter Newall collection]*

Glen Line at its zenith

Notwithstanding the questionable economics of the *Glenogle* experiment, the early 1880s saw Glen at the peak of its powers. Swire, Holts' agent in China and the architect of the Far East freight conference, was perhaps the most knowledgeable observer of developments in the business. Throughout the period, he believed that the Glen vessels displayed the best mixture of size and speed, and had continually badgered the conservative Holts to order larger and faster vessels for the Ocean Steamship fleet. Writing to Philip Holt in September 1880, he bemoaned the fact that *Glenlyon* had just beaten Ocean's *Ulysses* by one week from Foochow and eight days from Hong Kong, and that *Glenearn* had taken only 47 days outwards to Shanghai compared to 55 days for *Stentor*. A month later he wrote to Philip's brother Alfred that the Glens, in his view, had 'the best working plant in the trade', and were 'the greatest favourites with shippers'. In September 1881, he was still labouring the same point, forwarding a letter from Shanghai which included the statement: 'Glens, as the most desirable conveyance, are obtaining more than their share of cargo.'

The delivery of *Glengarry* in May 1883 and *Glenelg* two months later marked something of a watershed in fleet development. The two sisters were to be the last iron-hulled, compound engine equipped ships built for the company. No further vessels would be added for more than three years, and when the next ship was ordered, the firm had moved to steel construction and triple expansion engines. In twelve years, McGregor, Gow had introduced a total of 16 ships to their service, of which 14 had been built to their specification by London and Glasgow's Govan shipyard. At the end of 1883, fleet strength stood at 14, and with the oldest vessel just over ten years old, the company was apparently well-equipped to run a regular and highly competitive twice-monthly service for some time to come.

It was at this stage that marine misfortune first impacted on the company in a significant way. Glen had enjoyed a very fortunate introductory decade in the Far East trade, free of loss or even major accident. Maritime losses effectively ended Thomas Skinner's attempts to establish his Castles as serious rivals to Holt, Glen and Jenkins' Shires. Having lost *Drummond Castle* (1,985/1871) and *Cawdor Castle* (2,173/1873) in shipwrecks in the 1870s, he then lost *Braemar Castle* (2,182/1873) to a collision in 1880, *Fleurs Castle* (2,472/1874) to shipwreck in 1882, whilst in 1883 *Kenmure Castle* (1,951/1873) foundered in a gale and *Minard Castle* (2,460/1882) was wrecked. Even the more staid Holt line did not escape loss entirely, losing *Hector* (1,956/1871), *Orestes* (2,021/1875) and *Sarpedon* (1,949/1870) in quick succession in 1875 and 1876. In the 1880s, however, fate seemed to start catching up with McGregor, Gow and Co.

On 18th June 1884, *Glenfruin* suffered a broken propeller shaft in the Indian Ocean whilst homewards bound to the UK with tea. Such accidents were fairly common in the late nineteenth century, and *Glenfruin*, which proved almost unmanageable under sail, was fortunate to fall in with her sister *Glenavon* carrying another tea cargo (although this time for New York) after eight days. *Glenavon* towed *Glenfruin* for 900 miles until the shaft was repaired, and then stayed with her another several days to be certain that the repaired shaft would hold. This incident produced an interesting piece of legal precedent. *Glenfruin's* tea cargo was valued at £158,000, more than double the value of the vessel and her own stores (£70,000), and there was obviously scope for a salvage claim. The two ships were nominally owned by the same company, and each in fact had 19 of their 20 sixty-fourth shareholders in common. Mr. Justice Butt, sitting in London in March 1885, held that the owners of *Glenfruin* were liable, but that as they were also the owners of *Glenavon*, only the one shareholder in the latter vessel not common to the former was entitled to salvage. This gentleman was awarded £40, while the Master of *Glenavon* was granted £50 and her crew £250.

Just after the damaged *Glenfruin* finally made port, a more serious accident in home waters resulted in the first loss from Glen's steam fleet. *Glenelg* was only one year old when she set out from London for the Far East with passengers and a general cargo including £10,785 worth of military stores. During the night of 29/30th July she struck an isolated rock off Ushant and stuck fast with her fore and main holds flooded. Everyone was got away safely and spent the night in boats alongside the ship before making for land in the morning. The Master stayed alongside in hopes of being able to save the vessel, but within a day the vessel broke in two and became a total loss.

Glen was lucky to escape from the mid-1880s without further losses. The brief war between France and China in 1884-85 resulted in *Glenroy* being detained by the French for several days until 50 tons of lead, considered contraband, was removed. More seriously, *Glenfinlas* was moored at Foochow when the French Navy bombarded the Arsenal and Chinese warships anchored off it. One burning Chinese vessel sank right across her bows carrying away both anchors, while another sank under her quarter, having been under shellfire from the French almost up to the time of her sinking. International disturbances, however, brought more than just increased risk. War in Egypt and the threat of war with Russia resulted in the Admiralty chartering a number of fast merchant ships as transports and armed merchant cruisers. One of these was *Glenogle*, which, as we have seen, earned far more from her brief sojourn under the white ensign than she did in several years of normal commercial service. Simultaneously, the Far East end of Glen's normal business was embroiled in the short war between France and China.

The most serious incident in the Far East had nothing to do with war. On the morning of 17th October 1885 the somewhat accident-prone *Glenfruin* was leaving Hong Kong bound for London with a cargo of tea, when she was rammed amidships by the Netherlands India Steam Navigation Company's steamer *Camorta* (2,097/1880). With her hull split open just in front of the engine room, *Glenfruin* began to fill rapidly, but her Master managed to beach her in Belcher's Bay before her fires were put out and forward momentum lost. There she quickly settled on the bottom with her forefoot out of the water and her entire aft section submerged. Thanks to the Master's quick thinking, salvage proved fairly straightforward, and the ship was successfully raised on 7th November and docked locally for repairs the next day. The Hong Kong Supreme Court found *Glenfruin* entirely free of blame, *Camorta* being held to have entered the fairway improperly, the vision of both ships being blocked until it was too late by an anchored vessel.

These misfortunes did not seriously dislocate the service. McGregor, Gow still made occasional use of chartered tonnage in 1885 to fill temporary gaps in the service. In April of that year they advertised the steamer *Kut Sang* (2,311/1881) for despatch from their London berth, and in October, the same owner's *Lee Sang* (1,697/1885) also took one outward sailing. These were vessels on their delivery voyages for the Indo-China Steam Navigation Co. Ltd. In the same year an interesting experiment in cooperation between rivals began when McGregor, Gow agreed to place a small number of Ocean's vessels on the London berth for outward sailings. Holt ships made sporadic sailings from London for more than a year before the experiment was allowed to lapse. Holts, with their west coast ships 'only getting half cargoes' would not agree to Glen placing one of their 'smaller boats' on the Liverpool berth, while Glen for its part were soon turning down requests for more London sailings because 'cargo is becoming exceedingly scarce here.'

As the 1880s wore on, complaints about inadequate cargoes became more and more common. The homeward trade from the Far East gradually lost its mainstay and major earner as China tea was supplanted in western markets by stronger tasting Indian varieties. It became more and more common for ships to spend parts of their voyages coasting in the Far East. By the end of the decade, Glen ships were being increasingly diverted away from China in search of homeward cargoes. Some vessels were sent on to Japan to load part cargoes before returning to China to fill up. In February 1888 *Glenearn* was sent from China to the Philippines to load for the UK. She was followed the next month by *Glengarry*, and two further vessels were similarly diverted in June and July. In general, an improving British export trade to the Far East tended to increase outward business to compensate for falling homewards cargoes, but even this did not always provide adequate revenues for what was now a much larger and efficient British steam fleet.

One of Glen's earlier rivals did not survive the sharpening of competitive conditions in the middle of the decade. Skinner's Castle Line never really recovered from the expensive failure of *Stirling Castle* and the rash of accidental losses in the early 1880s. No further ships were added after 1882, and in 1887 three of the surviving four ships were sold, leaving only *Bothwell Castle* to trade on into the 1890s. The other major lines all survived, but it was clear that the glory days of the China trade were over, and that future profitability would require both hard work and substantial investment in new tonnage.

After the mid-decade breathing space, Glen returned to the builders in 1886. London and Glasgow delivered a new *Glengyle* in October 1886 (the first occasion on which a ship's name had been repeated in the steam fleet). She was followed in March 1887 by a sister, *Glenshiel*. Each of this pair was ten feet longer and some 400 tons larger than the *Glengarry/Glenelg* pair of 1883. More important than the slight increment in size, however, was the simultaneous introduction of steel construction and triple-expansion steam engines to the fleet. While this did not render the existing fleet obsolete at a single stroke, it was an indication that the combination of new technology and changing trade conditions would dictate the need for more new ships before very long.

The naming of Glen ships provides an interesting aside on the main themes of the company's history. The early Glen names all had a decided McGregor emphasis, and the company was to stick with Scottish glen names except for a brief Irish hiatus in 1917-1920 (see pages 80-81). Many of these names would be re-used for new ships as the originals were replaced. The company, however, appears to have shared a fairly common shipowners' aversion to repeating names that had proved unlucky. Neither of the names of the first two steam ships to be lost (*Glenelg* and *Glencoe*) was ever repeated. There does not seem to have been any policy of requiring new owners to change names when Glen ships were disposed of on the second-hand market. Four nineteenth century disposals (*Gleniffer*, *Glenfinlas*, *Glenfalloch* and *Glenearn*) and one early twentieth century disposal (*Glenogle*) were operated by their new owners without change of name. This was not originally a hindrance to naming new ships, but it would become so when the British government introduced a regulation to forbid more than one British ship trading under the same name. In the event, two ships (*Glenfalloch* and *Glenogle*) would continue to trade under the red ensign for years after they left the fleet, effectively denying the company re-use of their names.

Fading glory
It is impossible, even with the historian's hindsight, to mark the time when the Glen Line's hitherto almost uninterrupted story of success began to ebb away. The company was still very much at the peak of its powers in the first half of the 1880s, and the fleet reached its nineteenth century apogee in terms of number of ships (15) and total tonnage (41,500 grt) in 1887 with the arrival of *Glenshiel* in 1887. By the end of the decade, however, business was under pressure and the fleet was beginning to contract. The changing trade conditions referred to above clearly had a lot to do with the change in fortunes. So too did the requirement for a new generation of ships. These factors alone do not explain Glen's decline. It was, in fact, precisely at this time that the company's greatest rival, Holts' Blue Funnel Line, shook off a prolonged bout of

managerial conservatism and technological backwardness to build a fleet that would form the basis for twentieth century pre-eminence. Glen's decline was really a product of developments within its own management.

James McGregor had been the driving force behind the Far East steamship business since its inception. While the Gow family remained important partners into the twentieth century, their active participation in the management of the business faded after Leonard Gow returned to Glasgow in 1884. At that time James McGregor was still a vigorous man in his late 50s, and very capable of running a business he understood as well as any in the trade. Two problems were developing, however, that would bedevil the company in the near future. The first was that McGregor harboured extremely conservative ideas on steamship ownership. His grandson, Cameron McGregor, reported that he reacted with extreme hostility to early ideas of seeking new capital through floating a limited liability company. 'My grandfather,' he wrote, 'would not hear of it, holding the view, which he never changed, that a Limited Company meant limited honesty and that a proper Shipowner should own 64/64ths in his ship. He had a supreme contempt for what was called a managing owner.' McGregor followed this idea through in his dealings with his existing sixty fourth shareholders. Progressively through the successful years of the 1870s and 1880s, he followed a policy of buying these out, gradually narrowing the investor base as he did so.

This would not of itself have spelt trouble if the McGregor and Gow families had maintained the will and the wealth to continue building up the business. This unfortunately was not the case. Gow's interest in the Glen Line waned after the mid-1880s, and although he remained a significant investor in the business, his energies were devoted more and more to the developing shipping interests of A.C. Gow and Co. in Glasgow. Business relations between the two family senior statesmen appear to have remained cordial. Not only did Leonard Gow continue to take shares in new Glen steamers, but James McGregor also invested in Gow's new Glasgow-registered tramp steamers. In 1879, he took five sixty fourth shares in *Waterloo*, the first vessel built for the new venture, and in 1881 he took 13 in *Austerlitz*, the second new building.

The reciprocal partnership appears to have waned with the second generation of each family. McGregor had four sons, three of whom, Allan, Donald and Bertram, would eventually enter the firm. Their interest in and aptitude for the business, however, does not seem to have matched their father's, and they seemed as much interested in enjoying the fruits of wealth as in creating it. In addition, McGregor himself appears to have taken a significant amount of money out of the business to invest in a lavish lifestyle. As a result of all this, by the time the 1890s brought a need for fresh investment in new ships, the Glen Line had become too heavily dependent on one family whose wealth had been

Average voyage profits, 1882-1898			
Year (voyages)	£	Year (voyages)	£
1882 (22)	3,673	1891 (15)	1,795
1883 (18)	3,296	1892 (21)	1,388
1884 (14)	3,837	1893 (18)	2,096
1885 (16)	3,234	1894 (16)	1,990
1886 (14)	5,136	1895 (17)	2,279
1887 (19)	1,085	1896 (16)	969
1888 (20)	2,375	1897 (17)	1,617
1889 (20)	3,875	1898 (12)	4,620
1890 (11)	1,348		
Number of surviving voyage accounts on which average is based is given in brackets after each year.			

partially dissipated and whose second generation was not entirely ready to face the challenge of building afresh.

The profitability of the Glen Line began to slip in the second half of the 1880s. Only some two thirds of the voyage accounts for the period survive, but these are sufficient to paint a fairly clear picture. After a good year in 1886 (bolstered by receipts from the Admiralty charter of *Glenogle*), profits fell to well below the average for the previous ten years and stayed at these depressed levels in every year except 1889. The 1890s were even worse than the second half of the previous decade. The apparent recovery in 1898 is almost certainly a product of the survival of only a small number of voyage accounts, as the year in question was actually one of the worst of the decade for freight rates in the Far East.

Fleet replacement
Up until 1889, the development of the Glen Line fleet had been a story of fairly uncomplicated expansion. The first two steel-hulled, triple expansion ships, *Glengyle* and *Glenshiel*, delivered in 1886-1887, had been the seventeenth and eighteenth steamships to join the fleet since the first *Glengyle* had left the same Glasgow builder's yard in 1871. Only two vessels, the pioneering *Glengyle* and the unsatisfactory speculative purchase *Gleniffer*, had been sold, and only one ship, *Glenelg*, had been lost. The other 15 ships were all still in service, and the fleet had been maintained at a strength of 13-15 vessels since the early 1880s. The older ships, however, were now obsolescent, and were in any event reaching the end of what might have been considered their normal economic lives. With the pace of new building having slowed in the second half of the 1880s, the company faced the need for a major modernisation programme.

Before any such programme could be put in place, Glen suffered its second maritime loss, a disaster which was to prove the worst in terms of human cost of its entire history. *Glencoe* sailed from Liverpool for London in ballast on 2nd February 1889 to load for a new voyage to the Far East. She was sighted off Portland Bill two days later, but never arrived at London. On 6th February, the Glasgow-registered barque *Largo Bay* (1,255/1878) had been towed into Portsmouth with severe bow damage, having reported being in a collision with a large unknown steamer off Beachy Head on the night of the 4th. When *Glencoe* failed to arrive, fears arose that she had been the victim, and were rapidly confirmed when a fishing vessel picked up one of her lifebuoys near the collision site, and a part of one of the ship's doors washed ashore near Dieppe. Nothing was ever heard of any of her crew, all 54 of whom (including two pilots) had perished.

Knowledge of the circumstances of the collision was necessarily based entirely on reports from the crew of the *Largo Bay*. *Glencoe* had been proceeding up the Channel at speed, her captain undoubtedly anxious to make an early arrival on the London berth having been slowed down by bad weather in the Irish Sea. She had encountered *Largo Bay* coming down the Channel fully laden, and, almost simultaneously, another (unidentified) sailing ship, sailing northwards across the courses of both ships. *Glencoe* had attempted to cut between the two ships, but had misjudged the distances and been rammed on the port side by *Largo Bay*. Inevitably, there was some conflicting evidence. The weather was variously reported as clear and snowy, the steamer was described by some as having three masts and by others as having four, and was reported to have sunk immediately or simply to have disappeared from sight. At the enquiry in London on 1st April, *Largo Bay* was cleared of all blame, and *Glencoe* held entirely responsible. McGregor, Gow appealed against this decision, but the appeal was dismissed on 5th December. The Appeal Court judges were highly critical of *Glencoe*, one of them stating that 'a more flagrant wrong was never done by any ship than by this steamer.' In retrospect, this seems unduly harsh, as only one side of the story was ever heard, and the third vessel involved in the incident was never even identified. Whatever the rights and wrongs of the issue, nothing can diminish the extent of the tragedy. Glen had lost one of its most successful ships and her entire crew, almost within sight of British shores.

By the time the final judgement on the *Glencoe* case was handed down, several other ships had departed from the fleet, albeit under less tragic circumstances. Two of the oldest vessels were sold to the same British owner late in 1889. The former record-holder *Glenartney* went to G. Tweedy and Co. of London as *Chongar* in October. She was followed a month later by *Glenroy*, which was renamed *Gonchar* (an anagram of her sister's new name). Another ship of the same generation followed a year later, *Glenfinlas* going to Newcastle owners without change of name. All three ships would be gone by 1895, the first two scrapped, and the third foundering in the North Sea under Swedish colours.

There were to be two further disposals in the early 1890s. *Glenlyon* and the newer and larger *Gleneagles* were both sold to the same French owner in 1892-3. The second of these vessels was four and a half years newer than the first, and some 20% larger, but the difference in selling price was only £750 (£9,250 for *Gleneagles* and £8,500 for *Glenlyon*), proof that the entire group of vessels was really out of date. Despite this fact, the other 1870s-built ships all sailed on into the second half of the 1890s. *Glenfalloch* was never modernised, and became the first in what was to prove a long series of transfers to Far East owners when she was sold in Singapore in 1896. The other two survivors, *Glenearn* and *Glenorchy*, made it nearly to the end of the decade, both having had their lives extended by having their engines modified to triple expansion. The economics of major engine modifications to ageing vessels seems questionable. Fitting triple expansion engines to *Glenearn*, for example, cost McGregor, Gow £10,763 in 1895. If the second-hand prices achieved for her sisters are a reasonable benchmark, this was in excess of her unmodified second-hand value. When she was sold four years later, she realised only £8,000, and it does not seem likely from surviving voyage accounts that she actually managed to recover the cost of her modernisation before her sale.

The reason why McGregor, Gow embarked on the modernisation of some of their old ships was almost certainly that they could not afford to replace all of the obsolescent vessels with new tonnage. The new building programme was never able to meet the full needs of fleet regeneration. The first new acquisition, a second *Glenartney*, was an opportunistic purchase from the Sunderland yard of J. Laing. Significantly smaller and slower than the late 1880s arrivals from London and Glasgow, her major advantage appears to have been her relatively low cost (£47,218 on completion in December 1889). She was not to prove a great success and would last less than 15 years in the fleet. She was followed by two other similarly uninspired new buildings. The 3,500 ton *Glenesk*, delivered in June 1891 for £49,000, was another single purchase from a northeast shipyard. *Glenfarg*, delivered by London and Glasgow in June 1894 for £48,778, was another vessel of similar size, and marked no real improvement over the ships built by the same yard in the late 1880s.

Between 1889 and 1895, one vessel had been lost and five sold, but only three new vessels had joined the fleet, none of which offered sufficient increase in speed or carrying capacity to compensate for the decease in numbers. It would not be correct to blame the flagging pace of replacement on increasing capital costs. Shipbuilding costs tended to fall over the last quarter of the nineteenth century, as building itself became more efficient and more competitive. *Glenshiel*, built in 1887, had cost roughly the same as the smaller *Glencoe*, built nine years earlier. *Glenfarg*, built seven years after *Glenshiel*, and roughly equivalent in size, cost almost 25% less. Two related developments inside the company were almost certainly behind the shortfall in capital investment: the failing health of the company's managing owner and the constriction of the firm's access to capital that his policies had brought about.

Glenesk delivered by a Newcastle yard in June 1891 She was one of the few Glen ships of the nineteenth century not built on the Clyde. *[J.and M. Clarkson collection]*

Glenfarg which ran trials in June 1894. Note the steam pipe abaft the funnel. *[Peter Newall collection]*

Families and finances

James McGregor turned 65 in 1891, and soon thereafter his health began to fail. He developed diabetes, and then liver disease, and was in generally poor health before he finally died in his Hampstead home at the age of 69 on 23rd January 1896. Most of his wealth was tied up in shares of the ships of the Glen Line, and these were left in equal portions to his sons, of whom Allan, the eldest, became the firm's manager. By this time, McGregor's original partner, Leonard Gow, had long since retired to Glasgow, leaving his interest in the company in the hands of his son, Leonard Gow Junior. It was thus the younger generation of both families that had to take Glen into the new century.

They were forced to do so from a capital base that was far narrower than that from which the firm had originally

been launched. James McGregor's belief in full private ownership had gradually placed most of the burden of investment on the two founding families. Many original investors had been bought out. A minority retained their shares until death or retirement, but there had been no serious attempt to find others. A brief analysis of the sixty-fourth share ownership books for the vessels in the fleet reveals the extent of this narrowing of ownership. For the seven vessels entering the fleet before 1880 whose share registers survive, the McGregor and Gow families owned only 25% of the shares. For nine of the ten vessels to enter the fleet between 1880 and James McGregor's death in 1896, the share went up to 49%. For the seven vessels in the fleet when the company finally adopted limited liability, the proportion had gone all the way up to 82%.

Thus fleet modernization had to be funded almost entirely by the two founding families. In reality, the burden fell disproportionately on the McGregor family. From the time of Leonard Gow Senior's retirement to Glasgow in the mid-1880s, the Gow family's involvement in McGregor, Gow and the Glen Line began to wane. Increasingly capital was directed into the family's developing tramp ship interests, a development which culminated in 1895 with the amalgamation of the old firm of A.C. Gow with the fleet of D.H. Dixon and Harrison to found Gow, Harrison and Company. The Gow stake in Glen became more and more of a sleeping partnership. This drift away was exacerbated by poor relations between the younger generations. Leonard Gow Junior does not appear to have approved of the rather feckless managerial approach of the younger McGregors, who found themselves having to share a larger and larger part of the financial burden.

Competition grows

While both the capital base and freight rates were contracting, competition was increasing. In 1896, the rapidly expanding Japanese firm Nippon Yusen Kaisha commenced a service between its home island and Europe. Initially restricted to Middlesbrough and Antwerp, its fleet had grown to such an extent by 1898 that it was able to negotiate Conference loading rights at London. The Japanese had originally hoped to make Liverpool their British terminus, but such was the hold of Blue Funnel on that port that they chose London as their target instead. While the major inhabitant of that berth, P&O, was strong enough to continue to make its way, the other British companies, Glen, Shire and Ben, were far smaller and more vulnerable.

The foreign threat intensified in 1898 when Germany's Hamburg-Amerika Line also entered the Far East trade, initiating a joint service with the incumbent Norddeutscher Lloyd. Equally serious, however, were developments within Great Britain itself. Holt's Blue Funnel Line had been something of a sleeping giant throughout the 1880s, with fleet development held back by the conservatism of its founders. In the 1890s, however, the company began to invest heavily in new tonnage. At the beginning of the decade, the Blue Funnel fleet had totalled 34 ships of 78,200 grt; by its end, the fleet had gone up to 41 vessels, and total

gross tonnage had risen to 165,600 grt. In 1902, furthermore, Blue Funnel bought out its Liverpool rival, China Mutual, adding another 13 ships to its fleet. While the East and West coast services were separate, and there was never any real chance of Holts attacking the London berth directly, there was competition for a significant part of both outward and homeward trade, and pressure on Glen could only increase.

All this notwithstanding, 1896, the year of James McGregor's death, did see the arrival of two new ships under Glen colours. This pair, named *Glenlochy* and *Glenturret*, were each built by London and Glasgow at a cost of £57,915 a vessel. Unlike the fleet additions earlier in the decade, these vessels did represent a real step forward in size at 400 feet in length and just under 4,700 tons gross register. As such, they were broadly competitive with the ships that competing fleets had begun to introduce to the Far East trade. Interestingly enough, neither ship made its maiden voyage from the UK direct to the Far East. Both sailed to New York to load for China and Japan, a sure sign that life on the London berth was becoming more and more difficult.

Unfortunately, the new ships did not represent a permanent increase in fleet size. The 1873-built *Glenfalloch* was sold out of the fleet in the same year they arrived. She was followed in 1881 by the more modern *Glenfruin*, which in an interesting twist of fate became a running mate of her old Skinner rival *Bothwell Castle* (2,542/1881) in the Australian coastal fleet of McIlwraith, McEachern and Co. A year later, the veteran *Glenorchy*, built in 1871 and a dependable Glen servant since 1876, was finally sold, to spend her last five years under Italian colours. Finally in 1899, the last of the first generation of vessels, *Glenearn*, was also disposed of. Her initial owners were Glasgow-based, but following salvage after a serious grounding in the Clyde estuary, she also went to Italian owners, who would lose her in a Mediterranean storm in 1902.

The difficult years after the founder's death were marred by a run of serious accidents. In September 1896 *Glenartney* suffered a major cargo fire while transiting the Suez Canal outward bound, and was forced to unload and sail home for repairs. In January 1897 *Glenesk* grounded badly at Las Palmas and in August of the same year *Glengyle* had to be temporarily beached by a salvage steamer near Gibraltar after a collision in the Straits had left her with a

Glenturret of 1896 on the River Thames on 28th February 1914. Note the splendid counter stern. *[F.W. Hawks/Roy Fenton collection]*

flooded engine room. Finally in December 1897, *Glenartney* was in the wars again, being towed into Malta by a German steamer after losing her propeller in heavy weather.

The depletion of the fleet was accelerated in 1898 by Glen's third marine loss - and their first, after nearly three decades of service, in Far Eastern waters. *Glenavon*, built in 1881 and tripled ten years later, would almost certainly have been sold out of the fleet anyway (her sister *Glenfruin* had gone in 1897), but she saved her owners the problem of finding a buyer by striking Linting Rock on 29th December 1898 soon after leaving Hong Kong on a homeward voyage. Captain Pithie turned back for Hong Kong, but the ship filled rapidly and sunk in deep water an hour after striking. She may not have represented a significant material loss to the company, but four of her crew, including the first mate, drowned in the accident and a quartermaster died of exhaustion after swimming ashore.

Apart from these trials and tribulations, there were signs that the new managers were finding competitive pressure and poor trading conditions so harsh that they were considering abandoning the service. If we compare fleet dispositions in 1900 with those in 1895 (the year before James McGregor's death), we find the depleted Glen fleet only partially committed to the Far East conference berth. In 1895, Glen steamers made 18 sailings for China and Japan from UK and continental ports (usually Antwerp, Middlesbrough and London) and one more direct from New York. In 1900 they made only eight from the UK and Europe and two from New York. Two ships, *Glenesk* and *Glengyle*, spent the first third of the year on Boer War charters between the UK and South Africa, and one, the elderly *Glenogle,* spent the entire year tramping back and forth across the North Pacific. All of the vessels spent some time away from their normal trade. Most of these deployments were short-term tramping assignments in the Far East, but *Glenlochy* made two round trips across the North Atlantic, and *Glenshiel* at one stage actually sailed to the Black Sea.

By the end of the century, the addition of *Glenlochy* and *Glenturret* needed to be balanced against the departure of five older vessels, *Glenavon* through loss and four others through sale. The managers, however, were able to find the finances to make another two additions in fairly quick succession. In February 1901, London and Glasgow delivered a new *Glenroy*, a near sister to the pair built in 1896. She was joined two months later by one of the company's rare second-hand purchases. In December 1899, Houlder

Brothers' *Denton Grange* had stranded badly at Las Palmas whilst on a government charter to South Africa. Early attempts to refloat the vessel had failed and she was abandoned to the underwriters. She was finally re-floated six months after her accident and towed to Tyneside for repairs. There McGregor, Gow bought her in a damaged state for £46,000. Repaired and renamed *Glenlogan* she entered service in April 1901, becoming the first vessel in the fleet to match the 1882-built *Glenogle* for length. The arrival of these two ships brought the fleet back up to 11 vessels, almost enough to maintain a regular twice-monthly service. Unfortunately, the fleet would not stay this size for very long.

The Russo-Japanese War of 1904-1905 stimulated a sharp rise in demand for second-hand tonnage from Far East buyers, mostly Japanese. Glen's management decided to take advantage of good prices to dispose of the older part of the fleet. This sell-off saw the disposal of all of the surviving vessels built in the 1880s. *Glenogle* actually went before war clouds gathered, being sold to Burmese owners in July 1903. She had never really been a commercial success, but had given 21 years of faithful service, all but the last few of them as the largest vessel in the fleet. *Glengarry*, sold to the Japanese in January 1904, was the only other survivor from the era of iron hulls and compound engines (although she like *Glenogle* had been tripled in the early 1890s), and there can be little question that she had reached the end of her useful life with the company. The other three vessels sold, *Glengyle*, *Glenshiel* and *Glenartney*, all of which went to Japanese owners in April-May 1904, were more modern vessels built with steel hulls and triple expansion engines. As they were built between 1886 and 1889, none were in their first flush of youth, but under normal circumstances one might only have expected their sale if a new generation of replacements was already on the builder's stocks.

This was not the case. After the completion of *Glenroy* and the commissioning of the re-built *Glenlogan* in 1901, the company's fleet renewal programme slowed almost to a stop. *Glenstrae*, a near sister of the last London and Glasgow ships, delivered by Hawthorn, Leslie in March 1905, was actually the only other ship built to Glen's order during the remainder of the decade. Her arrival only brought the fleet up to a strength of seven vessels, half the number that had been operated at its peak in the early 1880s, and only half the number required to run a regular twice-monthly service on the London-Far East service.

Glenlogan was unusual for Glen in being a second hand purchase. Purchased from the underwriters after stranding when only three years old, she remained the largest ship in the fleet until 1914. *[Peter Newall collection]*

Through most of the first decade of the twentieth century, the Far East service was only maintained on a tenuous basis. Both the South African and the Russo-Japanese wars had presented good opportunities for short-term profits from government charters, but the withdrawal of Glen vessels from the regular berth only tended to do further damage to the company's weakening grasp on its traditional trade. The pattern of vessel employment remained erratic. Sporadic outward sailings to the Straits, China and Japan were maintained, but these voyages were frequently interspersed with tramping voyages often around the Pacific littoral. Cameron McGregor's memoirs speak eloquently of the lack of energy and direction in the company's affairs at the time.

'… our berth business outward had declined in an alarming way and homewards had become almost extinct. The three brothers were never in agreement as to whether the vessels should remain and take their chance on the berth or go tramping to Rangoon, Saigon or Dalny; for some time the tramping idea flourished, but at the expense of the old established business….

In 1907 I entered my Father's office, after three years in the office of Messrs. T.A. Bulmer and Co., Middlesbrough, and fresh from a trip to the Far Eastern ports. I was very surprised to find in the City an office devoid of energy. Nobody seemed to me to have any idea, or desire for that matter, to try and improve things; the policy of drift seemed to be installed in most minds. I met opposition on all sides. The activities of the N.Y.K. and Ben Line had been studied by me during my time in Middlesbrough where we acted as agents. Even this information seemed of no interest. The idea of running the Service on a regular schedule seemed just too much bother.'

Ellerman arrives, and departs

Against this background, it was hardly surprising that Glen experienced its first brush with takeover. Sir John Ellerman was one of the most aggressive and successful participants in the wave of takeovers which transformed British liner shipping in the years around the turn of the century. Having established a strong presence in the Atlantic and Mediterranean through acquisition, he had then taken over two well-established businesses in the UK-India trade, the Glasgow-based City Line and the Liverpool-based Hall Line. The Far East trade was a logical extension of these businesses and an obvious target for the next wave of expansion. While Glen Line's principals do not appear to have been actively entertaining ideas of selling out themselves at this stage, their shortage of both capital and vessels did present Ellerman with an opportunity to take a stake in the business, and to position himself as preferred buyer should a sale eventually be mooted.

With the fleet depleted by the 1903-04 sale of its older vessels, only one new vessel entering service, and no capital available to build more, Allan McGregor was favourably inclined to allowing Ellerman a stake in the business in exchange for badly needed

tonnage. The basic arrangement, worked out in late 1905, involved the transfer of Ellerman ships to Glen colours and management in return for a two-fifths share of the trade. Formally, the transferred ships were sold to Glen, but as Glen did not actually have the money to buy them, the 'sale' was underwritten by a mortgage from Ellerman, the transfer of ownership was actually only nominal. Although the transferred ships adopted Glen names and colours, and were managed by McGregor, Gow and Co. on the regular London-Far East berth, Ellerman's Hall Line continued to supply the masters and crew.

Initially, the transfer of four or five vessels was discussed, with the possibility of more to come if the business went well. Trade conditions, however, continued to be poor, and Ellerman's actual opening commitment was only two ships. The 4,460 ton *Netherby Hall*, building for the Hall Line at Swan, Hunter and Wigham Richardson of Newcastle was renamed *Glenearn* while still building and delivered straight to the Glen ownership in December 1905. She was joined at the beginning of 1906 by her slightly smaller and older sister *Branksome Hall* which was renamed *Glenavon*. The arrangement was now intended to last two years, with Ellerman having the right to a seven-year extension, and *Glenearn* took the first outward sailing for the new service on 15th January 1906.

The experiment did not prove a successful one. General trading conditions remained poor, and Glen's competitive position was not sufficiently strengthened by the addition of two ships to make a significant difference. By the summer of 1907, Ellerman appears to have come to the conclusion that he would do better deploying ships in other trades, and with the agreement of McGregor decided not to extend his commitment. The formal Glen-Ellerman arrangement expired in early 1908, but relations between the two firms remained congenial, and both of the loaned vessels stayed with the Glen fleet on charter until late 1910 when they finally returned to their old Hall names and ownership.

Ellerman's departure left Glen in a parlous state with an ageing fleet of only seven vessels, and little prospect of acquiring fresh tonnage. A decade of generally poor trading had sapped both the financial reserves and the will of the partners to carry on, and the pressure to sell was becoming irresistible. Allan McGregor appears to have maintained the family commitment to private ownership as long as he possibly could, but he was now almost completely isolated. One brother, Douglas, had withdrawn from the business several years before and moved to China, putting even greater

Glenavon (left) was acquired as part of a joint venture with Ellerman, but after only four years with Glen was returned to her former owners in 1910. To the right is British India's *Dilwara* (5,441/1891). *[G.R. Scott collection]*

Glen fleet - final sixty-fourth shareholders, 1910							
	Glenesk	*Glenfarg*	*Glenlochy*	*Glenturret*	*Glenlogan*	*Glenroy*	*Glenstrae*
A.G. McGregor	17	9	16	16	5	1	24
B. McGregor	12	8	15	16	0	0	10
A.G. and B. McGregor	2	1	0	0	0	0	0
Cockburn and Ferguson	11	6	15	16	42	43	0
L. Gow's trustees	0	18	6	6	16	16	16
Total for managers	42	42	52	54	63	60	50
Other investors	22	22	12	10	1	4	14*
	64	64	64	64	64	64	64

*The other investors' holdings in *Glenstrae* include six shares owned by Miss J. McGregor, a sister of the managers.

pressure on Allan and Bertram. Relations between the brothers and the other major shareholder, Leonard Gow, Junior, never appear to have been congenial, and the latter began to push harder and harder for a move to limited liability as a means both to protect his immediate interest and to provide him with a way out of something which had become little more than a drain on capital.

If we return to the 64th share registers at the time of the final move to limited liability, we find the two families controlling 369 of the available 448 shares, but of the 369 shares, 291 were in McGregor hands and only 78 in Gow hands. In addition, a large part of the McGregor family shares were no longer actually controlled directly by the two brothers who were still in the business, but were actually in the hands of their bankers.

With the business continuing to flounder, the McGregor brothers came under increasing pressure from both the Gow family and their own bankers to restructure. According to Cameron McGregor's memoir, the family tried hard to maintain its independence, searching for new trades onto which it might more profitably deploy its ships, and hoping for a general improvement in freight rates. In the end, however, the pressure proved irresistible. On 12thAugust 1910 the business was incorporated as a private limited liability company under the name of Glen Line (McGregor, Gow and Co.) Ltd., with a capital of £225,000. The choice of name was dictated by the fact that conference rights were held not by the Glen Line (which hitherto had only been an informal trading name) but by the old managing partnership of McGregor, Gow and Co. The capitalisation might have seemed modest for such a long established business, but in truth the fleet was small and ageing, and goodwill had been eroded by fifteen years of harsh competition. Indeed the new company was only cleared of the outstanding liabilities of the old business through the inclusion and liquidation of the private assets of the original McGregor shareholders.

Takeover and renewal

The move to limited liability had been designed from the start as a platform for the sale of the Glen Line, and this sale followed rapidly after the change in corporate structure. The decade and a half before the Great War saw a wave of takeovers and mergers in the British liner industry. Many family-run businesses had suffered as badly as Glen from low freights and increased competition, and the descendants or executors of the founding generation were often all too ready to sell out to a new group of entrepreneurs who were moulding fragmented assets into large shipping groups. The Glen Line appears to have attracted early interest from two of these, Sir John Ellerman and Sir Christopher Furness, but neither was prepared to make an offer attractive enough to satisfy the bankers who were the real arbiters of the sale process. A third offer from Sir Owen Philipps, was accepted, and Glen followed other great names of British liner shipping such as Elder Dempster and Pacific Steam Navigation into the Royal Mail Group.

The alliance of Sir Owen Cosby Philipps (later enobled as Lord Kylsant), Chairman of Royal Mail, and Lord Pirie, Chairman of the shipbuilder Harland and Wolff was to transform a large part of the British liner trade in the years leading up to the First World War. Buoyed up by a resurgence in the shipping market after more than a decade of recession, the two men forged a huge empire and began a large programme of rebuilding in search of market dominance. Ultimately their brand of expansionism was to prove disastrous for group companies and shareholders alike, and Kylsant himself would fall as precipitously as he had risen. In the short term, however, his intervention revitalised businesses that had been sliding into decline. This was very much the case for the Glen Line.

The sale of the McGregor family's share to Philipps' Elder Dempster was reported at a directors' meeting on 17th January 1911 (the same meeting, poignantly enough, at which the death of Leonard Gow senior, the surviving founder of the Glen enterprise, was recorded). At that date, the Glen Line owned a fleet of just seven vessels, of which only two, *Glenroy* and *Glenstrae*, had been completed after the turn of the century. Business conditions were beginning to pick up, a previous meeting in October 1910 having heard from the chairman 'that the Freight Market was improving… and he looked forward to a year or two of better times.' If the company was to capitalise on better business conditions and begin to restore its position within the Far East trade, it was clear that it would need fresh tonnage.

The process of renewal took some time to gather momentum. The existing management were still not convinced of the attractions of the liner business, particularly on the homeward berth. A directors' minute of 6th March 1911, for example, recorded: 'The subject of loading homeward was discussed and it was resolved that at the present it was advisable to secure best possible employment homeward, not necessarily by taking the berth but by chartering for whole or part cargoes if securable.' A month later, *Glenfarg* was reported to be taking coal cargoes along the Asiatic coast because the China homeward berth was 'not offering any inducement to load from there.' As late as October 1912 the directors were considering offers to purchase all five of the 1890s-built ships in the fleet. The new owners, however, clearly had no intention of breaking up the business. The response of Philipps to the sale proposition was that he was 'unable to see way clear to disposing of any steamers till advised how the Board intend to maintain a regular service until new boats arrive.'

The oldest ship in the fleet, the 1891-built *Glenesk* was eventually sold at the end of 1912 to Japanese owners for £16,000 (more than double her depreciated book value), but a month later a lucrative charter of £2,750 a month for three months for *Glenlogan* was turned down because she was 'needed on berth'. By this time, one very important step in the rebuilding process had already been completed. Royal Mail had first acquired an interest in Glen's old rival, the Shire Line, in April 1907, taking an equal third stake with the original managing company Jenkins and Co. and T. and J. Brocklebank (which had itself bought into the business the year before). Three months later, Royal Mail and Brocklebank had bought out Jenkins and Co. entirely, and in 1911 Royal Mail had bought out Brocklebank to become the sole owner of the Shire Line. The Royal Mail Group thus owned both Glen and Shire, but at this time the two businesses were still managed operationally by their original brokers, McGregor, Gow and Co. (already owned by Royal Mail) and Norris and Joyner. In order to facilitate the merging of the two services, Sir Owen Philipps bought Norris and Joyner in 1912, merging it with Glen's broker to form McGregor, Gow, Norris and Joyner Ltd (a firm which assumed its final form in 1917 as McGregor, Gow and Holland Ltd. following the appointment of Charles Holland as managing director). The two shipping companies maintained their separate identities, with Shire ships flying the Royal Mail flag, but henceforth their service to the Far East was run jointly under common brokerage.

New tonnage for both companies followed the amalgamation of interests. A total of six large steamships were ordered, four for Shire (which was even shorter of tonnage than its old rival) and two for Glen. To help accelerate the rebuilding process, three further ships were bought on the stocks, two for Shire and one for Glen. The first arrival in the Glen fleet, and the only addition before war broke out, was the vessel bought on the stocks. Bartram and Sons of Sunderland was building a group of three steamers for the Aberystwyth-based tramp firm of John Matthias and Co. In 1913, Philipps bought all three. The first two, which had already been launched as *Salopian* and *Reptonian*, went to Shire as *Radnorshire* and *Merionethshire*. The third, which was briefly assigned the name *Salopian* after the sale of her predecessor, was purchased on the stocks and launched as *Glenearn*, joining the fleet in January 1914. The new vessel, which was roughly the same size as the *Glenlochy/Glenturret* pair of 1896, but two knots slower, was obviously something of a stop-gap. Originally designed for the higher end of the tramping business, where owners looked to earn superior returns through charters to liner companies, she was adequate for the trade but no more. As a result of general ship price escalation, she was actually slightly more expensive than the 1896 ships, costing Glen £60,500. This investment, however, was small compared to that being made in the ships building to the company's own design.

It was normal Royal Mail Group practice to build as many ships as possible at the Harland and Wolff yards controlled by Lord Pirie. These, however, were fully occupied with other orders (mostly from other Group companies) and the pre-war Glen/Shire orders went to outside yards. Workman, Clark and Co. of Belfast built all four Shire vessels, while the two Glen orders went to Hawthorn, Leslie and Co. of Newcastle. The new Glen ships, to be called *Glengyle* and *Gleniffer*, represented the largest step forward in design, power and carrying capacity the company had yet undertaken. The ships were 500 feet long with a gross tonnage of 9,400 and deadweight capacity of 13,175. In capacity terms they were roughly twice the size of any other vessel in the fleet except the second-hand *Glenlogan*. In addition they were the company's first twin-screw ships, powered by two triple-expansion engines with a service speed of 12-13 knots and a top speed of 15 knots. Needless to say, such size and power did not come cheaply, each vessel costing in the region of £180,000, three times the cost of any other vessel in the fleet.

Glen did not have the money to pay for these expensive new ships. As a result, the new owners undertook a significant expansion of the capital base. In 1914, the authorized share capital was increased from £225,000 to £1 million. The money to take up these new shares came not from the general public, but from other companies within the Group. Glen's public share base had been very narrow when it was taken over, and remained that way throughout its time in the Royal Mail Group. The Group as a whole was raising significant funds from the public and from banks to fund both fleet expansion and further acquisitions of existing companies. This would eventually prove its undoing, but financial ruin was still far in the future in the heady days leading up to the First World War. For Glen itself, the important consideration in the short term was simply that its shareholders were making funds available to expand and modernize the fleet.

Perils of war

The onset of the First World War found Glen only just beginning to rebuild its fleet and its Far East service. With the arrival of *Glenearn* at the beginning of the year, the fleet had gone up to seven, but four vessels had been built in the mid-1890s, and the arrival of the first of the Royal Mail sponsored new buildings would not have produced a long-term increase in size even under peacetime conditions. With the capital base having been expanded, there were sufficient resources to add further new vessels. These were to appear during the war years. Unfortunately, losses between 1914

Glengyle running trials in 1914. She represented a massive step forward in size and was intended for a service from the UK to the Far East and on to the west coast of North America. *[Ian Rae collection]*

and 1918 were to prove sufficiently severe to delay the completion of the fleet renewal process until the end of the decade.

The new *Glengyle* arrived in October 1914. By that time, two ships had already been lost. Neither, paradoxically, had actually been sunk by the enemy. The 20-year old *Glenfarg*, the oldest ship in the fleet, left Moji for Woosung at the beginning of a homeward voyage on 13th August. Early the next morning she struck an uncharted rock off the Shirose Lighthouse. The forward holds filled rapidly, and an hour and a half after the initial impact number 2 bulkhead appeared to give way. All hands were safely evacuated into the boats, which had already been lowered and in just over a quarter of an hour the ship sank. The entire crew was picked up by a nearby Japanese steamer and landed at Nagasaki, where a naval court subsequently exonerated Captain Williams and his officers from any blame for the loss.

In the same month, the company lost the services of its newest vessel when *Glenearn* was trapped in Hamburg on the last leg of only her second voyage. It appears that German authorities did not allow the ship the 24 hours laid down by the Hague Convention to clear their waters after the outbreak of war, and seized *Glenearn* illegally. One way or the other, the vessel was lost to her owners, who abandoned her to the underwriters under the War Risks scheme in the following year. This piece of bad luck was partially balanced by one extremely large slice of fortune. On 28th October, *Glenturret* was stopped and boarded by the German cruiser *Emden* off Penang. *Emden* had just sunk the old Russian cruiser *Zhemchug* inside the harbour and would undoubtedly have added the Glen ship to her tally had not another Allied warship happened on the scene. The German boarding party was recalled, and *Glenturret* escaped into Penang harbour while *Emden* busied herself sinking her new quarry, the French torpedo-boat *Mousquet*.

The second of the large new steamships *Gleniffer* joined the fleet in June 1915. While she was still fitting out, however, the company had lost a third ship, once again to marine hazard. *Glenroy* was on the homeward leg of a voyage from Portland, Oregon and Vladivostock when she stranded on the Falloden Shoal near Singapore on 4th April 1915. The vessel had been proceeding at speed and was badly holed, settling immediately on the reef, where strong tides soon completed the work of destruction. Although the whole crew was rescued and some cargo eventually salved, the vessel herself began to break up within days and had to be abandoned as a total loss. On this occasion, the Court of Enquiry was highly critical of the ship's officers, who were held to have navigated their vessel in a highly rash fashion in dangerous coastal waters. The Master, H.W.E. Holman, had his certificate suspended for six months, and the First Officer, P.L. Sanders, had his suspended for three.

Beyond these early misfortunes, the war only touched lightly on the Glen Line until 1916. Government use of merchant shipping for military and naval purposes was fairly intensive, but fell unevenly across the British mercantile marine. Throughout the war, only two of the company's older vessels were requisitioned. The first of these, *Glenturret*, served briefly as a supply ship in August 1914 and then did not return to government service until October 1915. She would then serve in a variety of other roles until her loss in 1918. The second vessel, *Glenlochy*, did not become a military transport until February 1916. She too would then stay on a variety on different government roles for the remainder of her time in company ownership. The rest of the fleet remained on the Far East service, which was now being run in conjunction with the Shire vessels which were under Royal Mail ownership. Advertised as the 'Glen and Shire Joint Service of Steamers', it generally appears to have been able to maintain at least monthly departures from UK ports (although not, as ads carried as late as January 1916 appeared to suggest, from Hamburg and Antwerp!). While there was no significant enemy threat to the ships in distant waters after Germany's overseas warships were sunk in 1914-1915, the shipping routes nearer home were to become increasingly dangerous with the growth of the U-boat offensive.

Enemy submarines were not just to become a dangerous threat to British shipping in home waters and the North Atlantic. In 1915, the German admiralty began to transfer U-boats to the Mediterranean to operate not just in Turkish waters, but also from Austro-Hungarian naval bases in the Adriatic. These boats were able to prey on the concentration of Allied shipping passing through relatively restricted but largely unprotected waters with great effectiveness, and it was one of them which registered the enemy's first submarine success against Glen.

Glengyle, homeward bound from her second Far East voyage with 12,000 tons of general cargo, left Port Said for Genoa and London on 30th December 1915. At 1.50 in the afternoon on New Year's Day 1916, she was proceeding at 12½ knots some 240 miles east by south of Malta when a torpedo was sighted only 50 yards off the port beam. There was no time for evasive action, and following a 'tremendous explosion' which killed four Chinese engine room personnel, the ship at once began to heal over. A panic broke out while manning the boats and before five were got away, three European and three Chinese crewmen were drowned. Soon afterwards a second torpedo struck the ship on the staboard side and broke her back. After this, the assailant, *U 34*, surfaced and fired about 35 shells into *Glengyle* before taking her Master briefly on board for interrogation. The stricken ship remained afloat, and the German commander used the Master's boat to put bombs on board her which set fire to the cargo. Further shells were then fired into the vessel which finally sank at 5.20 pm. The survivors were picked up by *HMS Minstrel* without further casualties, about an hour after the enemy had departed. There was, however, to be one further casualty of what was to prove Glen's worst war loss when the firm's Managing Director, Allan McGregor, died suddenly soon afterwards. It was widely believed that it was the shock of *Glengyle's* loss which had caused his death.

Gleniffer was the second of the big new ships, and would enjoy a long life, surviving both world wars. *[Ambrose Greenway collection]*

Glenamoy was the second motor ship to join the fleet, and was the only one of the first generation of diesel-powered ships to have a full career with Glen Line. *[J. and M. Clarkson collection]*

The company remained chronically short of tonnage, and this may have helped push it into the vanguard of British development of the new motorship technology, which had just begun to make a commercial impact when war broke out. Harland and Wolff held a licence to produce diesel engines to the pioneering Burmeister and Wain design, and its chairman Lord Pirrie was a convinced enthusiast for the new machinery. He had some difficulty, however, in finding buyers among British firms sceptical of alternatives to steam propulsion. Glen appears to have been sufficiently desperate to take the risk, although according to Cameron McGregor, they actually had to retire their Superintendent Engineer to get around his objections! The Harland and Wolff/motorship connection was cemented soon after when Pirrie was appointed to the Glen board to replace the deceased Allan McGregor, and shortly thereafter elevated to chairman.

The first two motorships to enter the fleet were actually laid down for other owners. *Glenartney* was purchased for £171,000 in September 1915 after only four months service as Elder Dempster's *Montezuma*. She was followed up by a new *Glengyle*, a smaller ship completed as Leyland's *Bostonian* in December 1915 and bought by Glen for £150,000 three months later. It seems likely that both sellers were quite willing to dispose of vessels which Pirrie's considerable powers of salesmanship had persuaded them to take against their better judgement in the first place. For Glen, however, they marked the beginning of a revolution which would propel the firm to the forefront of British motorship development, and make them for a short while owner of the largest motorship fleet under the red ensign.

These new ships were joined by two further new recruits in the summer of 1916. The first, *Glenogle*, was a 6,800 gt steamship from the same Hawthorn, Leslie yard that had produced the slightly larger *Glengyle* and *Gleniffer*. She was actually to prove the last steamship ever built for the company. Other steamships would enter the fleet after both world wars, but these would all be second-hand standard ships bought as stopgaps. The second, *Glenamoy*, was a motorship, and like her sister *Glenartney*, a product of Harland and Wolff. Price inflation was not quite the problem it would become in the second half of the war, and the new ship cost Glen only £14,000 more than her sister.

The year ended on a sour note with the loss of a second ship to an enemy submarine while homeward bound through the Mediterranean. The victim in this case was the ageing *Glenlogan*, which Glen had brought back to life after

her stranding in Houlder colours during the country's previous experience with war. In a near repetition of the loss of *Glengyle* ten months before, *Glenlogan* was torpedoed without warning by *U 21* some 10 miles south east of Stromboli while on the Port Said to Genoa leg of a homeward voyage. The old ship sank within 35 minutes of being hit, but the entire crew of 73, together with 8 passengers, got away safely in the boats and were picked up within two hours by a French hospital ship.

1916 had been a year of mixed fortunes, with two losses and the tragic death of the managing director being balanced by the arrival of four splendid new ships. Sadly, some of the new ships were not destined to serve the company long. U-boats sank two further Glen liners in 1917, and in early 1918 claimed a third. All of the vessels lost were on the regular commercial service, and two of them came from the ranks of the new mid-war additions.

In an unpleasant echo of earlier losses, the first of the new group of casualties was another ship lost while still almost brand new. Indeed, *Glenogle* was the shortest lived of all of the losses. When intercepted by *U 24* outward bound from London on 27th March 1917, she had been in service for only seven months. Two torpedoes struck the ship simultaneously some 207 miles south west of Fastnet at 4.15 in the afternoon. Luckily this large almost new vessel took an hour to sink and the entire crew got away safely. The Master and 53 men were picked up by the British steamer *Ilvington Court* (4,217/1911) quite quickly and were landed at Falmouth on the 29th, but the Chief Officer and 21 others spent five days adrift before being rescued by a trawler. Like *Glenearn* and *Glengyle* before her, *Glenogle* was on her second Far East voyage when lost.

Four months later one of the pre-war veterans was lost in the same waters. *Glenstrae* was inward bound southwest of the Scilly Islands on 28th July when a submarine (subsequently revealed to be *UC 62*) was sighted on the surface 1½ miles off the port bow. The Master turned towards the enemy but was unable to avoid a torpedo which struck abreast number 3 hatch. All hands except one casualty of the explosion were got away safely in the boats before the ship sank and were picked up the following morning by a British destroyer, to be landed at Plymouth.

February 1918 very nearly brought a double disaster in the dangerous waters of the Mediterranean. By this time, merchant ships were being taken through the Mediterranean in convoy, but this proved no guarantee of safety for

Glenamoy and *Glenartney*, which sailed together from Alexandria on the last day of January. On the next day *Glenamoy* was torpedoed in number 3 hold by *U 33* 240 miles from Alexandria. The ship made it safely back to her port of origin under her own steam and was beached awaiting repair. *Glenartney* was not so lucky when the convoy was attacked again on 6th February some 30 miles north east of Cape Bon. One torpedo from *UC 54* struck the ship amidships just before midnight, and a second may well have hit simultaneously aft. The ship settled rapidly, but due to the proximity of escorts, the only lives lost were two men killed in the original explosion.

By this time two of the Shire vessels employed on the joint service had also been lost, both sunk in the Atlantic by the commerce raider *Möwe* within a few days of each other in early 1917. A third ship was sunk by a U-boat in May 1918. By this time, Glen itself had suffered its last loss to the enemy, but not its last casualty of the conflict. The company was lucky not to lose the veteran *Glenlochy*, which suffered a fire in her cargo of nitrates off the east coast of America in late May. The vessel was actually abandoned with the flames setting off the ammunition of her aft-mounted deck gun, but the fire died down and the crew was able to re-board and take the ship into Newport News. Her sister *Glenturret*, however, was lost in apparently less dangerous circumstances less than two months later. This last wartime casualty was a result of the pressures of war rather than of any form of enemy action. *Glenturret* arrived at St. Nazaire on 23rd July with a full cargo of wheat from South America, and was ordered into the port to lighten the ship before making the passage up the Loire to Nantes. Three days later, with the process not completed, she was ordered to sail despite the protests of the master and subsequently stranded in mid-river. The ship proved to be hopelessly stranded, and defied all attempts to get her off. In a tidal river with a strong current flowing, she quickly broke her back. Although a caretaker crew was left aboard and further attempts were made to re-float her, she finally broke in two and was scrapped after the war.

The four losses of 1917-1918 were only balanced by two new arrivals. These were a mismatched pair of motorships, again from Harland and Wolff. The 5,000gt *Glenavy*, delivered in September 1917 at a cost of £212,000, was easily the smallest of her type to join the fleet. She was followed a year later by *Glenapp*, broadly similar in dimensions to the *Glenartney/Glenamoy* pair, but powered by two eight-cylinder diesels rather than the six-cylinder machinery of her near sisters.

Glen's war losses pale into insignificance compared to those suffered by some larger companies. They did, however, represent a fairly large percentage of the company's available tonnage, including three large new ships which never really had a chance to realise their potential. The company was very lucky with loss of life, with only one vessel losing more than one or two crewmen, and even she only a fraction of the lives at risk. The positive side of the whole experience came from membership in a large shipping group. Had Glen still been independent, there must have been a very real risk that losses would have driven it out of business. Under the dynamic Kylsant-Pirrie leadership this was never a risk, and the funds for new tonnage of very modern design were made readily available. Whether the business could really stand the cost of such capital expansion was still a question to be answered. When the guns finally fell silent in November 1918, Glen's managers could look forward to the future with the confidence that the fleet rebuilding campaign dislocated by the war would soon give it the ships to rebuild a fully competitive Far East service.

Rebuilding to reconstruction

The war years had hit Glen very hard. Apart from five ships sunk by U-boats, the company had lost another three to marine hazard, as many as it had lost in more than 40 years before 1914. In addition, the captured *Glenearn* had been abandoned to the underwriters and returned to the British flag with another

owner. Only the 22-year old *Glenlochy* remained of the pre-war fleet. The company took advantage of the hugely inflated prices prevalent in the post-war shipping market to dispose of her on very favourable terms. In June 1919 she was sold to a Greek owner for £160,000, almost three times her original building price. She was destined to have an unhappy end, as her owner, financially stretched like so many who had bought during the short-lived boom, resorted to desperate measures to meet his creditors. Her wreck in the Azores in 1921 was deemed by the underwriters to have been deliberate, and the courts backed up their refusal to pay insurance.

Beyond *Glenlochy*, McGregor, Gow had only five war-built vessels sailing under their flag at the Armistice, the steamship *Gleniffer* and the motorships *Glenamoy*, *Glengyle*, *Glenavy* and *Glenapp*. They were a heterogeneous group, the first two having lost their sister ships, the last three never having had any. Reinforcements, however, arrived quickly, both through the completion of ships laid down during the war, and from post-war purchases and new buildings. Glen's post-war rebuilding was really part of the far larger effort set in hand by its parent group. Lords Kylsant and Pirrie embarked on one of the most ambitious building and buying sprees in shipping history in an effort to prepare the Royal Mail Group for the expected peacetime return to prosperity. This effort was eventually to end in ruin for the Group and its chairman, poor post-war trading conditions providing insufficient revenues to support the massive capital cost of expansion at boom prices. Glen was to end up with a balance sheet as badly stretched as its sister companies. In 1920, its authorized share capital was increased again, this time from £1 million to £5 million. This was not fully called up, but the firm's issued capital still rose to £2.3 million. As before, these shares were taken up by other Group companies. The general public held only about $\frac{1}{2}$ % of Glen's shares, with all the rest being held by Royal Mail and Elder Dempster. Their investment was to prove a poor one, but in the short term at least Glen finally got the ships it required to resume the Far East trade on a comprehensive basis.

Post-war tonnage basically came from four different sources. Glen got its share of the Group's huge purchase of war standard ships, 76 of which were brought to the Shipping Controller at a total cost of just over £15 million. The four Glen purchases were sisters from the pre-fabricated *War N* class, purchased at a total cost of just over £1 million, or £250,000 per vessel. They were hardly ideal vessels for the Far East trade, being too slow, and possibly too small, for optimal use, but they were readily available and could at least fill a gap until better ships could be built. Although the war had temporarily removed German competition from the east coast and European berths, the Japanese liner companies had emerged from hostilities stronger than ever, and the need for tonnage was acute. The four *War N*s were all given Glen names beginning with S, with a mixture of Scottish and Irish origins, *Glenspey*, *Glenshane*, *Glensanda* and *Glenstrae*. Only the last of these was a traditional company name, and only it would ever be used again.

The second group of ships, again a quartet, were already on the stocks of Harland and Wolff's Govan yard, the same yard that as London and Glasgow had built most of Glen's nineteenth century vessels. Twin-screw, 405-foot motor ships of some 6,750gt, they had been laid down for other group companies, but were launched for Glen with Glen names. Apart from Glen's own tonnage shortage, the transfer appears to have been motivated by a decision to concentrate the Group's motor ships in one company. The new vessels entered service between July 1919 and April 1920, all carrying new Irish glen names: *Glenade*, *Glenariffe*, *Glentara* and *Glenluce*. Although more modern in concept than the war standards, they suffered the same operational drawbacks. Experience was to show that they were really too small to be optimal for the route. In addition, and in common with most of the early Harland and Wolff motor ships, they were really too slow (10½ knots) to be competitive with modern foreign tonnage. They were also very expensive, costing the company an average of £371,360 per vessel.

Three components of Glen Line's post-First World War reconstruction programme.

Right: the war standard N type *Glenshane* – small and slow. *[J. and M. Clarkson collection]*
Middle: the intermediate-sized motor ship *Glenade* of 1919 was one of a class of four found to be too slow for the company's services. *[Ambrose Greenway collection]*
Bottom: *Glenogle* of 1920 was part of the quintet of large ships which formed the core of the inter-war fleet. *[Roy Fenton collection]*

The third source of tonnage was Glen's sister company, the Shire Line. The remains of this fleet had actually been integrated from an ownership point of view into Royal Mail, and some of the ships were employed on Royal Mail American routes. In order to maintain Shire's old Far East conference rights, of which Glen Line was the beneficiary, it was desirable to employ some on the Far East service. There were seven shire-named steamships in the Royal Mail fleet, three assorted former war standards and two pairs of large 1913-1915 built vessels from the yard of Workman, Clark. All but one of these ships was to feature on the Glen-Shire Far East service at some time during the interwar period, but two were to be a permanent feature. With the disregard for homogeneity that characterised fleet deployment throughout the period, the two chosen were not sisters, but one each of the 470- and 500-foot Workman, Clark pairs. *Pembrokeshire* and *Carnarvonshire* would remain under Royal Mail ownership until 1933, but from 1920 were functionally on permanent charter to Glen. Unlike the other immediate post-war recruits, they were large enough for the service. They were, however, a bit on the slow side, and more importantly were relatively expensive to run.

Although *Carnarvonshire* was a sister ship of *Gleniffer*, none of the first ten post-war additions to the Glen fleet were post-war designs drawn up to the company's own specifications. The fourth and last group of additions were designed from the first to be Glen vessels, and were to provide the core of the fleet through the 1920s and 1930s. There were five vessels in this group, *Glenogle, Glenapp, Glengarry, Glenbeg* and *Glenshiel*, names which marked a pleasing and what was to prove a final move back to traditional Scottish Glen names. (*Glenapp* was actually laid down with an Irish name, *Glenfarne*, but was renamed when the first ship of that name was transferred to Elder Dempster, while *Glenshiel* was initially planned as *Glencree*.) They were actually part of a larger group of ten, all built by Harland and Wolff's various yards, the other five being destined for the joint Royal Mail/Holland America service to the west coast of North America. It would actually take four years to get the entire group into service. *Glenogle* and *Glenapp* were completed on schedule in August and December 1920, but the construction of the next two was delayed after launch by severe material shortages, and they would not enter service until February and April 1922. *Glenshiel* was a later addition to the programme and did not appear until May 1924.

Purpose built 485-foot twin-screw motor ships with extensive lifting gear for use in underdeveloped eastern ports, the *Glenogle* class were at the forefront of British marine technology, and undoubtedly very good ships for their time. They were not, however, without their flaws. The biggest operational difficulty was their modest turn of speed. Until fitted with superchargers at the end of the 1920s, they could only manage a modest 12½ knots, better than most of the rest of the fleet, but still too slow to be competitive with the most modern ships in other liner fleets. Relatively low power to size ratios was a characteristic of early diesel design, but there is evidence that the shipbuilders themselves were not fully aware of the speed requirements of the service. In this regard, Cameron McGregor's unpublished memoir provides a fascinating insight into the genesis of the *Glenogle* class.

I remember a meeting at Cockspur Street, in Harland and Wolff's office, when Lord Pirrie spread out some plans on his desk and, pointing with pride and satisfaction at these blue prints, said – 'Now, Gentlemen, look – there's the type of boat that will make Blue Funnels sit up – cargo capacity in relation to deadweight never seen before – and mark the low consumption' – but it took us a little time to ascertain what the speed was going to be. Lord Pirrie wanted to build half-a-dozen then and there. Fortunately for us Sir Owen said (no doubt with a thought to the financial side) – 'Very nice, but we must look into it.' We all then turned our eyes on to the plans again, and the silence was suddenly broken by our Marine Superintendent, Captain Willy, saying in that very quiet way he had – 'Well, My Lord, these are not the kind of ships to make anybody sit up.' Lord Pirrie's Irish eyes flashed and he said, 'Pray, why not?' and Captain Willy retorted – 'Because they would only be useful in a tortoise race.' A tense moment ensued. The trouble was at that time Harland's designers wished to build a ship that would be attractive to shipowners as a whole, and we on the other hand knew that the only way to get the better paying measurement cargo was by speed, which could only be forthcoming at the expense of cargo capacity and deadweight. Eventually, after many meetings, Lord Pirrie agreed, I think a little reluctantly, to fine down the model, reduce the cargo capacity and give us 12½ knots instead of 10½ knots with an increased consumption.

As modified, the *Glenogle* class would be solid, if not spectacular, performers that would produce the best voyage results of the first decade and a half of peace. The real problem with the ships, however, was again their cost. Early motorship technology was undoubtedly much more expensive than tried and tested steam propulsion, and the new vessels were also large and complex in design. They also suffered from being built at the height of the post-war boom, when shortages of everything from shipyard space to labour and raw materials pushed prices to hitherto unimagined heights. The average cost to Glen of each of the first four vessels was a staggering £623,446. *Glenshiel*, built after prices had returned to more normal levels, still cost the firm £434,532, almost two-and-a-half times times the cost of the roughly equivalent steamship *Gleniffer* of 1915. Such high capital costs could only have been sustained if the ships were able to operate in sustained boom conditions. If written down over 20 years, allowing roughly £25,000 for scrap, *Glenogle* and her first three sisters would each have had to earn voyage profits of £30,000 per annum just to cover depreciation, and even more to cover interest costs and overheads, and to provide a dividend for shareholders. The 1920s and 1930s were not to prove an ideal environment in which to meet such demanding financial requirements.

By the time *Glenshiel* was delivered in May 1924, the fleet had reached something approaching its normal peacetime shape. As mentioned, some of the early post-war additions had been short-term measures, and, as the large motor ships arrived, there were some disposals to bring the fleet to its desired size. As was the case with the allocation of Shire Line tonnage to the Far East service, there was something slightly random and arbitrary about this process of rationalisation. Two of the war standards went fairly quickly, *Glenstrae* to the sister group company Union Castle as *Banbury Castle* in August 1920, and *Glenspey* four months earlier to take up tramping with King Line (not a group company, but managed by one of the chairman's other businesses). In the same year, the war-built motor ship *Glenapp* was sold to another group company Elder Dempster, to be converted into the passenger liner *Aba*. Finally, in 1923, four of the smaller motorships were sold to yet another Group company, Pacific Steam Navigation. The war-built *Glengyle* and *Glenavy* became *Lautaro* and *Lagarto* respectively, while two of the immediate post-war quartet, *Glenade* and *Glenariffe*, became *Loreto* and *Loriga*.

This left Glen with a far more heterogeneous fleet than might have seemed necessary. Apart from the five large new motor ships, there was one other motor ship of only slightly smaller size, the 1916-built *Glenamoy*, and the two survivors of the post-war quartet, *Glenluce* and *Glentara*. The

Glenluce (1920) was chartered to the Pacific Steam Navigation Company for one year in 1924, later traded in the tramp market and was sold in 1936. She was only marginally profitable. *[G.F. Shotter collection]*

only other owned vessels were the last two war standards, *Glenshane* and *Glensanda*, and the large steamship *Gleniffer*, which was joined on charter from Shire by her near sister *Carnarvonshire* and the slightly smaller *Pembrokeshire*. The Glen service thus missed the chance to operate an entirely motorship service, and was forced to make do with what was roughly a mixture of four different vessel types. In some senses this mixture made little real difference, as operational experience would show that, apart from the new motorships, only *Glenamoy* was really a profitable proposition in difficult trading conditions. The apparently mixed nature of the disposal process was, however, a reminder of two factors which loomed large in Glen's fortunes at the time. The first was that the optimal vessel size and configuration was far less clear than it had been in pre-war days when there was only one basic form of propulsion available. The second was that the company's asset acquisition and disposal decisions were not being taken independently. All of the disposals were to other group companies, whose needs might have loomed larger in group management's priorities. All of the new buildings came from a shipyard that was also within the group structure and that might have had a superior call on the collective drive for profit. There is no evidence to suggest that Glen was penalised in financial dealings with other parts of the group. The sale of four ships to Pacific Steam Navigation for £550,000 in 1923, for example, certainly caused Glen a significant capital loss, but the culprit was falling asset prices and it is doubtful if the ships would have realised any more if sold to an outsider. Similarly, the high cost of construction in the immediate post-war period was a general problem, and there is no suggestion that Glen could have acquired its ships significantly cheaper from other builders. It is fair to say, however, that the investment decisions taken were made in the context of a larger (and as time would prove, misguided) Group strategy, and were not necessarily optimal for the company itself.

While the composition of the fleet might not have been optimal, and the cost of creating it was to prove prohibitive, the fact remains that Glen was once again in a position to offer a full liner service to the Far East. This had not been the case for the past twenty years, and indeed the fleet had not really been as strong or as competitive since the 1880s. There was some juggling of the less satisfactory

vessels in the fleet. *Glenluce*, two of whose sisters had been sold to PSNC as 'rather slow for Company's service' was herself chartered to the same firm for a year in 1924. On her return, she was actually run as a tramp for a while with a reduced crew before returning to her regular service. The Shire steamer *Carmarthenshire*, sister to the already employed *Pembrokeshire*, came over on charter in 1923 and remained on the service until sold by her owners in 1929. Both of these ships, as well as the larger *Carnarvonshire*, were converted back to coal from oil in an attempt to reduce their very heavy fuel bills.

Economic problems

Glen experienced great problems in earning a satisfactory operating return from its enlarged fleet during the 1920s. It faced three basic problems: running costs had increased significantly, available freights did not come up to initial expectations, and competition from both British and foreign lines simply became tougher and tougher.

Larger ships required larger crews and consumed more fuel. Crew wages had increased significantly and so had the cost of other stores. A comparison put before the Management Committee in 1924 showed that on *Pembrokeshire*'s most recently completed voyage the average cost of stores consumed per day had been just over £19. By contrast, the same figure for *Glenlogan* over three voyages in 1913 had been between £10 and £11. Increasing costs would have been bearable if they had been matched by increasing revenues, but unfortunately this was not the case.

Freight revenues fell sharply over the first few years of the decade, and recovered only slightly thereafter. As the table overleaf demonstrates, Glen earned only just over half the total net freight in 1923 that it had been in 1920. For the remainder of the years before the Great Depression struck in 1929, revenues stagnated further for several years and then only crept back up towards 1921-22 levels. Aggregate tonnage of freight carried actually increased, although there was a distinct stagnation in the generally more remunerative measurement cargo. Partially as a result of this, but also because of increasing competitive pressure, average freight rates declined sharply. In addition, some of the normal sources of cargo seemed to be drying up. In 1924, for example, it was decided to omit both Hong Kong and Shanghai from two successive homeward voyages 'due to stagnant market', with the ships proceeding straight from Vladivostock to the Straits and Singapore. This was largely a result of problems with a Chinese economy damaged by increasingly severe internal conflict. Not surprisingly, revenues from homeward voyages declined far more sharply than was the case for the outward leg of the trips.

General economic problems were behind much of the decline in revenues, but increasing pressure from other operators was also to blame. As early as August 1924, Glen's management committee was talking about the desirability 'that the British lines should be in thorough agreement, so as to be able to present a united front to the Germans.' Far bigger problems in the early post-war years, however, were presented by other competitors that had not been temporarily removed from the scene by the war or the loss of tonnage through the Armistice. In November 1924, for example, Glen carried only 9% of UK tea shipments from Shanghai, compared to 22% by Ellerman and 52% by Blue Funnel. In the first half of 1925, Glen carried only 3% of all UK and continental European cargo from the same port, compared to 30% for Blue Funnel, 14% for Nippon Yusen Kaisha, 10% for P & O,

8% for Hamburg Amerika and 5 to 6% each for Messageries Maritime, Norddeutscher Lloyd and Ellerman. Part of Glen's difficulty stemmed from the larger size of some of the competing fleets, but the company was also suffering as a result of the slow speed of its ships. In 1925 management calculated that the average voyage time to Shanghai was 40 days for P&O and 41 days for N.Y.K. In contrast, its own average time was 47 days. Even the best performers, the *Glenogle* class, only managed 44 days. The large Shire steamers took a day longer, but the *Glenluce* and *Glentara* took 51 days and the ex-war standards 56 days.

A comparison of the operating profitability of the various ships in the fleet in the 1920s gives an interesting insight into the viability of the different sizes and propulsion systems employed. The basic situation was clearly that diesel was more profitable than steam, that larger size was more economical, and that speed made an important difference. The war standards were consistently loss-making throughout, confirming their status as unsatisfactory stop-gaps. The larger steamships, all purpose-built for the route, were only just able to cover costs in the generally difficult trading conditions of the time. The smallest motorships did only marginally better on average, although one did significantly better than the other. The larger motorships were actually the only ships to provide a consistently satisfactory operating return. It is interesting here, however, to note that the mid-sized *Glenamoy*, did almost as well as the larger and newer *Glenogle* class. This is particularly relevant when one considers that *Glenamoy*, at a building price of £185,000, cost less than half of what *Glenshiel* was built for, and less than a third of the price of the other four ships of the class. The comparison is not quite fair as there was significant price inflation between 1916 and 1920-24, but it does raise questions as to whether the *Glenogle* class were actually a bit too big for the trade. The whole issue becomes more germane when one considers the issue of covering depreciation. *Glenamoy* was actually the only vessel in the whole fleet to show a profit after depreciation in the 20s. The far more expensive *Glenogle*

Tonnage carried and net freight receipts, 1920-1928

	Number of sailings	Total carried (tons)	Average carried per voyage (tons)	Receipts £	Average receipts per ton £	Average receipts per voyage £
Outward						
1920	22	201,867	9,178	799,815	3.96	36,355
1921	24	142,312	5,930	503,282	3.54	20,970
1922	24	173,070	7,211	479,115	2.77	19,963
1923	26	202,048	7,771	497,201	2.46	19,123
1924	25	213,428	8,537	516,509	2.42	20,660
1925	25	192,495	7,700	441,597	2.29	17,664
1926	27	261,301	9,678	573,673	2.20	21,247
1927	26	266,211	10,239	573,010	2.15	22,039
1928	30	309,327	11,897	611,000	1.98	20,367
Homeward						
1920	21	158,515	7,548	1,125,587	7.10	53,599
1921	25	220,168	8,807	735,342	3.34	29,413
1922	28	254,044	9,073	561,247	2.21	20,045
1923	28	243,810	8,708	501,150	2.06	17,898
1924	25	242,056	9,682	456,570	1.89	18,263
1925	27	256,011	9,482	512,614	2.00	18,986
1926	30	286,249	9,542	532,819	1.86	17,761
1927	31	294,699	9,506	608,399	2.06	19,626
1928	28	256,414	9,158	545,550	2.13	19,484
Combined						
1920	21.5	360,382	16,762	1,925,402	5.34	114,867
1921	24.5	362,480	14,795	1,238,624	3.42	50,556
1922	26	427,114	16,427	1,040,362	2.44	40,014
1923	27	445,858	16,513	998,351	2.24	36,976
1924	25	456,286	18,251	973,079	2.13	38,923
1925	26	448,506	17,250	954,211	2.13	36,700
1926	28.5	547,550	19,212	1,106,492	2.02	38,824
1927	28.5	560,910	19,681	1,181,409	2.11	41,453
1928	29	565,741	19,508	1,156,550	2.04	39,881

Vessel profitability by type, 1924-1929

Vessel	Average profit per voyage (£)	Average profit per year (£)
War standard steamships		
Glensanda	- 1,131	-2,262
Glenshane	-301	-653
Radnorshire	-2,908	-4,362
Other steamships		
Gleniffer	759	1,517
Carnarvonshire	176	352
Pembrokeshire	295	590
Carmarthenshire	1,150	2,510
6,750 ton motorships		
Glenluce	331	606
Glentara	2,266	4,532
7,300 ton motorship		
Glenamoy	6,328	11,602
9,500 ton motorships		
Glenogle	6,718	13,435
Glenapp	7,598	16,462
Glengarry	6,495	14,073
Glenbeg	8,213	16,426
Glenshiel	6,850	13,157

class, despite higher voyage profits, were not actually covering their capital costs.

Given the low profitability of some of the less satisfactory members of the fleet, it is not surprising that Glen began to make some disposals towards the end of the decade. One of the war standards, *Glensanda*, was the first to go, being sold to the London tramp owners Meldrum and Swinson for £35,000 in 1928. The asymmetric pattern of fleet composition continued, however, as the next departure was not her sole remaining sister, but one of the smaller motorships. Sister Group company Elder Dempster found themselves temporarily short of appropriate tonnage following a marine loss, and bought *Glentara* from Glen at the beginning of 1929. *Glensanda* proved a reasonable success in the tramp role to which she was more suited by design, and sailed on as *Essex Lance* until sunk during the war, but *Glentara* did not prove a good buy for Elder Dempster, who sold her after four years, most of which was spent laid up.

The most interesting development of the period, however, was a sale that did not take place. In early 1929, Glen received an offer of £85,000 for *Gleniffer* from a whaling company. The large Glen/Shire steamships were ideal for conversion to whale factory ships, and two Shire vessels, *Carmarthenshire*, which had served on Glen charter from 1924, and *Cardiganshire*, which made a far briefer appearance in 1928, were actually sold by Royal Mail to Christian Salvesen for this purpose at the same time as Glen received the offer. On the surface, the offer was an attractive one. *Gleniffer* was 14 years old, and unlike the other vessels disposed of in the 1920s had been depreciated to a value (£50,000) where her sale would result in a capital gain rather than a loss. Management, unfortunately, felt that they had to turn down the offer, on the grounds 'that at such a figure no similar vessel of the same speed can be acquired, and the sale would disorganise the Service.'

The failed *Gleniffer* sale gives an indication of the biggest problem facing Glen at the end of the first post-war decade. Competition had been stiff, rates had been under pressure, and the fleet had not been ideally equipped to meet these challenges. Nonetheless, the company as an operating business was in reasonable shape, and was holding its own far better than some other British shipping lines had been doing. Its finances, however, had been stretched to the breaking point by the exorbitant cost of fleet reconstruction and new building in the early 1920s. Glen could not afford to sell *Gleniffer* because it could not afford to buy an adequate replacement. After the earlier disposals, the company was actually operating close to its limit, and needed to resort to occasional short-term charters to maintain a regular service. In 1929-30, no fewer than seven sailings were taken by non-regular ships, one each by *Cardiganshire* and *Montgomeryshire*, two by *Radnorshire* (all Royal Mail-owned vessels making their last Group sailings before sale), one by *Meissonier* from elsewhere in the Group, and one each by two Court Line tramps, the steamer *Quarrington Court* and the motor vessel *Aldington Court*. It was not a satisfactory position, as is evidenced by the fact that only two of these seven voyages actually registered a profit. Glen needed new tonnage, but did not have the means to buy it. In addition, the assets it did own had become seriously overvalued. The report submitted by the directors in July 1931 included a chilling note.

In submitting this balance sheet attention is drawn to the fact that the value of the Assets as they stand in the Books is in excess of present values. The matter has been under consideration, and a substantial writing down will ultimately have to be made.

Glen by this time was caught up in two larger, overlapping crises: the Great Depression and the collapse of the Royal Mail Group. Ultimately the latter was to have a far greater bearing on the future of the company, resulting as it would in a second change of ownership and a second 'rebirth' of the fleet. Before finding its saviour, however, Glen had to survive the sharpest contraction of trade the Far East trade, and indeed the whole industrial world, had ever faced.

The early 1930s witnessed economic catastrophe everywhere. For the British shipping industry, it brought the mass lay-up of vessels, the temporary extinction of some trades, the implosion of profits, and a wave of business failures. In many ways, Glen actually survived better than most. The fleet remained largely in commission throughout the period, and regular sailings were maintained, with only a slight drop in frequency. Unlike some of its sister Royal Mail Group companies, Glen was not burdened with excess tonnage, and there was actually only one further disposal during the depression years themselves, the last war standard, *Glenshane*, finally leaving the fleet. Only *Carnarvonshire* and *Glenluce* were ever actually laid up, the first in the second half of 1932 and the second for two shorter periods in 1934. All this notwithstanding, the company had to contend with a savage reduction in revenues.

The extent of the collapse in business can be appreciated from looking at the fortunes of the outward service between 1928 and 1934. In 1928, Glen made 30 sailings from its British and European terminal ports to the Far East. At its lowest ebb in 1931, the service still managed 23 departures. Cargo carried and freights earned contracted much more sharply. The lowest annual outward cargo carried (in 1932) represented only 39% of the 1928 total, while the lowest annual outward freight earned (in 1931) was only 35% of the 1928 equivalent. While things improved slightly after 1931-32, cargo carried in 1934 was only just over half that carried in 1928 and freights earned were still less than 50% of the pre-depression level.

Tonnage carried and net freight receipts 1928-1934						
Year	Sailings	Total (tons)	Average per voyage (tons)	Receipts (£)	Average per ton (£)	Average per voyage (£)
1928	30	309,327	11,897	611,000	1.98	20,367
1929	28	302,696	10,811	595,643	1.97	21,273
1930	24	173,185	7,216	347,837	2.00	14,493
1931	23	133,451	5,802	215,194	1.61	9,356
1932	24	121,430	5,056	232,482	1.91	9,687
1933	26	162,326	6,243	287,249	1.77	11,048
1934	26	176,688	6,796	294,337	1.67	11,321

With most voyages being undertaken with vessels only half full, profitability inevitably suffered. The large motorships suffered the least, with average voyage profits not falling to much less than 75% of 1920s levels. The rest of the fleet, however, suffered badly, with most voyages barely breaking even, and a significant proportion registering losses (see table overleaf).

Apart from chartered in tonnage, one other vessel joined the fleet in this period. Even although trading conditions were very bad, the company still felt able to run a regular service. With the sale of Royal Mail owned Shire tonnage, however, it was short of ships, with only *Carnarvonshire* and *Pembrokeshire* still available after 1930. Glen was not actually in a position to buy a new ship, but a workable short-term solution was found through the acquisition of the 1930-built motorship *Tolten* from her builders, Lithgows of Port Glasgow. *Tolten* had been ordered by Chilean owners, but had been left on the builder's hands after Compania Sud Americana de Vapores had run into financial difficulties. In an agreement dated 29 June 1933, Glen agreed to purchase the ship from Lithgows for £120,000, with the sum to be payable fifteen months after the contract date. Over the interim period, Glen paid a monthly sum to the builders of £1,467.4s.8d, of which £100 was regarded as part payment of the ultimate purchase price. This 'hire-

Vessel profitability by type, 1929-1934		
	Average profit per voyage (£)	Average profit per year (£)
War standard steamships		
Glenshane	-1,691	-3,383
Radnorshire	-2,651	-5,301
Other steamships		
Gleniffer	173	404
Carnarvonshire	-1,167	-2,528
Pembrokeshire	724	1,690
5,350 ton motorship		
Glenearn	591	1,181
6,750 ton motorship		
Glenluce	-2	-4
7,300 ton motorship		
Glenamoy	2,412	5,627
9,500 ton motorships		
Glenogle	5,015	11,703
Glenapp	5,721	12,396
Glengarry	4,434	9,606
Glenbeg	4,096	10,240
Glenshiel	5,296	12,357

purchase' arrangement suited both parties, as it got the ship off the builder's hands and gave Glen some badly needed tonnage without exposing them to an immediate capital spending requirement. *Tolten* was renamed *Glenearn* and entered service in the second half of 1933. She was not to prove a tremendous success. Like the *Glenluce* class she was really too small and too slow. The 'hire-purchase' period was extended to 1935, but the sale was never completed, and after five round trips to the Far East, *Glenearn* was returned to Lithgows.

While the Glen Line was struggling through the depression years, momentous events were unfolding at the corporate level which would ultimately result in a change in the company's ownership. The collapse and restructuring of the Royal Mail Group was a long and drawn-out process, complicated not just by the depths of the Group's insolvency and the extent to which public money and public confidence was involved, but by the intricate web of cross shareholdings and debt finance on which Lord Kylsant had built up the business. It was clear from the outset that much of the share capital of the shipping companies themselves was gone, tied up in expensive tonnage that could never pay for itself. The ultimate objective of the Trustees responsible for tidying up the mess Kylsant had created was to extract each company from the tangle of obligations and debts, and set it on its feet as a going concern without triggering insolvency and legal winding up. This inevitably meant the writing off of most existing share and debenture capital, and the sale of the business to new owners.

The shipping lines of the Royal Mail Group fell into two basic categories, those which were unable to meet their immediate financial obligations and were technically bankrupt, and those which were still viable businesses providing their overvalued assets could be written down to realistic values and fresh capital could be found to finance the slimmed-down balance sheet. The Glen Line, which had continued to make an operating profit (albeit a slim one insufficient to cover realistic depreciation and interest charges), fell into the second category. As had been the case when the business was first put up for sale more than two decades before, there were a number of shipping companies interested in acquiring the Line. Both P & O and Furness, Withy expressed an early interest. The most serious potential buyer from the very outset, however, was Glen's old rival in the Far East trade, Alfred Holt and Co., now under the dynamic leadership of Richard Holt, the nephew of one of the founders.

Holt's Blue Funnel Line had continued to dominate the Far East trade to and from the west coast of Britain, and had built up a diverse network of supporting businesses. The acquisition of the Glen/Shire franchise would give the access to the UK east coast trade. As early as August 1930, Richard Holt was writing to Walter Runciman, Chairman of the

Glenearn, the former *Tolten*, was at best a stop gap, acquired on terms akin to hire purchase. She returned to her former owners when Glen Line was restructured after the collapse of the Royal Mail Group. *[Ambrose Greenway collection]*

Seen in the Thames, *Glenshiel* was felt by Richard Holt to be 'rather too large', but this group was successful, if over-priced. Delivered several years after her four sisters, *Glenshiel* was almost a third cheaper. *[J. and M. Clarkson collection]*

Trustees, to express guarded interest. His letter gave an interesting analysis of the strengths and weaknesses of Glen after two decades of Royal Mail ownership.

> Our conclusion is that the five *Glenshiels* and the *Pembrokeshire* are good boats tho' the *Glenshiels* are rather too large – the others are poor property and not really suitable for the trade.
> I consider £1,200,000 as a full valuation for the eleven ships with their goodwill in the China trade.
> … it seems to me that speaking roughly the account balances on the basis of the shares, reserves and insurance fund being valueless. The concern has not been well managed for a long time and is now handicapped by unsuitable ships but I think with proper management it could be brought round.

Holt originally proposed buying 60% of Glen, but Runciman informed him that 'it would have to be the whole or none.' In January 1931, Richard Holt offered £1,250,000 to acquire the whole business. The Royal Mail Trustees were reluctant to accept this and other early offers for Group companies, believing that better terms could be arrived at by resisting the urge to sell under crisis conditions. In the event, their optimism over price was to prove misplaced, but such was the complexity of the overall group crisis that any early sale would almost certainly have proved impossible to execute. Although Holt was still in touch with Sir William McClintock (who had succeeded Runciman after the latter took a cabinet post) in early 1932, serious negotiations did not resume until 1934.

By this time, the tidying up of other Royal Mail assets had actually led to Glen acquiring two ships. *Carnarvonshire* and *Pembrokeshire* had been under Glen management on the Far East service since 1920, but had remained in Royal Mail ownership. The ongoing restructuring of Royal Mail required that these vessels be sold like the other Shire ships not deployed on the Glen/Shire route. With Glen's fleet down to only nine vessels, of which one (*Glenearn*) was unlikely to be retained in any re-structuring, the two ageing Shires were necessary to maintain a full list of sailings, and Glen therefore purchased them outright in March 1933. At the same time, Glen also formally acquired the Shire name and conference

rights. The combined price was a mere £15,000, an indication of the extent to which second-hand values had fallen in the depths of the Great Depression. Both ships were near the end of their economic lives and would actually be sold for scrap within a couple of years. These final sales, however, brought in just over double what Glen had paid two years before, and were the only capital transactions of the whole unhappy period in which the company did not register a loss.

A report on the Glen fleet prepared for the Trustees in early 1934 confirmed the extent to which the ships were overvalued. Excluding *Glenearn*, which any buyer could be expected to return to her builders, the 10-strong fleet was valued at only £350,000 compared to a book value of £3,062,603. Interestingly enough, the same report estimated that the cost of building up-to-date ships on a like-for-like basis would be £1,870,000, just over 60% of the fleet's book value, and roughly equivalent to the original aggregate purchase price of only the three most expensive ships.

Valuation of Glen Line fleet on 23rd March 1934 (prepared by C.H. Rugg and Co.)		
Vessel	**Age at 31st December 1933 (years-months)**	**Market value**
Glenshiel	9-9	£60,000
Glenbeg	11-10	£54,000
Glengarry	12-0	£54,000
Glenapp	13-2	£50,000
Glenogle	13-6	£49,000
Glenluce	14-1	£30,000
Glenamoy	17-4	£20,000
Gleniffer	18-8	* £11,750
Pembrokeshire	18-10	* £9,500
Carnarvonshire	19-11	* £11,750
		* UK break-up value

When negotiations resumed, Holt was still intent on taking only a controlling stake in Glen, but the Trustees continued to insist on a full offer. Finally in November Holt made an offer of £450,000 for Glen Line and £100,000 for its management company, McGregor, Gow and Holland, after Lloyd's Bank had agreed to advance £500,000 to the Ocean Steamship Co. to finance the purchase. This was significantly better than a rival offer from Lord Inverforth's United Baltic Corporation, whose threats to attack Blue Funnel's routes if it bought Glen were quickly squashed by government intervention. Negotiations continued, with Holt being forced to include Glen's unwanted Shanghai office building in the bid, and a final formal offer of £652,300 was finally made on 2nd March 1935. This was accepted, and on 29th April Ocean formally took over the Glen Line. The total amount written off in the reconstruction associated with the takeover was just under £3 million, wiping out all of the original share capital and a significant part of the firm's other liabilities.

Economic recovery
Writing to Walter Runciman in 1930 during the early stages of their negotiations over Glen, Richard Holt had talked of having 'a first class team who could easily do more work' and of preferring 'good new ships to second hand inferior ships.' When he finally completed the takeover four and a half years later, he proved as good as his word on both scores. There were numerous parallels between the two takeovers of the Glen Line in 1910-11 and 1934-35. In both cases a large and dynamic parent stepped in with far greater access to capital than its predecessor, and in both cases the new owner was fortunate in arriving at a time when trading conditions were beginning to improve after a prolonged slump. On each occasion as well, war was to intervene before post-takeover rebuilding was complete. The key difference between the first and the second takeover was that the second was initiated by a company with unrivalled expertise and a long record of success in Glen's own trade. The Glen and Shire Lines had been a relatively small and peripheral part of the rambling Royal Mail empire, a business in which most energy was concentrated on the far larger American and African shipping lines. The Holt business was more concentrated, and able from the start to devote sufficient expertise and capital to rebuild a business which was strongly complementary to its own. It was also of critical importance that Holt's west coast Far East business was relatively free from competitive challenge in its home port. As a result, the new owners actually gave Glen priority in the provision of new ships.

From the start, Glen was maintained as a separate operating entity within the Ocean group. It had its own London-based board of directors and managed its fleet under its own colours through McGregor, Gow and Holland. While cargo management remained with the London office, however, ship design, maintenance, routing and crewing were handled centrally from Liverpool. The existing managing directors, Cameron McGregor and Ernest Hills, stayed at the helm in the short term, but in 1937, a senior Ocean employee C.E. Wurtzburg was brought back from Singapore to take over management. Wurtzburg would remain as Glen's Managing Director through the Second World War until his death in 1952, and would be the man most closely associated with the firm's revival.

The keystone for revival was the provision of ships better able to meet the competitive requirements of the trade than the motley assortment with which Glen had sailed through the 1920s and early 1930s. The rebuilding process fell into two stages: a first in which completely unsatisfactory ships were replaced on a temporary basis by vessels transferred from the large Blue Funnel fleet, and a second in which new purpose-built ships were provided. The first stage was completed within a year of the takeover, but the second was only half way to fruition when the Second World War broke out.

When the ink dried on the takeover documents the Glen Line fleet had stood at 11 vessels. Of these, no fewer than five were disposed of in 1936. *Glenearn*, which had been excluded from the terms of the agreement, was returned to her builders under the terms of the original hire-purchase agreement after completing her fifth voyage at the end of

1935. *Glenluce*, the last of the unsatisfactory quartet of medium-sized and slow Harland and Wolff motor ships of 1919-20, completed an interrupted 30th and final voyage in February 1936 and was sold to Newcastle owners. Both of these vessels would have further careers, the first sailing under four different names until finally scrapped in 1967, and the second being torpedoed in 1941 as the Swedish *Korshamn*. The other three all sold to British owners, but all were ultimately destined for the breakers' yards. One of the paradoxes of the Scrap and Build scheme introduced by the government in an attempt to rationalise and modernise the British merchant marine was that some interested owners were actually short of old tonnage to offer for demolition. This produced a short-term upswing in the market for ageing second-hand tonnage, and ready buyers for the large old ships Glen could offer. Two of the three vessels disposed of were the former Shire Line steamships that Glen had only purchased as a stopgap in 1933. *Carnarvonshire* completed her thirty-first voyage in August 1935 and was then laid up until sold in January 1936. *Pembrokeshire*, always the more profitable of the two, lasted slightly longer in service, completing her thirty-third voyage in January 1936, but was sold in the same month. The final disposal was the war-built motorship *Glenamoy*, which completed her thirty-seventh voyage in July 1936 and was sold immediately afterwards. *Glenamoy* had been the most successful of the first generation of Harland and Wolff motorships, and the only one to come close to paying her way. She was, however, 20 years old, had survived torpedo damage in 1918 and a serious grounding in 1924, and would have required replacements for her outdated diesel engines. All three vessels were re-sold and broken up (in three different countries) within months of their disposal.

These disposals left Glen with only the five middle-aged *Glenogle* motorships and the veteran steamship *Gleniffer*. The latter, built in 1915, was a slightly unlikely survivor, but she was probably in better condition than the similar Shire vessels that were disposed of, and it would in any event only have been intended to keep her sailing for another few years until new tonnage could be built. In the event, the onset of war was to grant her a reprieve, and she would soldier on until 1947. She was not destined to be the only steamship sailing under Glen colours. While plans to order new tonnage went ahead, other ships were provided from Holt's large Blue Funnel fleet to keep the service running at full complement.

The first Blue Funnel vessel to make a Glen voyage since the nineteenth century was actually *Peisander*, which took an eastbound sailing in August 1935. Several other ships would also make single sailings to fill in gaps in the service (*Idomeneus* in 1936, and *Autolycus* and *Neleus* in 1938), but these were all voyages undertaken on what was essentially an internal charter basis. A more permanent measure of service maintenance was undertaken through the transfer of four other vessels to Glen colours. Of the ships involved, three were near sisters. *Elpenor*, *Machaon* and *Dardanus* were all members of a large group of 7,500-7,900 ton steamships built for Holts by a variety of builders over a period of some fifteen years. *Elpenor*, the oldest of the Glen recruits, had been completed by Hawthorn, Leslie in 1917, while *Machaon* had come from Caledon in 1920 and *Dardanus* from Workman, Clark in 1923. They were joined in Glen colours by one of Blue Funnel's relatively small number of motorships, the 1923-built *Tantalus*, a vessel of almost identical size and capacity despite her different appearance and power plant. None of these vessels were in their first flush of youth, and they were no faster than the ships Glen already had in service. They were, however, all products of Holt's famous policy of building ships to a higher standard than those of any competitors, and were of a size better proven to be economical on the trade than their often-larger Glen equivalents. *Dardanus*, renamed *Flintshire*, was the first to change her funnel from blue to red, sailing under new colours in August 1935. She was followed in October by *Glenfinlas* (ex-*Elpenor*) and in December by *Glenaffaric* (ex-*Machaon*). The quartet was completed in March 1936 when *Tantalus* was renamed *Radnorshire*.

Two of the four second hand ships transferred from the Blue Funnel fleet in the1930s.

Top: The steamer *Elpenor*, completed in 1917 was the oldest of the transfers.

Middle: *Elpenor* became *Glenfinlas* in October 1935. At some time her funnel was reduced in height and she served Glen Line throughout the war.

Bottom: The Blue Funnel motor ship *Tantalus* was transferred to Glen in 1936 and renamed *Radnorshire*. She reverted to Blue Funnel ownership and her original name in 1939.
[all B. and A. Feilden/J. and M. Clarkson]

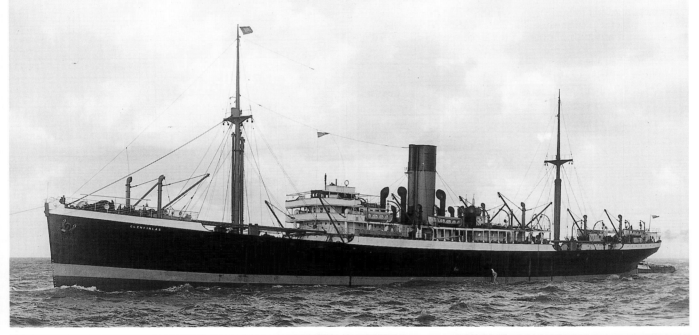

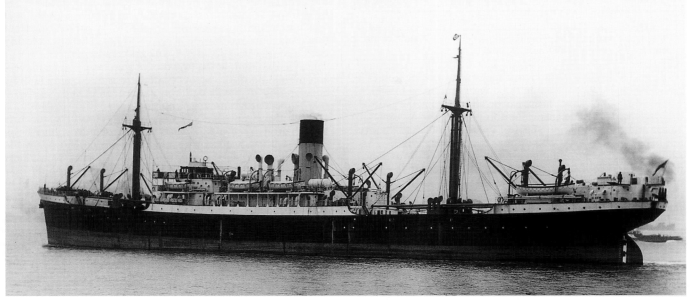

The choice of names for the transferred vessels had several interesting aspects. While any organizational remnant of the Shire Line had by now disappeared, the company still held the old company's east coast conference rights. To help maintain these, a minority of new fleet additions would henceforth always be given Shire names. New management seems from the start to have had a greater sense of history than its predecessor, and the two names chosen were those of two of David Jenkins' first three steamers of the 1870s. The maintenance of tradition was also apparent in Glen nomenclature. There were to be no repeats of the Irish Glen names introduced during the Pirrie-Kylsant years, and the new *Glenfinlas* bore a name which had also first been used in the 1870s. In this context, the fourth choice of name, *Glenaffaric*, was something of an anomaly, as it was one of only two new names introduced to the fleet during the last 35 years of its existence. It was at least a Scottish glen name, even if it was one that was frequently mis-spelt!

The revitalised Glen business began to show positive results in 1936. 1935 was actually a poor year, with average voyage profits coming in below those of 1933-34 and modest profits from most voyages being eroded by large losses on others. Business, however, was picking up, and 1935 was the year of maximum disruption from fleet changes. In 1936, average voyage profits reached a level not seen since 1929. After that the business really got back into its stride, and with trade experiencing the beneficial effects of the pre-war boom, average voyage profits in each of year from 1937 to 1939 were more than double those of the best year (1927) of the late 20s.

Voyage results, 1926-1939			
Year	No. of voyages	Aggregate profits	Average profits
1926	30	£100,312	£3,344
1927	31	£151,724	£4,894
1928	28	£124,559	£4,449
1929	31	£145,308	£4,687
1930	25	£46,611	£1,864
1931	25	£18,947	£758
1932	24	£12,867	£536
1933	26	£75,604	£2,908
1934	28	£59,823	£2,137
1935	25	£23,954	£958
1936	26	£78,882	£3,034
1937	26	£274,300	£10,550
1938	25	£324,502	£12,980
1939	27	£280,141	£10.376
Aggregate profit for 1932 includes loss from one vessel lay up and for 1934 from two vessel lay ups.			

There were a number of factors at work behind this recovery, and it is impossible to be very precise as to which was the most important. There can be no doubt that the general improvement in trade made the job of the new owners far easier and offered the prospect of profits which had simply not been possible over the previous decade and a half. This said, there can be no doubt that results must have profited not just from the professionalism and experience of the Holt organization, but also from its extensive and well-developed network of agencies and business relationships. Finally, the fleet, while not completely modernized, had been purged of its least efficient units, and enhanced by vessels that were at least solid earners even if they were some way short of being fast or modern. Analyzing voyage results on a vessel-by-vessel basis provides some interesting insights into this last issue. The ex-Blue Funnel steamships did not earn as much in aggregate or on a per voyage basis as the *Glenogle* class

motorships. The latter vessels, however, were not only larger but also far more expensive units, and even if the good results for 1936-39 could have been perpetuated over a 20-year period, only *Glenshiel*, which cost roughly a third less to build than each of the other four, would have come close to covering her capital cost. The most profitable vessel in the fleet on a per-voyage basis was *Radnorshire*, the only ex-Blue Funnel motorship, which would appear to give an indication of the optimal mix of size and propulsion.

Voyage profits by vessel, 1936-1939			
	Voyages	Aggregate profit	Average profit
Glen - steam			
Gleniffer	8	£51,752	£6,469
Glen - motor			
Glenogle	10	£99,902	£9,990
Glenapp	10	£119,552	£11,955
Glengarry	9	£92,289	£10,254
Glenbeg	10	£120,441	£12,044
Glenshiel	10	£112,864	£11,286
Ex-Blue Funnel - steam			
Flintshire	9	£68,246	£7,583
Glenfinlas	10	£42,857	£4,286
Glenaffaric	10	£82,331	£8,233
Ex-Blue Funnel - motor			
Radnorshire	7	£95,580	£13,654
Excludes four single voyages by Blue Funnel ships and six voyages by new (1938-39) motor ships			

Not one of the vessels in the table above had been built after 1924, and by 1937 the average age of the fleet was roughly 15 years. By 1937, however, plans were well-advanced to completely transform the nature of the fleet. Although the Blue Funnel fleet itself was aging, it was still in a very strong position operating from its Liverpool base, and the group managers gave priority to modernizing its new acquisition which was far more exposed to competition on the east coast and continental berths. No fewer than eight modern motorships were planned for the Glen fleet. These were to be splendid 18-knot 9,000 ton ships which could lay fair claim to being the most advanced cargo liners of their day. They would when completed be sufficient to operate the core twice-monthly service to the Far East without any help from the older vessels already in service. Sadly, war was once again to intrude in the early stages of fleet modernization, and the new service was not to become a reality until almost a decade after it was first envisaged.

By the time the first orders were ready to be placed, a combination of the recovery in merchant shipping and the acceleration of naval building as part of Britain's general rearmament programme was putting severe strain on Britain's shipbuilding capacity. The shortage of berth space was aggravated by the fact that some old yards had been permanently closed during industry rationalization in the Depression. To date, a very large percentage of Glen's fleet had been built at Govan, but new ownership brought new loyalties, and only one of the new vessels was actually built anywhere on the Clyde. Three of the orders went to Caledon at Dundee, and one to Scotts' at Greenock, both which had been building ships for Blue Funnel for many years. The other four went overseas, one each to Holland and Denmark, and two to the Taikoo Dockyard at Hong Kong.

If the builders had changed, the choice of names for the new vessels indicated that new management was still keen to foster a sense of history. Two ships were given Shire names to maintain the important Shire element of the conference rights. *Denbighshire* (the Dutch-built ship) and *Breconshire* (one of the Hong Kong buildings) both had names which had first featured in the Jenkins fleet in the 1870s. The six Glen names chosen were also traditional ones first employed in the 1870s and 80s. *Glenearn, Glengyle* and *Glenartney* were the Caledon-built ships, while *Glenroy* came from Scotts. The second ship delivered from Hong Kong was christened *Glenorchy*, while the name assigned to the vessel being built by Burmeister and Wain at Copenhagen was *Glengarry*. This name, of course, was being carried by one of the old Harland

and Wolff motorships, but the latter vessel was renamed *Glenstrae* to free it up for a more illustrious successor.

The new ships marked the largest capital expenditure programme since the ill-fated rebuilding programme of the early 1920s, and the fact that Glen was in a position to undertake it was due as much to the re-capitalisation of the business by its new owners as to the improving freight rates of the late 1930s. As the table overleaf makes clear, there was considerable variation in the cost of vessels depending on the location of the yard. The British-built ships were the most expensive, while the two Hong-Kong-built vessels

The Caledon built *Glenearn* on trials. *[University of Dundee GD324/6/3/60/17]*

Glenroy, photographed in the Mersey by Basil Feilden. *[B. and A. Feilden/J. and M. Clarkson collection]*

benefited from far lower wage rates in the Far East. Even the most expensive, however, was less than three-quarters as expensive as a *Glenogle* class equivalent of the early 1920s, despite having roughly equivalent carrying capacity and far greater power.

First cost – Glenearn class motorships			
Ship	Delivered	Builder	First Cost
Glenearn	December 1938	Caledon, Dundee	£440,500
Glenroy	December 1938	Scotts, Greenock	£442,750
Denbighshire	July 1939	N.S.M., Amsterdam	£428,600
Breconshire	July 1939	Taikoo, Hong Kong	£365,900
Glenorchy	December 1939	Taikoo, Hong Kong	£366,500
Glengyle	April 1940	Caledon, Dundee	£446,500
Glengarry	April 1940*	B&W, Copenhagen	£384,560
Glenartney	September 1940	Caledon, Dundee	£465,580
* Seized by Germans while awaiting delivery			

The first two new ships, *Glenearn* and *Glenroy*, commenced their first commercial voyages twenty days apart in December 1938. Each had already begun its second round trip to the Far East before the next pair entered service, *Denbighshire* in July 1939 and *Breconshire* a month later. Prior to their arrival, the two Shire named ex-Blue Funnel ships *Flintshire* and *Radnorshire* were returned to their former colours and names (*Dardanus* and *Tantalus* respectively). *Glengyle* and *Glenorchy* would both be completed by the end of 1939, and *Glenartney* would follow early in 1940. Under normal circumstances their arrival would undoubtedly have triggered the return of the other two ex-Blue Funnel ships to their original owners. In September 1939, however, Britain had gone to war, and circumstances were anything but normal.

A second war

In the Second World War, as in the First, the greatest enemy of the British merchant marine was to be the German U-boat force. The new conflict, however, varied greatly from the old in scope and scale, adding a new threat from a much more potent aerial weapon, and ranging across all of the world's major oceans and seaways. Glen had maintained at least a skeleton service through the Suez Canal to the Far East throughout the 1914-18 period. In the new war, this service was first disrupted by the closure of the Mediterranean to all but very heavily escorted convoys from mid-1940, and then completely terminated by the Japan's entry into the war in

late 1941. There was one other key difference. Unlike, the First World War, during which government control of British shipping had never been more than partial, the entire industry effectively came under central control from the very beginning of hostilities in 1939.

This new and far more total war saw Glen's fleet more exposed to danger and loss than had been the case in the First World War. Paradoxically, the threat was actually increased by the modernity of the newest part of the fleet. The world-leading mixture of size and speed possessed by the new motorships suited them well not only for inclusion in fast convoys in particularly dangerous waters but also for service as naval auxiliaries. Of the seven *Glenearn* class ships that actually entered service between 1938 and 1940, four were requisitioned and commissioned as naval vessels. The greater paradox, however, was that the larger Glen fleet of 1939-1945 actually suffered lower losses than its smaller 1914-1918 equivalent. Only three Glen Line vessels were actually sunk by enemy action during the Second World War. All were lost in a period of less than six months in 1942, and not one of these fell prey to the modern successors of the German U-boats that had sunk five Glen ships between 1916 and 1918. One was lost to a different arm of each of the major enemy powers, the predators being successively German aircraft, a Japanese submarine and an Italian motor torpedo boat. In this respect at least, Glen's war experience was reflective of the wider range of threats that the new war brought to bear on Britain's merchant marine.

All of Glen's new ships were immediately requisitioned for government service after the war began, as were the older *Glenaffaric* and *Glenstrae*. *Glenearn* and *Glenstrae* were employed as transports helping with the move of the British Expeditionary Force to France in September and October 1939. *Gleniffer*, the oldest ship in the fleet, had perhaps the first reasonably close brush with the enemy, when a U-boat sank *Pyrrhus*, one of her Blue Funnel stable mates, from the outward convoy in which she was sailing in February 1940. *Glenaffaric* would become more closely involved in the war when in June she helped with the evacuation of British troops from St. Nazaire. The ship saved some 4,000 soldiers, surviving a night along the quayside while the town was under bombing attack and then sailing safely back to Britain unescorted after missing her convoy. By this time, four of the new fast ships, *Glenearn*, *Glenroy*, *Breconshire* and the brand new *Glengyle* were employed on government chartered service in the Atlantic between Trinidad and Liverpool. Soon thereafter, all four ships were formally taken over by the Admiralty, the three *Glens* for conversion into fast landing ships and *Breconshire* as a commissioned naval transport, a role which would make her one of the legends of the sea war before her loss.

By this time, the company had also lost the services of another of the new motorships, this time to the enemy. *Glengarry* was only a few days from completion at Copenhagen when the Germans invaded Denmark in early April 1940. Key

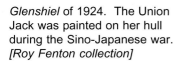

Glenshiel of 1924. The Union Jack was painted on her hull during the Sino-Japanese war.
[Roy Fenton collection]

crew members had actually been flown out to Copenhagen with Admiralty assistance in an attempt to get the valuable ship away early, but this gambit proved too late and simply resulted in the advance party being captured. In an echo of the previous war, Glen had lost one of its newest vessel to capture in an enemy port, although on this occasion, they would eventually get their ship back.

The first Glen liner actually to suffer damage at the hands of the enemy was *Glenstrae*, the former *Glengarry* which had been renamed in September 1939 to free her former name for the new motorship later captured by the Germans in Denmark. On 7th September 1940, *Glenstrae* was passing through London's Royal Albert Dock on her way to berth in King George V Dock when the first major Luftwaffe bombing raid on the capital commenced. One bomb near missed her to port while a second passed straight through the ship and exited through number 4 deep tank. Luckily this bomb did not explode until the following day, by which time the ship had changed position. *Glenstrae* remained in dock throughout a succession of heavy German raids in the following days, but sustained no further damage, finally arriving at Hull for repairs at the end of the month.

The German bombing offensive against Britain's ports and coastal sea lanes exposed a number of other ships to danger and damage in the following months. Two of the new motorships, *Glenartney* and *Glenorchy*, were caught in the Liverpool docks during the fierce air raids of March 1941, and both were lucky to escape with only superficial damage. *Glenfinlas*, which had suffered slight bomb damage in London at about the same time, was on passage from Southend to Middlesbrough when she was attacked by an enemy aircraft off Felixstowe on the afternoon of 6th April. Attacking from cloud cover, the German bomber hit *Glenfinlas* twice before she or her escort could open fire. One bomb passed right through the ship without exploding, but the second detonated in the midships machinery spaces, killing the second and fifth engineers and eight Chinese crew members outright and fatally injuring another. Further attacks were successfully beaten off, but *Glenfinlas* was left dead in the water and was towed into Harwich only with some difficulty. Patched up there, she was later moved to the Tyne for full repairs, finally returning to service in January 1942.

By this time, the four new ships taken up for Admiralty service had all been heavily involved in the fierce air-sea war in the Mediterranean. It had originally been intended to use *Glenearn*, *Glenroy* and *Glengyle* as fast naval transports, but after the experience of the Norwegian campaign it was decided to convert them to infantry assault ships instead. Each equipped with its own flotilla of landing craft, all three were moved to the eastern Mediterranean in early 1941. *Glenearn* and *Glengyle* were involved in a commando raid on Bardia on 19-20th April, but thereafter all three ships were thrown into operations of a quite different nature as the German assaults first on Greece and then on Crete forced the Royal Navy into a series of highly dangerous evacuation exercises in the face of superior enemy airpower.

All three ships survived the campaign, but not without their fair share of misfortune and damage. *Glenroy* missed the first evacuation mission through running aground while leaving Alexandria harbour. *Glenearn* took a bomb hit on her forecastle north of Crete on 24th April, and then two days later was rendered immobile when a near miss flooded her engine room on a second run between Crete and the Greek mainland. The vessel was towed first back to Crete and then all the way across the Mediterranean to Alexandria for repairs. *Glenroy*, back in service after her grounding incident, was in turn damaged by air attack at the end of the month, leaving only *Glengyle* to complete the disastrous campaign unscathed. She continued to lead a charmed life; in June participating in a successful commando landing on the coast of Vichy Syria, but her two less fortunate sisters were to suffer further damage before the year was out. *Glenearn* was rammed by the burning *Georgic* during an air raid on the anchorage at Suez in July. More seriously, *Glenroy* was hit by an aerial torpedo during a supply run to the garrison at Tobruk on 23rd November and had to be beached before she could be successfully towed back to base.

While all this was going on, their sistership *Breconshire* was engaged in a series of operations that would ultimately lead to her loss. Unlike the three Glens, *Breconshire* was used as a fast supply ship, the purpose for which all four had originally been taken into naval service. As such, she was to spend almost all of her short life on arguably the most hazardous convoy duty of the entire war, the campaign to supply the embattled mid-Mediterranean island fortress of Malta. Her first Malta run took place in November 1940, before the real siege began. She was successfully brought out again in December. A second run in January 1941 encountered the full might of the Luftwaffe for the first time, and although *Breconshire* survived an inward voyage in which RN warships were badly hit, she was herself damaged by a near miss while unloading in Malta harbour and had to be repaired locally before sailing safely back to Alexandria. After a brief diversion to carry British troops to

Breconshire sailing from Gibraltar in late September 1941 to take part in Operation Halberd. Behind her to the left is HMS *Edinburgh*, part of the escort, and the French liner *Pasteur* to the right. *[Peter Newall collection]*

Glen Line ships during the Second World War.

Right: *Gleniffer* alongside with Blue Funnel's *Pyrrhus* outside of her in the Taikoo Dockyard on 14th October 1939. *[Ian J. Farquhar collection]*

MIddle: *Glenapp* of 1920 seen in South Africa in 1941. *[Ships in Focus]*

Lower: *Glenogle* at Port Chalmers, New Zealand, far away from her usual routes. *[Ian J. Farquhar collection]*

Left: *Glenshiel* with her wartime paintwork. *[Ambrose Greenway collection]*

Middle: *Glenearn* as *HMS Glenearn* fitted out as a Landing Ship Infantry Large. *[Imperial War Museum A.20532C]*

Bottom: *Glenartney* seen at Sydney at the end of the war. Note the two guns aft, Carley floats carried on deck and the gun tubs forward. *[National Maritime Museum P22832]*

Greece in March, she returned to the Malta run. She made one trip in April and another in May, returning from the latter in July this time to Gibraltar, from whence she returned briefly to the UK.

Breconshire sailed again for Malta in September in the Operation Halberd convoy. She was brought out in early December, returning on this occasion to her more familiar eastern Mediterranean base, but on this occasion was turned round in a week and was back in Malta by the 18th as a result of Admiral Vian's successful defiance of a greatly superior Italian fleet in the First Battle of Sirte. She left for Alexandria in January, during which time her sister *Glengyle* made a successful run to the island in a temporary role as a supply ship. The roles were reversed within a few weeks, with *Breconshire* once again making a supply run while the empty *Glengyle* was returned to Alexandria to revert to her more normal role. *Breconshire* herself was brought out in February through a wave of air attacks which all but eradicated a simultaneous incoming convoy. This completed *Breconshire's* seventh successful round trip to the island. Unfortunately, she was not to survive her attempt at an eighth.

Breconshire sailed from Alexandria for Malta on 20th March in convoy with three other fast merchantmen. Admiral Vian's escorting force once again saw off a greatly superior Italian surface fleet (the Second Battle of Sirte), but after the convoy had dispersed for a fast run towards their destination, German aircraft intervened to more deadly effect. *Breconshire* was hit and disabled only eight miles short of her destination on the morning of the 23rd, and heavy seas frustrated attempts to tow her into port. She only got as far as a roadstead on the south of the island. Here she was subject to repeated attacks, and after several more hits finally capsized and sank on the 27th.

Breconshire – Malta Convoy Operations, 1940-42

Convoy (Operation)	Ships in convoy	From-To	Sailed	Arrived
MW 4	4	Alexandria-Malta	23/11/40	26/11/40
ME 5A	4	Malta-Alexandria	20/12/40	23/12/40
MW 5.5	2	Alexandria-Malta	7/1/41	10/1/41
	1	Malta-Alexandria	23/1/41	26/1/41
(MD 2)	1	Alexandria-Malta	18/4/41	21/4/41
(MD 3)	1	Malta-Alexandria	28/4/41	30/4/41
MW 7B	2	Alexandria-Malta	5/5/41	10/5/41
MG 1	7	Malta-Gibraltar	23/7/41	26/7/41
GM 2 (Halberd)	9	Gibraltar-Malta	25/9/41	29/9/41
	1	Malta-Alexandria	5/12/41	8/12/41
	1	Alexandria-Malta	15/12/41	18/12/41
(MF 2)	1	Malta-Alexandria	6/1/42	8/1/42
(MF 4)	1	Alexandria-Malta	24/1/42	27/4/42
ME 10	3	Malta-Alexandria	13/2/42	16/2/42
MW 10	4	Alexandria-Malta	20/3/42	sunk

Glen's two other war losses followed within six months of *Breconshire's* loss, the first within just over a week. *Glenshiel* was on an independent passage from Bombay and Karachi to Australia when she was intercepted by the Japanese submarine *I-7* some 300 miles east of the Maldives on 3rd April. Hit by a torpedo on the port quarter, the ship began to sink slowly but the Master was able to get the whole complement safely away in the boats before the ship was sunk by a second torpedo and subsequent gun attack. All were rescued safely by the destroyer HMS *Fortune* later the same day, a fortunate escape given the fact that some Japanese submarines were already attacking survivors of their victims after they had taken to the boats.

The last war loss was another of the new motorships and again occurred on the highly dangerous convoy routes to Malta. *Glenorchy* was one of the fast merchantmen selected for Operation Pedestal, the largest, most costly and most famous of the Malta convoys. The convoy had already suffered heavy losses from repeated air, sea and underwater attacks (including the Blue Funnel motorship *Deucalion*) when the scattered remnants were attacked by a large force of motor torpedo boats between Cape Bon and Pantellaria on the night of 12/13th August. *Glenorchy* was struck simultaneously on the port side amidships by two torpedoes which flooded the engine room. The Chief Engineer was killed in the attack, and although the survivors got safely away in the boats, the Master, Captain G. Leslie, refused to leave his ship and was lost when she eventually capsized and the aviation fuel in her cargo exploded.

Captain Leslie's funeral pyre marked Glen's last war loss, but another ship came close to becoming a third victim of the Mediterranean air war before 1942 came to an end. *Glenfinlas* had participated in the invasion of French North Africa, arriving at Bougie on 11th November. The port was under fierce air attack, and the ship's gunners had already claimed one attacker before *Glenfinlas* was hit by three bombs in numbers 1 and 2 holds on the afternoon of the 13th. The ship settled on the bottom alongside the quay, only narrowly avoiding complete destruction when a burning French transport threatened to drift down on her and endanger explosives which had yet to be unloaded from the after holds. *Glenfinlas* was actually left on the bottom of Bougie harbour, with much of her crew drafted away to other duties, until April 1943 when she was refloated and taken to Oran for temporary repairs. Here she was almost lost again when an explosion of as yet unloaded aviation fuel in number 1 hold killed two US soldiers and forced the rapid sinking of the floating dock in which she was placed. Raised again, she finally made it back to Sunderland for permanent repairs on 11th October 1943, eleven months after she was first damaged. She finally re-entered service in February 1944.

Apart from these losses and near-losses, the other Glen ships that remained in commercial service all experienced busy and often dangerous wars. *Glenartney* rescued 109 survivors from the Armed Merchant Cruiser HMS *Comorin* in gale force conditions when the latter succumbed to an engine room fire on 6th April 1941. *Glenaffaric* narrowly avoided a submarine torpedo 240 miles south of Karachi on 4th October 1942. *Glenbeg* was one of a number of ships involved in the ultimately unsuccessful attempt to salvage the ex-French ship *Pierre Loti* (5,647/1913) (herself under Holt management) after the latter went aground near Libreville in December 1942. *Glenapp* was the Commodore's ship in SC 122, one of the convoys caught up in the last successful wolf pack attack on North Atlantic shipping in March 1943. *Glenogle*, which had spent the first half of the war on long-distance voyages to the Far East and Australia, arrived in the Mediterranean in August 1943 and made five successful trips to Malta (by then a far safer, but by no means peril-free, destination) in the following ten months. In the closing year of the war, *Denbighshire* and *Glenartney*, the two surviving fast motor ships not taken up for naval service, were both attached to the train for Britain's Pacific Fleet in the carrier-based campaign against Japan.

The other three modern motor ships remained in service as RN landing ships throughout the war, with at least one participating in each of the major British amphibious operations of the period. *Glengyle*, which had survived the disastrous early campaigns in the Mediterranean without damage, participated in the raid on Dieppe and then the landings at Oran in 1942. She then took part in the landings on Sicily and then Salerno in 1943, before being sent east to take part in a planned amphibious assault on Sumatra. This operation was cancelled, and the vessel returned to the Mediterranean to take part in the Anzio landings in January 1944. *Glenearn* and *Glenroy*, both of which had been damaged in the Mediterranean, were part of the D-Day invasion force in June 1944, during which the latter was mined, resulting in her being towed back to Portsmouth with a flooded engine room. *Glenroy* was repaired in time to be sent out to the Far East, where she took part in the assault on Rangoon. *Glenearn*, which had gone straight to the Pacific after the Normandy landings, took place in the invasion of the Philippines but was damaged by a petrol explosion in April 1945 and had to be docked in Sydney for repairs. *Glengyle* also arrived in the Pacific in the last year of the war, but hostilities ended before she could contribute to the campaign.

Beyond its own ships, Glen, in common with other British shipping companies, managed a number of vessels for the Ministry of Shipping and its successor the Ministry of War Transport. These were a mixed bag made up of one ex-French vessel, one Canadian-built 'Fort' and two US-built 'Ocean' ships, three British-built cargo vessels of different designs, two 'Sam'-named US Liberties on charter to the British government, and one German vessel captured at the end of the war in Europe and given an 'Empire' name. Three of these were lost to enemy action during the war, *Ville de Rouen* to a U-boat in the North Atlantic on 28th December 1942, *Fort McLeod* to a Japanese submarine in the Indian Ocean on 3rd March 1944, and *Empire Lancer* to a U-boat in the Mozambique Channel on 16th August 1944. Half the crew of the last vessel were lost, but in the other two cases the entire complement was rescued. A fourth vessel, *Samwater*, was lost to fire in January 1947 while still under Glen management.

Before bringing the story of the Glen Line's second experience of world war to an end, it is useful to look at a factor which had played such a destructive role during its first, the financial impact of wartime conditions. As we have already seen, asset inflation seriously undermined the company's financial strength during and immediately after the First World War. During the second, more systematic and fairer government control prevented a similar rapid escalation in shipping rates and ship values. Indeed a sample of Glen's wartime voyage and vessel-hire earnings suggests that the company was allowed to earn a stable and fairly generous return on its assets throughout. The company was paid an annual hire of between £44,000 and £45,000 for each of the three modern motorships serving as Royal Navy landing ships. As each annual payment was roughly equivalent to one tenth of the vessel's building cost, this represented a perfectly adequate return for a vessel with an economic life of 20 years and a generous one if economic life was stretched (as it was in each case) beyond 25 years. The voyage results of the vessels that remained in mercantile service also indicate that a good rate of return was earned. The total voyage earnings of *Glenartney*, one of the other modern motor ships, and of *Glenbeg*, one of the older generation, both show a similar pattern of a vessel being allowed to earn roughly twice what would be required to cover depreciation over a 20 year life.

Peace and prosperity

Glen emerged from the Second World War in far better shape than it had the First. Six of the eight new motorships around which fleet renewal had been planned before war broke out were still afloat. Of the older vessels, only one had been lost, leaving four of the ageing, but still useful Harland and Wolff motorships, together with the First World War vintage *Gleniffer* and the two ex-Blue Funnel steamships available for service. All told this was certainly a strong base from which a peacetime service could be re-constituted, a much stronger one, in fact, than was available to the Blue Funnel parent company which had lost roughly half of its ships to enemy action. Considerable re-fitting and re-construction work would, however, be necessary before the Glen Line could return to full commercial effectiveness.

The unconverted ships were all released to the company from requisition in 1946: *Denbighshire*, *Glenogle*, *Glenbeg* and *Glenfinlas* in March; *Glenaffaric*, *Glenstrae* and *Glenartney* in April; *Glenapp* in May; and finally *Gleniffer*

Voyage earnings, 1939-1945				
Glenartney — built 1940 — first cost £465,580				
Voyage	From	To	Days	Earnings (£)
1	30/9/40	16/2/41	140	23,304
2	17/2/41	3/6/41	107	21,323
3	4/6/41	6/11/41	156	28.198
4	7/11/41	3/5/42	178	35,901
5	4/5/42	30/8/42	119	28.158
6	31/8/42	4/11/42	66	14,556
7	5/11/42	20/12/42	46	10,976
8	21/12/42	18/3/43	88	17,850
9	19/3/43	28/5/43	71	12,485
10	29/5/43	4/7/43	37	10,755
11	5/7/43	13/11/43	132	25,890
12	14/11/43	7/3/44	114	24.045
13	8/3/44	6/1/45	305	70,281
14	7/1/45	11/5/45	125	19.918
15	12/5/45	5/11/45	178	52,632
Total (1-15)				396,272

Glenbeg — built 1922 — first cost £617,234 (1939 book value £199,700)				
Voyage	From	To	Days	Earnings (£)
40	12/6/39	18/11/39	172	8,574
41	30/11/39	13/5/40	166	31,463
42	14/5/40	5/11/40	176	38,551
43	6/11/40	25/4/41	170	43,153
44	26/4/41	11/12/41	230	44,086
45	12/12/41	6/3/42	85	12,971
46	7/3/42	11/6/42	97	17,249
47	12/6/42	10/11/42	152	29,786
48	11/11/42	15/6/43	217	29,825
49	16/6/43	16/9/43	93	(7,496)
50	17/9/43	24/4/45	586	78,652
51	28/4/45	18/9/45	144	14,413
Total (40-51)				341,227

in August. The three ex-Royal Navy landing ships all required extensive re-building to restore them to their designed configuration. With the heavy pressures on dockyard capacity, delays were inevitable, and *Glenearn* (reconverted by Smith's Dock) and *Glengyle* (reconverted by Vickers Armstrongs) did not re-enter service until December 1947 and March 1948 respectively, while *Glenroy* (reconverted by Silley Fox of Falmouth) was finally ready in May 1948. They were thus preceded into service by their long-lost sister *Glengarry*. *Glengarry* had survived the war in German colours, having luckily never been deployed in her first intended role as a commerce raider, and having ended the war as the training ship *Hansa*. Initially taken over by the British government as *Empire Humber*, her intended conversion to a Combined Operations Headquarters Ship had been overtaken by the end of the war. Glen had actually first taken possession of her by sleight-of-hand, sailing her away for re-conversion in contravention of a possession order from an Admiralty marshal, but their ownership was confirmed by High Court order in May 1946 and the vessel finally re-entered service under her original name in April 1947.

Glenroy, fitted out as a Landing Ship Infantry Large, at Malta on 23rd April 1946. *[Peter Newall collection]*

The original plan for the fast motorship service had been based on an eight-ship service. Two of these had been lost, but Holts remained committed to the concept and were able to provide two replacement vessels from within their own fleet. The two vessels in question were actually follow-on orders to the original eight ship order, sister ships to the *Glenearns* intended for the Blue Funnel fleet. Laid down originally by Caledon as *Priam* and *Telemachus,* the two vessels had experienced very different wars. *Priam* had been requisitioned before completion for conversion to an escort carrier but the decision was taken that work on her was too far advanced to make such conversion economical and she had been returned to her owners and completed to her original design. *Telemachus,* in a much earlier state of construction, was taken over instead and was actually completed as the carrier *HMS Activity.* Released after the war, she was transferred from Blue Funnel to Glen and rebuilt as a Glen cargo liner, entering service in October 1947 as *Breconshire.* She was joined the following year by *Priam,* which was transferred to Glen in October 1948 and given the name of the other wartime loss, *Glenorchy.* Thus, almost exactly ten years after the first ship of the class had entered service, the full eight-ship fast motorship service was finally completed.

The cost of re-assembling the modern motorship fleet was significant as it involved heavy expenditure on conversion work. The bill for returning *Glengarry* to her original designed configuration came to £570,229, almost a third again as much as the vessel had cost to build. The total cost to Glen of the new *Breconshire* was £864,685, of which £207,000 went to the Admiralty to acquire the vessel and £657,685 was spent transforming the vessel from an escort carrier back to a cargo liner. The new *Glenorchy,* only seven years old at the time of her transfer from Blue Funnel, cost a further £446,484. The balance sheet, however, was in a healthy state, and was supplemented by £367,700 from the Government Tonnage Replacement Scheme. Glen's management was able to make significant write-downs in the early post-war accounts to ensure that peacetime operations did not carry the same

burden of over-valued assets as had been the case two and a half decades before. The total fleet thus stood at only £2.5 million in the 1948 parent company accounts, making up less than 50% of total assets of some £5.5 million, all of which were roughly 75% funded (£4.1 million) by shareholders funds.

The completion of the pre-war modernisation programme allowed for the disposal of older vessels. The war and the subsequent disruption of Glen's new-building programme had meant that the two ex-Blue Funnel vessels had remained in Glen colours far longer than originally intended. Both were returned to their former colours and names in 1947, *Glenfinlas/Elpenor* in January and *Glenaffaric/Machaon* in September. Between these dates, the 32-year old *Gleniffer* completed her 68th and final voyage and was sold to BISCO for demolition. Although never a particularly profitable vessel, *Gleniffer* had long survived all of the other large steamships built in the early Kylsant period, in the process compiling the longest record of unbroken service of any vessel yet to fly Glen colours.

Voyage results were generally very strong during the years when the commercial service was being built back up towards full capacity. Although civil war and the eventual communist victory kept Chinese ports off the itinerary in the short term, Southeast Asian destinations, Hong Kong and Japan all proved lucrative destinations and sources of cargo as the western Pacific rim recovered rapidly from war and embarked on several decades of dramatic industrial growth. Glen, like other British liner companies, benefited from a relative absence of competition in the early years as the merchant fleets of ex-enemies Japan and Germany, and to a lesser extent ex-Allies like the Netherlands, had to be re-built almost from scratch. Even although voyages tended to be prolonged by long stays in congested ports whose facilities were in need of re-building and modernisation, the following selection of voyage results from the first half of 1948 shows that the more modern Glen vessels were normally earning profits of roughly £50,000 on each five-six month round trip,

Priam from a builder's photograph. After the war she joined the fleet as *Glenorchy*. [University of Dundee GD324/6/3/79/14]

and that even the old 1920-22 vintage ships were making a more than respectable return on their more sedate passages.

After the resumption of the full commercial service, the late 1940s and early 1950s saw a series of transfers of ships back and forth between Glen and Blue Funnel colours. These were partially a product of attempts by Holt's management to fit ships best to the requirements of what was effectively an integrated Group service between the UK and the Far East. They were also driven by the decision to back up the premium fast service offered by the *Glenearn* class motorships, with a slower service covering a slightly different range of ports. The four surviving motorships from the early 1920s were transferred to Blue Funnel ownership in 1949, *Glenapp* becoming *Dardanus* in January, *Glenstrae* changing her name to *Dolius* in February, *Glenogle* to *Deucalion* in April and *Glenbeg* to *Dymas* in August. *Glenstrae/Dolius* only lasted until 1952 when a dockside collision resulted in an early trip to the scrapyard, but the other three sailed on until mid-decade before also being broken up. All had given long and distinguished service. Despite being deemed at times too large and too slow for their designed service, their commercial success had really only been blighted by the excessive cost of their initial construction.

Early transfers from Blue Funnel into the Glen fleet fell into three categories. The first was a single modern motorship, *Achilles*, one of the first members of the large A-class which formed the backbone of the parent company's post-war rebuilding programme. Her transfer was to provide the ninth ship which was needed for the Glen Line service because of port delays in the Far East. Renamed *Radnorshire*, she was to prove the longest lasting of the new recruits, flying Glen colours from May 1949 until 1962. The second category

Voyage earnings, January-September 1948*				
Vessel	**Voyage no.**	**Voyage length**	**Completed**	**Voyage profit**
Glenstrae	17	291 days	6th January 1948	£29,936
Glenogle	58	225 days	22nd January 1948	£38,375
Breconshire	1	154 days	11th February 1948	£50,888
Glenbeg	55	252 days	12th February 1948	£53,405
Glengarry	2	170 days	13th February 1948	£41,395
Denbighshire	24	145 days	24th March 1948	£55,680
Glenartney	21	156 days	28th April 1948	£51,040
Glenearn	13	179 days	2nd June 1948	£38,745
Breconshire	2	160 days	20th July 1948	£43,367
Glengarry	3	158 days	20th July 1948	£56,346
Glengyle	10	170 days	20th August 1948	£24,195
Glenogle	59	218 days	27th August 1948	£47,778
Denbighshire	25	156 days	27th August 1948	£63,027
Glenstrae	18	240 days	2nd September 1948	£57,669
Glenartney	22	155 days	30th September 1948	£61,793
*excludes first partial voyages of *Glengyle* and *Glenroy* after their return to service				

was made up of old steamships which generally only lasted for a year or two before going to the breakers yard. The first two of these were actually *Machaon* and *Elpenor*, which had served Glen as *Glenaffaric* and *Glenfinlas* between 1935 and 1947 and returned under the same names in May and August 1950 respectively. Their transfers were only short-term, the first vessel being handed over to BISCO for demolition in January 1951 and the second going the same way in June 1952. A third Holt veteran, *Lycaon* of 1913, completed this triumvirate. Transferred to Glen as *Gleniffer* in February 1951, she followed her sisters to the breakers in July 1952.

The *Glenogle* of 1920 was one of four ships transferred to Ocean in 1949, and is seen here as *Deucalion*. [*J. and M. Clarkson collection*]

The third category of new arrivals was made up of Liberty ships. Holts had bought eight of these in 1947 to provide short-term reinforcements for the war-ravaged Blue Funnel fleet. With Blue Funnel's own building programme beginning to provide faster and more useful liner tonnage than the 11-knot Liberties, some could be released for other duties, and no fewer than six of the eight served a term on Glen's new secondary service. Three were transferred in 1950, *Titan* (renamed *Flintshire*) in September, *Euryplus* (renamed *Pembrokeshire*) in November, and *Tydeus* (renamed *Glenbeg*) in December. When the old ex-Blue Funnel steamships were sent to the breakers, another two Liberties were transferred to Glen, *Eumaeus* (renamed *Glenshiel*) in March 1952, and *Eurymedon* (renamed *Glenlogan*) in October of the same year. The sixth and final ship of the group to change its funnel colour from blue to red arrived in March 1954 when *Talthybius* was renamed *Gleniffer* (making her the third vessel to bear the name in less than ten years).

Transfers to and from Blue Funnel were normally charged at the book value of the vessel at the time of 'sale' or a near equivalent. The almost new *Achilles/Radnorshire* actually became the most expensive fleet asset on Glen's books, being transferred to them at the cost of £606,630. The ex-Liberties were at the other end of the scale – indeed the six together were less expensive than the single A-class motor ship. The three 1950 Liberty transfers each took place at a value of £93,622, while the two 1952 transfers were charged to Glen at £76,179 and £76,186 and the 1954 one at £56,808. These prices were significantly below the market value of the vessels concerned, evidence not only of the strength of the shipping market but also of the good terms on which the ships had originally been bought and the progressive fashion they had been depreciated on the balance sheet. Finally, Glen made a significant gain on its brief ownership of the old Blue Funnel steamships. The total acquisition cost of *Machaon/Glenaffaric*, *Elpenor/Glenfinlas* and *Lycaon/Gleniffer* was only £32,209, while the combined price received on the sale of the three to BISCO for demolition was £247,000.

The Liberties formed the basis of Glen's secondary service through the mid-50s, supporting the primary service

which the *Glenearn*-class motorships maintained throughout. Two of them were involved in the company's brief brush with government requisitioning during the Suez Crisis. *Glenshiel* was taken up by the Ministry of Transport between 15th August and 21st December 1956, and Glen covered her absence by hiring *Tantalus* from Blue Funnel. *Gleniffer* was also called up on 7th September, but was released just four days later.

By 1957-58, the rebuilding of the overall Group fleet had reached a stage where the Liberties could be disposed of and more appropriate second-hand Blue Funnel ships drafted in to man Glen's secondary service. *Glenlogan* and *Glenshiel* were transferred to China Mutual in May and July 1957. *Pembrokeshire* and *Flintshire* were transferred to Ocean Steamship in September and November of the same year. The transfer value in each case was between £34,400 and £37,600, the values at which the ships then stood on Glen's books. The last two, *Gleniffer* and *Glenbeg*, were sold directly by Glen to foreign buyers in April 1958. The prices realised for the pair were £170,000 and £150,000 respectively – a handsome capital gain, and a further indication of how things had changed for the better since the latter days of Royal Mail ownership when Glen was frequently forced to sell over-valued ships at significant capital loss.

The vessels transferred from Blue Funnel to replace the Liberties were a much more heterogeneous group, but all had originally been built with the demands of the Far East liner trade in mind, and even the oldest represented an improvement over the ship she replaced. The first new arrival was very much the veteran of the group and was to spend the shortest time in Glen colours. *Ajax* had been built in 1930 and was a survivor from a class which had included *Deucalion*, lost in the same Malta convoy as *Glenorchy*. The 1929-30 Holt's motorships had been excellent vessels in their day, and although *Glenlochy* (as the vessel was renamed) was now 27 years old, she was not quite on her last legs. Transferred at a book value of only £28,650, she had £43,100 lavished on upgrading her. In the event, she only served Glen until November 1958 when she went back to Blue Funnel as *Sarpedon*. She lasted another four years before a fire hastened her final sale for scrap.

Further transfers from Blue Funnel.

Top: The almost new *Achilles* was transferred in May 1949 and as *Radnorshire* remained with Glen until 1962.
Middle: The Liberty *Euryplus* became the *Pembrokeshire* in September 1950.
Left: *Eumaeus* was renamed *Glenshiel* in March 1952 but remained with Glen for only five years before transferring to China Mutual and being renamed *Euryades*. [all J. and M. Clarkson]

Above: The *Ajax* of 1931 became the *Glenlochy* in September 1957 [Ambrose Greenway collection]

Right: *Glenfruin*, the former *Astyanax* in the River Thames on 4th March 1961 during her short Glen Line career. [Captain C. L. Reynolds/Roy Fenton collection]

Below: *Stentor* of 1946 photographed on 3rd June 1961 as the *Glenshiel*. She was a government, rather than a Holt's design. [Captain C. L. Reynolds/Roy Fenton collection]

The other five arrivals were newer vessels and more permanent additions to the Glen fleet. All were single screw motorships, roughly equivalent in power and carrying capacity to *Radnorshire*, the only survivor of the first batch of ex-Blue Funnel transfers. Of the four transferred in 1957, the oldest was *Telemachus*, built in 1943. The others, *Calchas*, *Astyanax* and *Bellerophon* had been built between 1946 and 1950. The four were renamed *Monmouthshire*, *Glenfinlas*, *Glenfruin* and *Cardiganshire* respectively, the first being the least expensive transfer at £98,169, the last the most expensive at £202,936. *Cardiganshire* was refrigerated immediately after her transfer to Glen at a further cost of £141,795. Despite these variations in cost and age, these vessels looked fairly similar. The fifth and final new arrival, which did not join until November 1958, was rather different. *Stentor* had been laid down as a large fast cargo liner for the Ministry of War Transport, and although completed by Holts, she did not have the classic Blue Funnel profile of the rest of the transfers. Renamed *Glenshiel*, she was actually the most expensive of the transfers at £239,273, although *Cardiganshire* with her new refrigeration plant was to cost the firm more in total. All this expenditure was actually quite modest considering the quality of the assets obtained. Glen, in any event, could well afford the cost, as the company was experiencing a decade of strong operating results, the like of which had had not experienced during the previous half century.

Glen's financial performance between 1949 and 1960 is summarised in the two tables below. The first shows profits and fleet book values for the ship-owning company itself. The second gives summary income statement and balance sheet figures for the consolidated Glen group, including associated agency earnings. The picture is a very positive one. Even in the poorest year, net consolidated earnings never fell below £750,000. The shipping company only once earned an annual return equivalent to less than 25% of the combined book value of the fleet employed and on several occasions reached more than double this figure. Throughout the period, the balance sheet was largely financed by shareholders' funds, without significant recourse to debt. With profits consistently strong, and earnings retention remaining reasonably high in line with normal Holt's practice, the net worth of the business grew steadily throughout the period from £4.7 million in 1949 to £11.6 million in 1960.

Cardiganshire, the longest lasting of the 1950 transfers, formerly Holt's *Bellerophon*, photographed in the Straits of Malacca by the late Peter Foxley. *[Roy Fenton collection]*

Glen Line, parent company earnings and fleet book values, 1949-1960

Year	Profit (£)	Fleet book value (£)	Profit/book value (%)
1949	774,234	2,870,526	26.97
1950	727,693	2,943,218	24.72
1951	1,061,544	2,698,270	39.34
1952	1,428,486	2,616,265	54.60
1953	1,090,161	2,406,964	45.29
1954	866,372	2,266,670	38.22
1955	626,348	2,085,336	30.04
1956	917,221	1,918,509	47.81
1957	1,876,533	2,430,057	77.22
1958	730,954	2,321,098	31.49
1959	676,917	2,133,410	31.73
1960	942,907	3,039,824	31.02

Glen Line, consolidated profits and balance sheet totals, 1949-1960

Year	Profit (£)	Total assets (£)	Shareholders funds (£)
1949	843,201	6,724,211	4,711,141
1950	815,553	7,583,771	5,376,952
1951	1,199,536	8,705,876	6,365,566
1952	1,636,801	9,546,127	7,446,263
1953	1,249,374	9,670,853	7,644,463
1954	996,031	9,746,482	8,103,383
1955	752,176	9,977,903	8,419,309
1956	1,094,761	11,161,295	9,193,970
1957	2,105,904	12,584,659	10,648,037
1958	849,733	12,599,679	10,816,135
1959	768,746	13,445,087	10,850,000
1960	1,043,650	14,052,878	11,583,244

Farewell to the Glens

There was no indication when the 1960s dawned that it would be the last full decade of the company's existence. The economic and structural pressures which would undermine the profitability not just of Glen but of much of the British shipping industry were to emerge fairly rapidly as the decade wore on, but although both the declining efficiency and productivity of British industry, and rising economic nationalism in the Far East were already causing problems as the 1950s came to an end, they had yet to assume critical proportions. Competition, however, was increasing from the low levels of the early post-war period, and fleet modernisation was a more pressing concern than it had been at any time since the initial rebuilding programme of the early Holt years.

Glen had not actually laid down any new vessels since the eight-strong *Glenearn* class had been ordered in the late 1930s as the Holt Group's rebuilding programme had concentrated on the war-ravaged Blue Funnel fleet. The six survivors of the *Glenearn* class were still in service, together with the two equivalent vessels transferred across from Blue Funnel as war loss replacements. Although all were now in, or about to enter, their third decade, they were still competitive and profitable fleet units, but this situation could not be expected to last much longer. The company's overall business position could not be maintained by further transfers from the Blue Funnel fleet as any such vessels could only be expected to maintain the secondary service and not compete head-on with the increasing number of fast, modern vessels that foreign and other British companies were putting on the East Coast and Continental berths for the Far East Conference service.

Although Blue Funnel too would soon need new vessels, the first moves towards modernization in the late 1950s and early 1960s were taken with the Glen fleet which remained more vulnerable to competition. Herbert McDavid, the Glen Chairman who had taken over from Charles Wurtzburg after the latter's death in 1952, was convinced that the company needed new specially designed vessels to maintain its position. While Blue Funnel, with seven to eight sailings a month, was carrying some 90% of west coast cargo to and from the Far East, Glen, with three monthly sailings was only accounting for about 25% of east coast freight on the same route. It had normally had to face approximately ten other sailings a month by British competitors alone. The most dangerous of these competitors were the Leith-registered ships of the Ben Line. Ben had been a participant in the Far East liner trade since the early days of steam, but had generally not competed for the higher end of the market. This began to change in the mid-1950s with the introduction of the 10,000 ton, 17-knot *Benreoch* class. Ben's competitive threat was to sharpen further with the arrival at the beginning of the 1960s with the 11,300-ton, 20-knot *Benloyal* class, arguably the first ships to be put on the berth which were clearly superior to the now ageing *Glenearns*.

Deliberations over new tonnage for Glen began in 1957 and came to fruition in March 1958 with the decision to order a class of four new motor ships for the company. These vessels were to be 11,900-ton, 540-foot thoroughbreds,

powered by 18,000 BHP Sulzer diesels giving them a service speed of 20 knots. The last vessels to be designed by Holts' long-serving Chief Naval Architect Harry Flett (who had been responsible for the *Glenearn* class two decades before), the ships of the *Glenlyon* class have a fair claim to be considered the ultimate British examples of the traditional engines-amidships fast diesel cargo liners. They had a more distinctively modern appearance than some of the earlier Holt motor ships, although they remained true to company tradition in maintaining a relatively tall, vertical funnel amidships. Beyond appearance, they also represented a potent combination of power and carrying capacity which should have earned them long and profitable careers if the industry conditions for which they were built had continued throughout their careers.

The combination of inflation and a step-change in size and power made each of the new ships more than three times as expensive as any previous new building. Each engine cost just over £370,000 (roughly the same as the total cost of each of the two Hong Kong-built ships lost in Malta convoys in 1942), and the final cost of each vessel was between £2.15 and £2.25 million (roughly equivalent to the total book value of the entire Glen fleet in 1947). With the large reserves built up through a decade and a half of good profits, Glen could afford the new ships without any real strain, but the new ships would have to work hard to earn a return commensurate with their high capital cost. Perhaps the most worrying aspect of their construction, however, was not their cost but the fact that only one British yard, Fairfield on the Clyde, could match tenders received from Dutch yards. Holts had built abroad before, indeed half the *Glenearn* class had come from outside Britain, but the reasons for earlier moves away from UK yards had not been primarily economic. The fact that British shipbuilding could only compete successfully for half of the *Glenlyon* class was a worrying sign for the future.

The *Glenlyon* class were introduced into service between September 1962 and January 1963. Their arrival allowed the return to Blue Funnel of the rather mixed bag of middle-aged vessels that had been supporting the *Glenearns* since the late 50s. Each delivery was attended by a transfer back to the parent company: *Glenfruin* in September, *Glenfinlas* in October, the long-serving *Radnorshire* in December, and *Glenshiel* in January. *Monmouthshire* was also transferred back in October 1963, leaving the refrigerated, 16-knot *Cardiganshire* as the only vessel in the Glen fleet outside of the *Glenearn* and *Glenlyon* classes.

With competition continuing to intensify, and the time approaching when the *Glenearn* class would have to be replaced, further new building was not long in coming. In May 1964, after a year-long delay to adapt specifications to changing market conditions, Holts placed an order for eight new ships, four, to be known as the *Priam* class, for Blue Funnel, and four, to be known as the *Glenalmond* class, for Glen. These vessels marked another major step forward in Group ship design, not simply through the adoption of an engines-aft configuration, and were to be the largest and fastest vessels ever to fly the Glen flag. Their conceptualization, however, had been a drawn-out process (the design was first

Glenlyon class motorships, 1962-3							
Ship	Builder	Launch delivery	Contract price £	Engines £	Spares £	Total contract £	Final cost £
Glenlyon	NDSM Amsterdam	17th March 19th October	1,667,900	370,440	31,940	2,070,280	2,156,750
Glenogle	Fairfield Glasgow	3rd May 28th September	1,778,830	370,140	31,940	2,183,910	2,229,500
Flintshire	v d Giessen Rotterdam	18th June 21st December	1,787,600	370,440	31,940	2,189,980	2,251,550
Glenfalloch	Fairfield Glasgow	3rd July 26th January	1,778,830	370,140	31,940	2,183,910	2,223,600

Glenogle, completed October 1962, the first of the *Glenlyon* Class. *[Peter Newall collection]*

Glenalmond, name ship of her class. *[J. and M.Clarkson collection]*

Breconshire, the former aircraft carrier *HMS Activity* of 1942, and others were sold for scrap in 1967 as new ships were delivered. *[J. and M. Clarkson collection]*

drawn up in the mid-50s), and their arrival was to be further delayed by problems with the British yards contracted to build six of the eight vessels. The problems with the building of the *Priam/Glenalmond* class lie more in the realms of Blue Funnel history than in the Glen story. Glen, in fact, received the two ships (*Glenalmond* and *Pembrokeshire*) built by Mitsubishi of Japan, which were only 12 months from keel-laying to delivery, and neither John Brown's *Glenfinlas* nor Vickers' *Radnorshire* were as badly delayed as several of the other Vickers' ships destined for Blue Funnel. Glen was also the beneficiary of the lower prices quoted by the Japanese yard, which meant that two of their vessels were almost 20% cheaper than the rest of the class. The delays and associated cost overruns, however, were not the biggest problem. While the ships would undoubtedly have earned the companies more had they been brought into service a year earlier at lower cost, the real tragedy of these vessels was that they were doomed to obsolescence by the advent of containerization at the very time they were being built.

Glenalmond class contract details

Yard	Yard number	Vessel name	Contract price
Mitsubishi	1613	*Glenalmond*	£2,409,000
Mitsubishi	1614	*Pembrokeshire*	£2,324,000
John Brown	731	*Glenfinlas*	£2,929,672
Vickers	188	*Radnorshire*	£2,804,690

The arrival of the 21-knot *Glenalmonds* triggered a final reorganisation of the Glen fleet, one that would take place progressively throughout the remainder of the decade. It was decided that only three of the new vessels would actually be required for the Glen service, with the result that *Radnorshire*, the last to be delivered, although she appeared in the Thames in Glen Line colours, was transferred directly to Blue Funnel ownership (see photograph page 188). In a departure from previous policy, she actually retained her old name, not being renamed *Perseus* until 1972. The entry of the other three new ships into service triggered the final

departure of three of the veteran *Glenearn* class. *Glenroy* was the first to go, being delivered for scrap in Japan in November 1966. She was followed in April 1967 by two more ships, *Glenartney* and *Breconshire*. The remainder of the class lasted a few more years. *Denbighshire* finally went to the breakers in May 1969 and *Glenearn*, the first of the class to enter the service, in December 1970. The other three vessels also left the fleet in 1970, although each received a brief reprieve through a transfer to Blue Funnel. *Glengarry* served only four months as *Dardanus* before a one-way trip to a Far East scrapyard. *Glenorchy* (renamed *Phemius*) and *Glengyle* (renamed *Deucalion*) lasted only a few months longer before making a similar last voyage, in their cases without reversion to former names or colours.

The passage of these splendid vessels, each of which had followed distinguished and dangerous war service with more than two decades of peacetime profitability, would rapidly be followed by the disappearance of the company that they had served. The three *Glenalmonds* and four *Glenlyons* did maintain a reasonably profitable service through to the end of 1972. The higher speed of these vessels was sufficient for each of the groups to contribute one sailing a month. One last batch of vessels was transferred in from Blue Funnel to maintain the secondary service. The 1952-built turbine-powered *Nestor* served between December 1968 and July 1970 as *Glenaffaric*. Three mid-50s D-class motorships arrived in 1970; *Demodocus* being renamed *Glenroy*, *Diomed* becoming *Glenbeg*, and *Dolius* becoming *Glenfruin*. They were joined by one of the later A-class motorships, *Antenor*, which was renamed *Glenlochy*. These transfers were not a success. While the main service could still normally make a profit, the secondary one could not. Indeed as the figures below make clear, the so-called B Service was consistently, and heavily, loss making.

The overall results of trading in the early 1970s were not sufficient to justify the continuation of the business. Total voyage profits for the entire fleet in 1970 were only just over £80,000, as a result both of the miserable performance of the B Service and a disastrous fourth quarter. The figures for 1971, were again depressed by one bad quarter, this time the first, and continued losses from the B Service, improving only to £494,400. In 1972, the figure climbed to £740,600, but most of this

Glenbeg, formerly Holt's *Diomed* sailed in Glen Line colours for just under two years. *[R.J. Weeks]*

improvement came as a result of the B Service being discontinued in the third quarter. The B Service itself simply was not viable but, even without it, the business rationale of continuing to operate was questionable. The average cost of each of the seven modern vessels in the fleet was approximately £2.5 million, giving a total investment of some £17.5 million. In each of 1971 and 1972 these vessels earned their owners something in the vicinity of £1 million after depreciation, or just under £150,000 per vessel. This was a return roughly equivalent to that being earned in the early 1950s, when the new building cost of a vessel was only a quarter to a fifth of the current figure, and when the written down book cost of the fleet was between £2 and 3 million. Put simply, even the new ships were not earning their owners an adequate return on their investment.

The Glen Line, while still a separate legal entity, had been a far more closely integrated part of the Holt Group than it had been of Royal Mail before. Although cargo management activities had continued to be carried out in London, most other services were carried out from group headquarters in Liverpool, and the officering and manning of the vessels had been carried out from a common group pool. The only tangible manifestation of Glen's independent identity apart from the names

Voyage profits (after repairs and depreciation), 1970-72						
	A Service (*Glenalmond* class)		L Service (*Glenlyon* class)		B Service (other vessels)	
(£,000)	Total	Average	Total	Average	Total	Average
1970						
1st quarter	166.7	55.5	147.8	49.3	(79.4)	(26.4)
2nd quarter	168.1	56.1	88.2	29.5	(146.3)	(48.4)
3rd quarter	90.8	30.2	122.3	40.7	(165.5)	(55.2)
4th quarter	(50.0)	(16.7)	26.0	8.7	(288.6)	(57.7)
1971						
1st quarter	2.1	0.7	9.8	3.3	*(92.6)	(46.3)
2nd quarter	94.8	31.6	63.4	21.1	(124.4)	(41.4)
3rd quarter	173.7	57.4	214.0	71.3	(118.3)	(39.4)
4th quarter	153.9	51.3	219.6	73.2	*(101.6)	(50.8)
1972						
1st quarter	50.3	16.7	134.3	44.7	#(146.7)	(36.7)
2nd quarter	151.7	50.6	167.4	55.8	(122.3)	(40.7)
3rd quarter	268.7	89.6	213.3	71.1	**(42.4)	(42.4)
4th quarter	*27.3	13.6	22.3	7.2	-	
Three voyages per quarter except # four, * two, ** one						

Glenfinlas, the second of the Glenalmond class to be delivered and the last Glen Line ship built on the Clyde. *[Ships in Focus]*

and colours of its ships had been its east coast berth. When this latter ceased to be viable as a separate function within Holts' range of shipping services, Glen itself simply ceased to exist as a shipping company. There was no clear dividing point – indeed, the Glen Line might simply be said to have faded away.

The four vessels transferred to Glen in 1970 were all returned to Blue Funnel names and colours in 1972, and the B Service itself was wound up in the following year. By this time, even some of the modern ships had also left the fleet. With containerization continuing to make inroads into conventional services, there was less and less cargo left to be carried on the already overcrowded London berth. The three *Glenalmonds* were all transferred to Blue Funnel operating companies in 1972-3, each assuming a new name beginning with a P in line with their sisters already operating under those colours - *Glenalmond/ Patroclus, Glenfinlas/Phemius, Pembrokeshire/Phrontis (Radnorshire* which had actually been owned by Blue Funnel since commissioning, followed suit to become *Perseus*). At the same time, the remaining London-based management services of Glen were moved to Liverpool. Finally in 1974, all the remaining east coast conventional services of the Holt Group were combined with those of their former rival, the Ben Line, to form the Benocean joint service, managed from Ben Line's headquarters at Leith. Individual ships continued to be owned and manned by the component companies, but under this arrangement there was little need for a separate Glen identity.

The four *Glenlyons*, the last representatives of a century-long tradition, were not actually sold out of the Group until 1977-78. Although they retained their names until final sale, they were deployed on a variety of charters or on assignments elsewhere in the group route network as well as on the Benocean service. *Flintshire* was transferred to Blue Funnel's Dutch flag subsidiary in 1974 and eventually sold in 1978. *Glenfalloch* was transferred to Elder Dempster in 1975 and sold in 1977. *Glenlyon* was also transferred to Elder Dempster in 1975, but returned to Glen ownership later in the same year. She and *Glenogle*, which remained under nominal Glen ownership throughout, were both sold in 1978. *Glenlyon* and *Flintshire* were both scrapped within a year of sale. *Glenfalloch* and *Glenogle*, however, were both to enjoy long second careers under the flag of the People's Republic of China. Both vessels were still reported to be afloat at the end of the century, although they have since been deleted by Lloyd's Register. The Glen Line name also survived to enter its third century, but long before that time it was nothing more than a company name, sold by its original owners and purchased by new entrepreneurs to act as a banner for an entirely different venture. To all intents and purposes, the real Glen Line ceased to exist with the disappearance of its remaining vessels into the Benocean joint venture in 1974, exactly 100 years after the first *Glenartney* established the company's reputation by winning the China tea race.

End of the line: *Glenlyon*, one of the last two Glen Line ships. *[F.R. Sherlock/Roy Fenton collection]*

GLEN NAMES

James McGregor, the founder of the Glen Line, originally used the names of glens associated with the Clan McGregor although, as the company expanded, other Scottish glen names with no real McGregor association were employed. During the First World War the company began to use Irish glen names, presumably at the behest of Lord Pirrie, the chairman of Harland & Wolff and one of the most influential forces in the management of the Royal Mail Group to which the Glen Line then belonged. The company returned to Scottish glen names after the war, and this trend was confirmed following the Blue Funnel takeover in the 1930, most of the names being used thereafter being original McGregor ones.

Glenade
A valley in the Darty Mountains running down to Donegal Bay.

Glenaffaric/Glenaffric
A forested valley west of Loch Ness in the Highland region through which the River Affric runs northeast to join the River Glass near Cannich.

Glenalmond
The valley of the River Almond in Perth and Kinross running southeast and east from the south of Loch Tay to the Tay Estuary just north of Perth.

Glenamoy
A valley in the north west of County Mayo.

Glenapp
A valley in South Ayrshire running inland from Ballantrae.

Glenaray
A narrow valley in Argyll and Bute running into the head of Loch Fyne at Inveraray.

Glenariffe
A valley in County Antrim famous for its waterfalls.

Glenartney
A narrow valley in central Perth and Kinross running eight miles northeastward from Glenartney Lodge to Cultybraggan, following the course of the Water of Ruchill until it joins the River Earn near Comrie.

Glenavon
More commonly called Strathavon, this is the valley of the River Avon which rises in the Cairngorm mountains and flows 22 miles east then north from Loch Avon to join the River Spey at Ballindalloch; one of the villages in the glen is Tomintoul, the birthplace of James McGregor.

Glenavy
A valley and village in County Antrim on the eastern shores of Lough Neagh.

Glenbeg
A variety of candidates: (1) a small valley north of Granton-on-Spey in the central Highlands, (2) a coastal village in Ardnamurchan on the northern shores of Loch Sunart in the western Highlands, and (3) a valley and lake on the Beara Peninsula in County Cork.

Glencoe
A narrow pass some 10 miles long between Loch Leven and Rannoch Moor, made infamous by the 1692 massacre of the Macdonalds by Campbell soldiers in government service.

Gleneagles
A valley running through the Ochil Hills which takes its name from a 12th century chapel (eagles being the Gaelic for church) but is now more famous for a internationally renowned hotel near Auchterarder and two championship golf courses.

Glenearn
More commonly known as Strathearn, this wide valley stretches over 30 miles from Balquidder in the west to the Firth of Tay in Perth and Kinross.

Glenelg
A village in a remote Highland peninsula across the Sound of Sleat from Skye subsequently made famous by Gavin Maxwell's book 'Ring of Bright Water'.

Glenesk
The most easterly glen in the Braes of Angus occupying the valley of the River North Esk which flows east and then southeast from the Grampians to the village of Edzell at its mouth.

Glenfalloch
A narrow glen in Argyll and Bute which runs north from the top of Loch Lomond to Crianlarich.

Glenfarg
A narrow glen in southern Perth and Kinross extending the length of the River Farg which runs north from the Ochil Hills until it joins the River Earn east of Bridge of Earn.

Glenfarne
A valley on the eastern side of County Leitrim near Lough MacNean.

Glenfinlas
A small glen running west from the banks of Loch Lomond south of Luss towards Glenfruin.

Glenfruin
A valley in the eastern part of Argyll and Bute running southeastward between the Gareloch to the east and Loch Lomond to the west, site of the one-sided battle between the Macgregors and the Colquhouns in 1603 which led to the proscription of the former.

Glengarry
Two candidates; (1) a valley in Atholl in highland Perth and Kinross running southeast from the Pass of Drumtocher to the Pass of Killiecrankie, and (2) a valley in the Lochaber district of the Highlands running eastward from the head of Loch Quoich to Invergarry on Loch Garry.

Glengyle
A valley running westward from Loch Katrine in Perth and Kinross, the site of Glengyle House, the birthplace of Rob Roy Macgregor.

Gleniffer
A small wooded valley just south of Paisley, associated with the weaver poet Robert Tannahill.

Glenlochy
The valley of the River Lochy in Argyll and Bute which runs southwest to join the River Orchy near Dalmally.

Glenlogan
A valley in Wester Ross in the northwest Highland region running down towards Kinlochewe.

Glenluce
A valley in Dumfries and Galloway which carries the Water of Luce south into Luce Bay.

Glenlyon
A valley in western Perth and Kinross carrying the River Lyon eastward from Loch Lyon to the River Tay between Aberfeldy and Kenmore.

Glenogle
A deep valley running northwestward for seven miles from Lochearnhead to the Lix Toll in Stirling Council area.

Glenorchy
A glen carrying the River Orchy southwest from the Bridge of Orchy to the head of Loch Awe.

Glenroy
The valley of the River Roy which flows south to join the River Spean at Roy Bridge.

Glensanda
A valley and village in the West Highlands on the Morvern peninsula, on the west shore of Loch Linnhe, now the site of one of the largest quarries in western Europe.

Glenshane
A valley in the Sperrin Mountains in Northern Ireland carrying the main road between Belfast and Londonderry.

Glenshiel
A valley in the Skye and Lochalsh area of the Highland Council area carrying the waters of the River Shiel northwesterly between the Five Sisters of Kintail and the Saddle from Loch Cluanie to Shiel Bridge and the head of Loch Duich.

Glenspey
More commonly known as Strathspey, this long valley carries the River Spey northeast from the Grampians to the North Sea at Kingston-on-Spey.

Glenstrae
A valley in Argyll and Bute carrying the River Strae southwest into the head of Loch Awe two miles northeast of the settlement of Lochawe.

Glentara
Not strictly speaking a place name but almost certainly refers to the Valley of Tara, northwest of Dublin which is the site of the Hill of Tara, the ancient seat of the High Kings of Ireland.

Glenturret
A glen in central Perth and Kinross running five miles northeastwards from Crieff into what is now the Loch Turret Reservoir.

GLEN LINE RECALLED - 1

Richard Woodman

Although the officers and engineers in Alfred Holt's employ were interchangeable throughout their fleet, there were particular advantages in serving under the red and black funnel of the combined Glen and Shire Lines. During the fifties and sixties the so-called 'Glen-boats' (it was too tedious to constantly refer to the Shires which were, in any case, fully integrated into the Glen service and only distinguished by their Welsh names) all ran on the main-line service to the Far East. On Glen boats there were no lingering periods of interminable loading on the Java coast, of serving on lengthy detachments on the De La Rama round-the-world service, or on the Singapore-Australia 'jags'. The only uncertainty in the ship's proposed voyage would rest with the time the vessel was on the China coast and the delays and frustrations inherent in coping with the hostile, centralised Communist regime. Even so, my memory of several voyages in Glen Line vessels between 1960 and 1966, were that we picked up the schedule and were rarely late home.

A second attraction was that the Glen Line employed Chinese in the engine room, the catering department and, significantly for us, on deck. The Chinese were almost entirely self-regulating under their senior petty officers who were men of some standing in their own right. I have an early image of the bosun of the *Glenartney*, on my first voyage in the winter of 1960, going ashore in London in full reefer uniform. It was extremely difficult, indeed impossible for a junior midshipman as I then was, to penetrate the hermetic world inhabited by the 55 Chinese who were accommodated under the poop. Daily contact was between the bosun and the chief officer, and in the engine room between the 'Number One' greaser and the second engineer. The catering department was run slightly differently with a British chief and second steward, and a Chinese 'Number One' steward who was the leading hand and ran the Chinese cooks and stewards. The master had his own personal steward who was known as 'The Tiger'.

With a master, four mates, ten engineers (including an 'Extra Third' who was responsible for the refrigeration plant), two electricians, a purser-cum-first radio officer, a junior radio officer, a doctor and the two British catering staff, plus four midshipmen, the ship's complement was 78 or so.

For us midshipmen the benefit of sailing in a Glen liner was that rather than working on deck alongside the crew we were more likely to get bridge watch-keeping experience even in a junior capacity. The large number of Chinese available to the chief officer meant that no recourse was necessary to the cheap labour provided by the presence of midshipmen to attend to jobs to which the British seamen in a Blue Funnel liner often objected. This was of enormous value to boys like myself who, going to sea at sixteen, had to teach ourselves astro-navigation and went some way to compensating us for the pretty awful half-deck accommodation which was a solitary deck house at the after end of the centrecastle between numbers 4 and 5 hatches. Instead of having to scrub out and tend the bridge, for example, a job which entailed a daily ritual of brass polishing and was the middies' especial duty in a Blue Funnel liner, the Glen ships bore three Chinese quartermasters who attended to this and, in port, manned the gangway. Nevertheless we were far from feather-bedded and undertook a variety of jobs around the decks when on day-work routine.

The food, always of interest to a hungry and growing youth, was magnificent with breakfasts of five courses, dinners of six or seven and a lunch in between. Despite this, however, my own weight remained under ten stones until I had obtained my second mate's certificate. I have early memories, once the ship arrived on the Malay coast and began cargo work, of being constantly tired. This was due to a combination of the unaccustomed heat and the lack of proper sleep – the half-deck was surrounded by derricks, their noisy winches and the shouts of numerous labourers handling our general cargoes.

I served in several Glen liners as midshipman: *Glenartney*, in which I did two voyages (my first and last under indentures), *Glenfruin*, *Glenorchy*, *Glenlyon* (her maiden voyage) and I coasted *Glenogle*. Later I served as Extra Third Mate in *Glenlyon* and *Glenearn*. In the latter the passengers were no longer carried and the officers occupied some of their former cabins on the promenade deck. The *Glenfruin* had been built as *Astyanax* and as midshipmen we were therefore accommodated in a half-deck on the boat deck which had the disadvantage of being over the engine room, so it was still noisy and hot. *Glenlyon* and *Glenogle* were new ships but, with the exception of *Glenfruin*, the others had been part of the rebuilding programme initiated by Holts in 1938 after their acquisition of the Glen Line from the Royal Mail Group. The *Glenorchy* had in fact been built as *Priam*, but she was not significantly different from the *Glenearn* class. Although I believe the twin Burmeister & Wain engines in the '*Glenearns*' caused the engineers some headaches, I cannot recall them letting the ships down and we were very proud of our 18-knot service speed in such ageing vessels. They were still capable of giving the Ben Liners a run for their money in the monthly 'London-direct' sailing from Singapore, even when Ben introduced a new class of ship in the *Benloyal*. Glen's answer was the four vessels of the *Glenlyon*-class: *Glenlyon* herself, *Glenogle*, *Glenfalloch* and *Flintshire*.

Under a good chief officer and bosun the ships were very well maintained. Homeward bound in Hong Kong extra work would be carried out by shore-gangs of contracted labour who were capable of chipping an entire mast, priming, undercoating and glossing it in four days with cargo work uninterrupted. The black topsides and pink boot-topping would also receive a coat of undercoat and gloss despite the junks, lighters, walla-wallas and sampans which might be lying alongside with cargo or plying for hire round the ship. This was long before the notion of health and safety at work and yet there were remarkably few accidents. In fact I recall more injuries occurring when loading tea in what was then Ceylon. The metal strips protecting edges of the plywood tea chests would often become partially detached and peel back, cutting the bare feet of the labourers as they stowed them. Since this was usually in the last of our available space, it could prove a tricky operation. A disinfectant wash and strip of elastoplast was rarely enough and treatment was never complete without the aspirin which was always demanded.

As the *Glenearn*-class carried passengers, they often bore over 101 souls and a ship's doctor was signed on. While these were often former junior housemen looking for a soft option and the chance to see a bit of the world before they settled into general practice, the *Glenartney*'s doctor was a long-service man, who never wore uniform but favoured a suit, white duck in the tropics. Dr Da Silva was rather a mysterious figure, of Portuguese origin, who spoke with an accent. 'We are the same, you and I,' he once said to me, 'both men from the forest'. I had just enough Latin to know what he meant, at least in the literal sense.

Our normal run was from London to Port Said, through the Suez Canal to bunker and barter at Aden. From there came the nine-day Indian Ocean passage - perhaps the halcyon part of the voyage if during the North East Monsoon - before we hit the coast at Penang and began our first serious discharging. From Penang we ran down to Singapore and a four-day 'work-out' in Keppel Harbour with mates and midshipmen on cargo watches from 07:00 to 23:00. One of the two senior midshipmen usually kept the night watch from 23:00 until 07:00 with the duty quartermasters and the security guards employed by the company. Such a relaxed regime did not pertain in Hong Kong where 24-hour cargo-working was the norm. Here, when outward bound, we berthed alongside Holt's Wharf with its own warehouses.

We would then sail for Japan to complete our discharge and then begin loading. Japan was the ship's company's Mecca and a frantic shore-bound night life was indulged in between cargo-watches in Yokohama and Kobe, with short stops at Shimizu and Nagoya in between, so that when we finally left the Japanese coast we were exhausted and ready to do penance among the puritan rigours of North China.

Under Mao the Chinese experience was never a happy one. Our first port was Hsinkiang, near Tientsin at the head of the Gulf of Chihli, where it was usual to keep the ship anchored for several days under armed guard on the Taku Bar. In the summer it was unbearably hot and in winter bitterly cold with perhaps 10° degrees Celsius of frost and pancake ice floating round the ship. We would be constantly on the alert to move the ship in to a berth, but after several false starts the moment would come, usually at 04:00 in the morning, when the Communist officials arrived alongside and passed us through a lengthy and intentionally humiliating immigration process. While we mustered in the saloon, our cabins were searched, our letters 'read' and our identities paraded. Since some of our Chinese crew came from Shanghai, they would be given a grilling to ensure they lost 'face', but much of this was posturing. After about four hours of our standing about unable to return to our cabins, the officials would allow us to proceed and the pilot would come board. Once alongside, cargo work would start; it was usually well organised and efficient. Our sole diversion ashore was the so-called Friendship Club where king prawns and Tsingtao beer were available, along with some handsome Chinese products such as carpets that are now fashionable in London stores at comparatively exorbitant prices.

Having loaded plywood, chemicals, titanium, canned goods and cameras in Japan, we now took aboard hides, hog bristle, human hair, antimony, talcum and tung oil in Hsinkiang, Tsingtao on the Shantung Peninsula, and Shanghai. In the sixties, just before the Cultural Revolution, Shanghai was a city frozen in time. Whenever we embarked a pilot aboard in Chinese waters the armed guards arrived with him and we were forbidden to use our radar (which meant anchoring in dense fog), to take photographs or be seen to undertake any activity conceived by the xenophobic Red Army soldiers to constitute spying. The midshipmen handling the Chinese courtesy ensign at morning and evening colours, had to be seen to do so with the utmost respect, otherwise a letter of grovelling apology had to be written to the entire Chinese nation. This grew much worse during the Cultural Revolution and resulted in several officers being removed from their ships and serving periods of imprisonment.

From Shanghai we returned to the cheerful and chaotic bedlam of Hong Kong where we secured to a buoy and awaited hundreds of small craft each with their lading destined for London, Hamburg and Rotterdam. We worked six hours on and six off, a punishing regime with the attractions of Hong Kong eating into our supposed rest periods. Without going ashore a three-piece suit could be had tailor-made for £15 in four days. Stories of inferior workmanship were false. The dinner jacket I bought in 1966 lasted until 1998 when I could no longer wear it owing to middle-aged spread. My son has now taken it over. In Hong Kong we loaded a considerable amount of produce which had originated in mainland China: more hides, furs, rattans, dried ginger and cotton piece goods, along with manufactured goods from the Crown Colony: toys, shoes, clothing, general cargo, personal effects and *ad valorem* consignments such as silks and, on one occasion, a splendid wooden yacht stowed as deck-cargo.

Our return by way of the Malay ports filled us with rubber, coffee, sawn timber, gum copal, desiccated coconut and more canned goods, topping off with tea in Ceylon. Here, in Galle, there were no tugs to bring the lighters of tea off to the ship at anchor in the natural harbour, so the senior midshipman received his first command, the ship's motor lifeboat, pressed into service as an extemporised tug-boat. When it broke down, as it inevitably did, he was usually blamed. Such injustices fuelled the customary constant warfare that separated the 'deck' from the 'engine room' and was a mixture of good-natured rivalry and misperceived class-dislike. (This diminished hugely when the passengers were removed from the ships and the departments enjoyed a more integrated social life. However this was fuelled by such circumstances as pertained on *Glenartney* in 1960 when the senior midshipman, with four years sea-time to his credit and who was 22, was unable to order a can of beer, while the 9th Engineer on his first voyage at 19 was. Both were in the motor lifeboat when it objected to heaving lighters!)

A little cargo was handled at Aden, but we were by now beginning to sense the impending onset of that sailor's disease, the Channels, a mounting excitement at coming home. Once through the Canal we might receive an order to proceed via Genoa, which entailed a passage through the Strait of Messina and the Tyrrhenian Sea, but our arrival in the English Channel soon followed. Arrival was always an anti-climax with the ever suspicious officers of HM Customs subjecting us to humiliations equal to - and somehow worse than – those of their Chinese counterparts. Paying off and receiving one's instructions from the superintendent either swiftly ruined your mood (if you were ordered to sail on the coast, you signed on again), or liberated you to a period of leave.

In recalling these voyages much of the detail has been lost. There was, of course, occasional bad weather, perhaps a typhoon skirted in the China Seas, or a full-blooded Biscay gale. There were joyous periods like the flying-fish crossing of the Indian Ocean in the North East Monsoon with the swimming pool erected on the foredeck abreast number 2 hatch. Then there was the noise, light and colour of Hong Kong; the stark beauty of the Japanese coast in winter with the little cluster of crew watching Mount Fuji's conical peak emerge above the horizon from the morning mist; the invasion of one's ship by coolie labourers, or the deep-tank cleaners – elderly women in black *samfoo* pyjamas with head gear made from cardboard and their drinks in old condensed milk cans. There were the young agent's runners, ex-public-school boys serving their own apprenticeship on the first and steeper ladder in commerce than our own; the sew-sew women who would darn one's long white tropical socks; the milk-girls who sold soft drinks in Singapore; the tailors, barbers and vendors who flocked aboard under the mistaken impression that we were wealthy. Then there was the Gully-Gully man, the conjuror who robbed us of money and credulity in the Suez Canal. All the images I associate with a skinny young man with an impressionable mind who is not quite myself. One forgets the long hours, the heat, the occasional flaring disagreements, the occasional illicit hangover, the mosquito bites and the dirt that had to be washed off the ship after every stay in port handling the break-bulk cargoes of those lost days.

Despite its close kinship with Blue Funnel, in many ways the Glen Line possessed its own identity. On appointment one was issued with a distinctive cap badge. Instead of the blue flag with its 'AH' monogram it showed a pilot jack with a red-and-white border surmounted by a blue pennant bearing a white maltese cross. The latter, one was told, was won in the steam tea races of the 1870s which superseded the better known tea clipper contests. This was rubbish, of course; the pennant was worn by auxiliary steamers above a company house flag to indicate they were steam vessels (a fact not readily clear if they had sails hoisted and their funnels obscured) and thus bound by the rule of the road to act as such. But such small myths, true or not, bound us to our ship and made us, at least for the time being, Glen-men.

Glenorchy, in pristine condition, sailing from the Mersey in 1948 after reconditioning following war service as *Priam*. She was a replacement for her near sister of the same name lost in a Malta convoy. *[Elsam, Mann & Cooper Ltd./Andrew Bell collection]*

GLEN LINE RECALLED - 2

Andrew Bell

Some of Glen's 'we are superior' attitude, dating from the 1920s and before the Kylsant crash, survived into the 1950s although there were only a few people who had worked for the original company. This 'we are separate and a superior part of Blue Funnel' attitude was engendered by the Glen Line management in London (based at the offices of Alfred Holt subsidiary McGregor, Gow and Holland located in St Helen's Place) even though the sea staff were entirely changeable with all the rest of the Blue Funnel fleet. Oddly, the Alfred Holt man responsible for running Glen Line was not automatically made a partner (usually known as a manager) of Alfred Holt but they did devolve independence to a considerable extent – after all in Ben Line and P&O they had real competition from the UK East Coast/North West Europe.

I only met one original Glen Line sea staffer, a master who had retired from deep-sea trips in 1953 but came back to 'coast' *Glenearn* to the Continent and back. He had style and had achieved popularity through his wont not to abide by the Alfred Holt directive that when at sea in UK waters double watches be kept – four on and four off. On joining a ship he would send a telegram to Liverpool saying that was what he was going to do and India Buildings never countermanded him. As one of the two cadets coasting *Glenearn* in the Coronation year summer this meant we had a virtual cruise to the Continent for a fortnight. Captain Symonds reminisced how, as a junior officer in Glen Line in the 1920s, their lifestyle in the terminal port of Shanghai was one of organized leisure – it was the local shore staff who discharged and loaded the ship.

The post Second World War reconditioning of *Glenroy* caused an Alfred Holt disdain of Falmouth Docks (at the

Glenartney at Singapore in 1959. *[Ambrose Greenway]*

time beneficially owned by P&O) that lasted for years. The conversion from a hard war that had ended with her as a Landing Ship Infantry resulted in a massive over-run of both time and cost. Nothing Liverpool could do would speed up the work and Falmouth Docks joined Holt's hate list, as did Vickers-Armstrongs, Newcastle over building some of the *Priam* class in the 1960s. These ships did not even get a proper launch as Holts declined to have a ceremony for them 'to show our dissatisfaction with the yard' – so the yard chose one of its own to launch each one of them.

The sustained high performance of the *Glenearn* class's complicated B & W main engines was the cause, by the mid 1950s, of round-the-clock maintenance throughout the time they were at the Glen Line berths in King George V Dock, London. As there was usually one of the class loading and another discharging this produced much visible activity and chief officers' distress in the mess.

It was common across the Glen Line fleet for all the ratings and petty officers to be Chinese. When I made my last trip as a cadet in 1955 three generations of one family were represented. Grandfather had been with the ship since her first post Second World War voyage, his son joined him

some years later and then a grandson. The Chinese crew were habitual gamblers, usually playing mahjong. Often the stakes were not doing look out duty on night time watches which did not enhance the wakefulness of the eventual loser. *Glenartney*'s chief officer did his best to stop this practice but without much success – as with everything else that a Chinese crew chose to do whether it was work practices or drying, foul-smelling foodstuffs on the poop.

At their mainline ports in the Far East, Glen Line usually had different agents from Blue Funnel. Where the Swire Group and Holt's own Mansfield company represented Blue Funnel, Jardines were Glen Line's agent: both were trading houses of great experience – the princely hongs. They could provide in-house cargoes in large and sustained quantities just as Swires do today to fill Cathay Pacific's large fleets of wide-bodied freight-only jets. As Mainland China recovered from its civil wars and as centralised Communism took over, trading patterns settled down and in the 1950s exports grew. As designed in the late 1930s the *Glenearn*s had number 3 as a refrigerated hold. In early 1955 serving on *Glenartney* we loaded a full reefer cargo of pork for Poland which was discharged at Hamburg and railed eastwards into the then Soviet colony. Even during the Korean War Glen Line had no second thoughts about being a plank of the Pan-Soviet empire's economics. Such was the growth of this trade that *Telemachus* (the 1943 prototype of the 28 *Anchises* class ships) was transferred to become *Monmouthshire* for she had a reefer hold and *Bellerophon* of the *Anchises* class had her number 4 hold converted to reefer space and became *Cardiganshire*.

The four cadets on each of the *Glenearn* class had the worst accommodation in the whole of the Alfred Holt fleet. The half deck was in a deck house at the after end of the centre-castle adjacent to number 4 hatch and above number 5. Although we ate with the passengers and the officers in the stately dining saloon, our hutch down aft comprised two small two-berth cabins separated by a cramped study plus a rudimentary bathroom and toilet. Surrounded by hatches and six winches, it had no ventilation system so it was hot in the tropics and cold in a Japanese winter. In port there was no escape from the noise of cargo being worked day and night. Thieving stevedores meant keeping the port holes closed. On some of the class more sympathetic chief officers (who were not in the majority in the 1950s) moved the cadets into passenger cabins as soon as the last had disembarked, usually at Hong Kong.

Thirty years after Ocean eliminated the entity of Glen Line they sold the identity to Curnow Shipping of Porthleven, Cornwall. When James Fisher and Son withdrew from a joint crewing venture in the Scottish Highlands and Islands in 1989, Curnow needed a replacement name and considered Glen Line with all its history to be appropriate. However, plans to enter that area of operation using a slow-speed purpose-designed and built catamaran were never realised.

Fleet List

G1. JANE LEECH 1867-1871 Wooden ship

O.N. 1262. 797g 797n 188.0 x 30.5 x 20.3 feet.

1854: Built by George Cox, Bideford.
25.3.1854: Registered at Liverpool in the ownership of John Leech, Staley Bridge.
7.1867: Acquired by Allan C. Gow and Co., Glasgow.
30.7.1867: Re-registered at Glasgow in the names of James McGregor and Leonard Gow.
29.3.1871: Foundered off the Canary Islands.
14.4.1871: Register closed.

G2. ESTRELLA DE CHILE 1867-1888 Iron barque

O.N. 58353. 582g 556n 171.5 x 28.1 x 17.0 feet.

1.10.1867: Launched by Laurence Hill and Co., Port Glasgow for Alan C. Gow and Co., Glasgow.
12.11.1867: Registered at Glasgow in the names of James McGregor and Leonard Gow, with the shipbuilder Laurence Hill owning 20/64 shares.
29.9.1868: Re-registered at Glasgow in the ownership of McGregor and Gow; Hill's shares having been purchased.
25.11.1888: Wrecked on Robin Rigg Bank, Solway Firth whilst on a voyage from Whitehaven to Rosario with a cargo of steel rails. One member of the crew of 15 was lost.
30.11.1888: Register closed.

G3. GLENAVON (1) 1868-1879 Iron ship

O.N. 60355 1,125g 1,080n 208.1 x 34.7 x 20.9 feet.

22.6.1868: Launched by Archibald McMillan and Sons, Dumbarton (Yard No. 146) for Alan C. Gow and Co., Glasgow.
24.6.1868: Registered at Glasgow in the ownership of James McGregor and Leonard Gow.
8.1879: Re-rigged as a barque.
11.1879: Sold to Robert Constable Hall, Rockcliffe, Black Rock, County Cork.
19.11.1879: Registered at Cork.
22.8.1887: Sailed from Astoria on a voyage to Liverpool with a cargo of salmon oil, flour and wheat.
22.12.1887: Spoken by the British sailing vessel CUMERIA in position 37 north by 33 west and not heard of again.
13.4.1888: Posted missing at Lloyd's.
11.5.1888: Register closed.

G4. GLENORCHY (1) 1868-1869 Iron ship

O.N. 60391 1,348g 1,286n 224.2 x 36.4 x 22.6 feet.

19.11.1868: Launched by Archibald McMillan and Sons, Dumbarton (Yard No. 148) for Alan C. Gow and Co., Glasgow.
16.12.1868: Registered at Glasgow in the ownership of James McGregor and Leonard Gow.
1.1.1869: Wrecked on Kish Sandbank, eight miles from Kingstown, Ireland whilst on her maiden voyage from Glasgow to Bombay with coal and general cargo.
7.1.1869: Register closed.

G5. GLENARAY 1869-1873 Iron barque

O.N. 60417 698g 661n 180.1 x 29.5 x 18.8 feet.

19.4.1869: Launched by Archibald McMillan and Sons, Dumbarton (Yard No. 151) for Alan C. Gow and Co., Glasgow.
13.5.1869: Registered at Glasgow in the ownership of James McGregor and Leonard Gow.
22.1.1873: Sold to James Spence, Melbourne.
1.3.1876: Wrecked at Black Gang Chine, Isle of Wight whilst on a voyage from Adelaide to London.
13.9.1876: Register closed.

G6. EASTERN ISLES 1869-1874 Composite screw brig

O.N.60473 600g 408n 170.4 x 26.0 x 12.6/19.5 feet (awning deck).
C.2-cyl. by J. and J. Thomson, Glasgow ($26\frac{1}{2}$" and 46" x 33"); 110 NHP.

20.10.1869: Launched by Archibald McMillan and Sons, Dumbarton (Yard No. 154) for Alan C. Gow and Co., Glasgow.
3.12.1869: Registered at Glasgow in the ownership of Leonard Gow.
24.4.1874: Sold to Edward Munster de Bussche, Ryde, Isle of Wight
6.5.1874: Sold to Peter Allan Anderson, London
23.10.1874: Sold to Lewis James Fraser, London (who commissions Charles Dunlop of Singapore to sell at that port for not less than £8,000 a day later).
12.1874: Sold to Massim Bur Sallay al Jooffree, Singapore.
29.12.1874: Registered at Singapore.
12.1882: Sold to Said Abdulla bin Mohrin Aldjeeffrie, Palembang and renamed KONSUL GENERAAL READ.
28.12.1882: Register closed.
1887: Dismantled.

G7. GLENGYLE (1) 1870-1881 Iron

O.N. 63790 1,667g 1,264n 274.2 x 32.9 x 24.4 feet.
C.2-cyl. by the London and Glasgow Engineering and Iron Shipbuilding Co. Ltd., Glasgow (34" and 60" x 39"); 185 NHP.
1886: T.3-cyl. by Blair and Co., Stockton-on-Tees ($21\frac{1}{2}$", 35°" and 58°" x 39"); 200 NHP.

27.8.1870: Launched by London and Glasgow Engineering and Iron Shipbuilding Co. Ltd., Glasgow (Yard No. 145) for Alan C. Gow and Co., Glasgow.
9.1870: Completed at a cost of £25,700.
10.10.1870: Registered at Glasgow in the ownership of James McGregor and Leonard Gow.
1880: Managing company became McGregor, Gow and Co.
4.1881: Sold to Arthur B. Forwood, Liverpool for £16,700 and renamed ALVENA.
2.5.1881: Registered at Liverpool.
1883: Owners became the Atlas Steam Ship Co. Ltd. (Leech, Harrison and Forward, managers), Liverpool.
1886: Engines converted to triple expansion.
19.1.1897: Sunk in collision with the steamer BRITISH QUEEN near Sandy Hook whilst on a voyage from New York to the West Indies and Honduras with general cargo.
2.2.1897: Register closed.

G8. GLENROY (1) 1871-1889 Iron

O.N. 63860 2,159g 1,411n 331.2 x 34.4 x 24.4 feet.
C.2-cyl. by London and Glasgow Engineering and Iron Shipbuilding Co. Ltd., Glasgow (40" and 70" x 42"); 250 NHP.

14.10.1871: Launched by London and Glasgow Engineering and Iron Shipbuilding Co. Ltd., Glasgow (Yard No. 154) for Alan C. Gow and Co., Glasgow.
11.1871: Completed at a cost of £36,800.
7.12.1871: Registered at Glasgow in the ownership of James McGregor and Leonard Gow.
1880: Managing company became McGregor, Gow and Co.
11.1889: Sold to G. Tweedy and Co., London for £13,000 and renamed GONCHAR.
12.11.1889: Registered at London.
10.7.1893: Sold to London Steamers Ltd. (P.W. Richardson, manager), London.
12.2.1895: Sold to John S. Turnbull, Glasgow and broken up at Bo'ness.
25.4.1895: Register closed.

G9. GLENLYON (1) 1872-1892 Iron

O.N. 68010 2,118g 1,373n 329.0 x 34.3 x 24.8 feet.
C.2-cyl. by London and Glasgow Engineering and Iron Shipbuilding Co.Ltd., Glasgow (40" and 70" x 45"); 275 NHP.

19.10.1872: Launched by London and Glasgow Engineering and Iron Shipbuilding Co.Ltd., Glasgow (Yard No. 163) for Alan C. Gow and Co., Glasgow.
11.1872: Completed at a cost of £41,310.
6.12.1872: Registered at Glasgow in the ownership of James McGregor and Leonard Gow.
1880: Managing company became McGregor, Gow and Co.
7.1892: Sold to E. Calliol et H. Saint Pierre, Marseilles, France for £8,500 and renamed VERCINGETORIX.
14.7.1892: Register closed.
5.5.1900: Wrecked on Rague Carro, near Marseilles whilst on a voyage from Rufisque to Marseilles with a cargo of ground nuts.

G10. GLENFALLOCH (1) 1873-1896 Iron

O.N. 68036 2,157g 1,419n 330.0 x 34.3 x 24.8 feet.
C.2-cyl. by London and Glasgow Engineering and Iron Shipbuilding Co. Ltd., Glasgow (40" and 70" x 45"); 275 NHP; 10 knots.
3.1889: T.3-cyl. by Hall, Russell and Co., Aberdeen ($21\frac{1}{2}$", 36" and 58" x 45"); 223 NHP.

12.5.1873: Launched by London and Glasgow Engineering and Iron Shipbuilding Co. Ltd., Glasgow (Yard No. 169) for Alan C. Gow and Co., Glasgow.
6.1873: Completed at a cost of £49,900.
27.6.1873: Registered at Glasgow in the ownership of James McGregor and Leonard Gow.
1880: Managing company became McGregor, Gow and Co.
3.1889: Engines converted to triple expansion.
18.9.1896: Sold to Lim Ho Puah (56 shares) and Lee Choon Guam (6 shares), Singapore for £6,500, name unchanged.
14.10.1896: Registered at Singapore.

30.3.1911: Sold to Lim Peng Siang, Singapore.
6.6.1913: Sold to Ho Hong Steamship Co. Ltd., Singapore.
3.1927: Broken up.
13.4.1927: Register closed,

G11. GLENARTNEY (1) 1873-1889 Iron
O.N. 68062 2,143g 1,400n 331.2 x 35.3 x 24.7 feet.
C.2-cyl. by London and Glasgow Engineering and Iron Shipbuilding Co. Ltd., Glasgow (44" and 79" x 45"); 320 NHP.
9.9.1873: Launched by London and Glasgow Engineering and Iron Shipbuilding Co. Ltd., Glasgow (Yard No. 170) for Alan C. Gow and Co., Glasgow.
11.1873: Completed at a cost of £55,136.
8.12.1873: Registered at Glasgow in the ownership of James McGregor and Leonard Gow.
1880: Managing company became McGregor, Gow and Co.
10.1889: Sold to G. Tweedy and Co., London and renamed CHONGAR.
12.11.1889: Registered at London.
10.7.1893: Sold to London Steamers Ltd (P.W. Richardson, manager), London.
28.9.1993: Sold to John S. Turnbull, Glasgow to be broken up at Bo'ness.
19.10.1893: Register closed.
12.1893: Demolition began.

G12. GLENEARN (1) 1874-1899 Iron
O.N. 68079 2,151g 1,410n 330.1 x 35.3 x 24.8 feet.
C.2-cyl. by London and Glasgow Engineering and Iron Shipbuilding Co.Ltd., Glasgow (44" and 79" x 45"); 320 NHP.
1.1894: T.3-cyl. by Gourlay Brothers and Co., Dundee (21½", 39" and 60" x 45"); 201 NHP, 1,350 IHP, 10 knots.
7.11.1873: Launched by London and Glasgow Engineering and Iron Shipbuilding Co.Ltd., Glasgow (Yard No. 171) for Alan C. Gow and Co., Glasgow.
2.1874: Completed at a cost of £55,324.
3.3.1874: Registered at Glasgow in the ownership of James McGregor and Leonard Gow.
1880: Managing company became McGregor, Gow and Co.
25.4.1884: Collided with and sank the steamer RAJAH BROOKE in Penang harbour.
1.1894: Engines converted to triple expansion at cost of £10,763.
16.3.1899: Sold to Mossgiel Steamship Co. Ltd. (John Bruce and Co., managers), Glasgow for £8,000.
10.2.1900: Grounded and partially submerged at Dunagoil Bay, Bute whilst on a voyage from Palermo to the Clyde with a cargo of boxed fruit. Abandoned to underwriters as a constructive total loss.
12.7.1900: Register closed.
7.1900: Refloated and towed to Greenock for repairs. Sold to George Brown, Greenock.
18.1.1901: Re-registered at Glasgow.
7.2.1901: Sold to G.B. Giacopello, Spezia, Italy and renamed ELENA.
12.2.1901: Register closed.
1902: Sold to Pietro Lagomaggiore fu. L., Genoa, Italy.
24.10.1902: Foundered in a gale in the Mediterranean 20 miles south of Bormetteo whilst on a voyage from Odessa to Cette with a cargo of corn and planks. Five of her 22 crew were lost.

Glenartney [London Illustrated News 1st August 1874/Ambrose Greenway collection]

Chongar, ex *Glenartney,* at Bo'ness for breaking up - the first ship to be scrapped there. [Peter Newall collection]

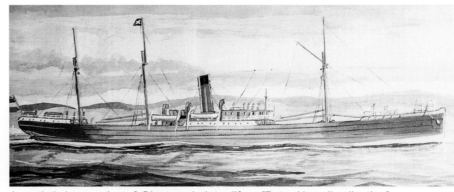

An artist's impression of *Glenearn* in later life. [Peter Newall collection]

G13. GLENFINLAS (1) 1874-1890 Iron
O.N. 68109 2,154g 1,409n 330.0 x 35.3 x 24.8 feet.
C.2-cyl. by London and Glasgow Engineering and Iron Shipbuilding Co. Ltd., Glasgow (44" and 79" x 45"); 320 NHP.
3.4.1874: Launched by London and Glasgow Engineering and Iron Shipbuilding Co. Ltd., Glasgow (Yard No. 174) for Alan C. Gow and Co., Glasgow.
5.1874: Completed at a cost of £56,126.
4.6.1874: Registered at Glasgow in the ownership of James McGregor and Leonard Gow.
1880: Managing company became

McGregor, Gow and Co.
12.1890: Sold to William J. Jobling, Newcastle-upon-Tyne.
15.9.1892: Owners became the Glenfinlas Steamship Co. Ltd. (William J. Jobling, manager), Newcastle-upon-Tyne.
7.1894: Sold to Charles W. and Frederick A. Harrison, London.
31.7.1894: Registered at London.
4.1895: Sold to K.O.F. Dalman, Gothenburg, Sweden and renamed ELFSBORG.
26.4.1895: Register closed.
8.12.1895: Foundered in the North Sea whilst on a voyage from Iggesund to London with a cargo of wood and iron.

G14. GLENORCHY (2) 1876-1898 Iron
O.N. 68382 2,788g 1,778n 321.3 x 39.6 x 21.2 feet.
C.2-cyl. by John Elder and Co., Glasgow (50" and 86" x 42"); 400 NHP.
7.1886: T. 3-cyl. by London and Glasgow Engineering and Iron Shipbuilding Co. Ltd., Glasgow.
8.3.1871: Launched by John Elder and Co., Glasgow (Yard No.132) for Stoomvaart Maatschappij 'Nederland', Amsterdam, Holland as WILLEM III.
19.5.1871: Damaged by fire off Plymouth whilst on a voyage from Den Helder to Batavia. Abandoned to underwriters at Plymouth. Later repaired
27.1.1873: Registered in the ownership of William MacArthur, London as QUANG-SE.
26.9.1873: Sold to William Houstoun, London.
20.11.1874: Owners became William Houstoun and James A. Steel, London.
2.2.1876: Acquired by James McGregor, London for £45,000.
17.2.1877: Renamed GLENORCHY.
28.2.1877: Registered at Glasgow.
1880: Managing company became McGregor, Gow and Co.
7.1886: Engine converted to triple expansion at cost of £15,100.
1.1898: Sold to G.B. Lavorello fu P., Genoa, Italy for £5,200 and renamed PINA.
13.1.1898: Register closed.
7.1903: Demolition began at Genoa.

G15. GLENEAGLES 1877-1893 Iron
O.N. 76737 2,798g 1,838n 367.1 x 37.1 x 26.4 feet.
C.2-cyl. by London and Glasgow Engineering and Iron Shipbuilding Co. Ltd., Glasgow (50" and 88" x 48"); 530 NHP.
15.1.1877: Launched by London and Glasgow Engineering and Iron Shipbuilding Co. Ltd., Glasgow (Yard No. 198) for Alan C. Gow and Co., Glasgow.
2.1877: Completed at a cost of £60,220.
16.2.1877: Registered at Glasgow in the names of James McGregor and Leonard Gow.

Gleniffer of 1878 was small, slow and soon sold. *[Ambrose Greenway collection]*

1880: Managing company became McGregor, Gow and Co.
3.1893: Sold to E. Calliol et H. Saint Pierre, Marseilles, France for £9,250 and renamed CHARLES MARTEL.
24.3.1893: Register closed.
15.12.1894: Rammed and sunk by the French steamer CAMBRAI (965/1875) while at anchor in the Gironde estuary nine miles below Bordeaux on a voyage from Algiers and Alicante. Abandoned as a constructive total loss.

G16. GLENIFFER (1) 1878-1882 Iron
O.N. 78599 2,165g 1,412n 291.0 x 34.7 x 24.6 feet.

C.2-cyl. by Earles' Shipbuilding and Engineering Co. Ltd., Hull (26" and 58" x 45"); 250 NHP.
6.11.1877: Launched by Mounsey and Foster, Sunderland (Yard No.83) as LADYBIRD.
Prior to completion sold to McGregor, Gow and Co. for £30,647 and renamed GLENIFFER.
9.5.1878: Registered at Glasgow in the name of James McGregor.
6.1882: Sold at Havre to Beslauer, Fils et Compagnie, France.
10.10.1883: Registered at London under same ownership.
3.1887: Sold to George C. Stewart, Liverpool.
31.3.1887: Registered at Liverpool.
1896-1898: Laid up at Antwerp.
11.1898: Sold to Verdeau et Compagnie, Bordeaux, France and renamed BURDIGALA.
11.11.1898: Register closed.
5.4.1899: Sailed from Cardiff for Marseilles with a cargo of coal and patent fuel and disappeared.
17.5.1899: Posted missing.

G17. GLENCOE 1878-1889 Iron
O.N. 80434 2,913g 1,901n 387.2 x 38.2 x 26.5 feet.
C.2-cyl. by London and Glasgow Engineering and Iron Shipbuilding Co. Ltd., Glasgow (48" and 88" x 60"); 550 NHP.
26.11.1878: Launched by London and Glasgow Engineering and Iron Shipbuilding Co. Ltd., Glasgow (Yard No. 209) for Alan C. Gow and Co., Glasgow.
12.1878: Completed at a cost of £63,319.
27.1.1879: Registered at Glasgow.
1880: Owners became McGregor, Gow and Co.
4.2.1889: Foundered in English Channel off Beachy Head following a collision with the barque LARGO BAY (1,255/ 1878; Hatfield, Cameron and Co. Glasgow) whilst on a voyage from Liverpool to London in ballast. The entire crew of 51 and two pilots were lost.
21.2.1889: Register closed.

Glencoe of 1878, a real thoroughbred, in contrast to *Gleniffer*. *[National Maritime Museum 58/1678/Peter Newall collection]*

G18. GLENFRUIN (1) 1881-1897 Iron

O.N. 84284 2,985g 1,936n 360.4 x 43.3 x 24.5 feet.

C.2-cyl. by London and Glasgow Engineering and Iron Shipbuilding Co. Ltd., Glasgow (48" and 88" x 54"); 530 NHP.

9.1891: T.3-cyl. by Wallsend Slipway and Engineering Co. Ltd., Newcastle-on-Tyne (25", 40" and 68" x 54"); 330 NHP, 1,700 IHP; 12 knots.

9.1917: T.3-cyl. by Central Marine Engineering Works, West Hartlepool in 1893 (23", 36½" and 62" x 39"); 239 NHP.

20.11.1880: Launched by London and Glasgow Engineering and Iron Shipbuilding Co. Ltd., Glasgow (Yard No. 216) for McGregor, Gow and Co., Glasgow.

1.1881: Completed at a cost of £56,114.

17.1.1881: Registered at Glasgow.

18.6.1884: Propellor shaft broke at sea in Indian Ocean. Towed by GLENAVON until repairs effected then safely made Suez.

17.10.1885: Run aground at Belcher's Bay, Hong Kong to prevent foundering after collision with the steamship CAMORTA.

7.11.1885: Refloated. Subsequently repaired at Hong Kong and returned to service.

9.1891: Engines converted to triple expansion at a cost of £12,369.

16.3.1897: Sold to Andrew McIlwraith, London for £16,500.

4.5.1897: Renamed KALGOORLIE.

11.6.1897: Sold to McIlwraith, McEachern and Co. Proprietary Ltd., Melbourne. Accommodation fitted for 130 saloon and 400 dormitory passengers, 2,980g 1,853n.

12.7.1897: Registered at Melbourne.

1909: Withdrawn from service and laid up at Melbourne.

12.11.1912: Sold to McAlister and Co. Ltd, Singapore. Stripped of machinery and reduced to a coal hulk.

2.2.1916: Registered at Singapore.

21.9.1917: Sold to the Ho Hong Steamship Co. Ltd., Singapore and re-engined with machinery from OSCAR II.

Top and middle: *Glenfruin* at the official opening of Tilbury Docks on 17th April 1886. *Glenfruin* was the first general cargo ship to enter the port. *[Top: NMM 58/1674/Ambrose Greenway collection, middle: Peter Newall collection]*
Below: *Kalgoorlie, ex Glenfruin.* She lasted in Singapore ownership until the 1930s *[Ian J. Farquhar collection]*

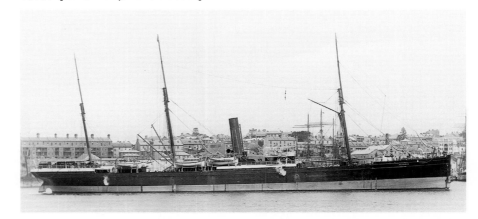

13.1.1919: Re-registered at Singapore and renamed HONG HWA; 3,081g 1,924n.

1.1925: Captured, looted and then set free by Chinese pirates whilst on a voyage from Singapore to Hong Kong.

1932: Laid up.

4.10.1932: Sold to Thomas C.S. Wilkinson, Singapore.

16.11.1932: Sold to Ho Hong Steamship Co. (1932) Ltd., Singapore.

11.1933: Sold to Midoni Shokai, Osaka, Japan.

21.11.1933: Register closed.

1.1934: Broken up.

Glenavon passing through the Suez Canal still crossing yards on her foremast. *[Peter Newall collection]*

Glenogle after the removal of one funnel. *[Ambrose Greenway collection]*

G19. GLENAVON (2) 1881-1898 Iron
O.N. 84305 2,985g 1,936n 360.4 x 43.3 x 24.5 feet.
C.2-cyl. by London and Glasgow Engineering and Iron Shipbuilding Co. Ltd., Glasgow (48" and 88" x 54"); 530 NHP.
2.1891: T. 3-cyl. by Wallsend Slipway and Engineering Co. Ltd., Newcastle-upon-Tyne (25", 40" and 68" x 54"); 330 NHP, 2,000 IHP; 12 knots.
16.2.1881: Launched by London and Glasgow Engineering and Iron Shipbuilding Co. Ltd., Glasgow (Yard No. 217) for McGregor, Gow and Co., Glasgow.
3.1881: Completed at a cost of £55,945.
12.4.1881: Registered at Glasgow.
2.1891: Engine converted to triple expansion at a cost of £12,010.
29.12.1898: Wrecked on Linting Rock, Sa Mun Group, China whilst on a voyage from Japan and Hong Kong to the UK with a cargo of hemp, tea, rice and general. Four crew were drowned and one died of exhaustion after swimming ashore.
25.1.1899: Register closed.

G20. GLENOGLE (1) 1882-1903 Iron
O.N. 85912 3,749g 2,000n 420.5 x 45.1 x 25.3 feet.
C.2-cyl. by London and Glasgow Engineering and Iron Shipbuilding Co. Ltd., Glasgow (59" and 83" x 60"); 700 NHP.
9-11.1890: T. 3-cyl. by London and Glasgow Engineering and Iron Shipbuilding Co. Ltd., Glasgow (32", 52" and 88³/₄" x 60"); 700 NHP, 4,000 IHP; 14 knots.
7.2.1882: Launched by London and Glasgow Engineering and Iron Shipbuilding Co. Ltd., Glasgow (Yard No. 224) for McGregor, Gow and Co., Glasgow.

4.1882: Completed at a cost of £90,123.
23.3.1882: Registered at Glasgow.
17.7.1883: Collided with and sank Italian barque ACHILLE off the Royal Sovereign Lightship, English Channel.
1885: Chartered at Hong Kong by Royal Navy as Armed Merchant Cruiser and present at the annexation of Port Hamilton, Korea.
9-11.1890: Engine converted to triple expansion at a cost of £15,000.
4.8.1903: Sold to Lim Chin Tsong, Rangoon, Burma for £17,500.
17.9.1904: Registered at Rangoon.
17.1.1919: Wrecked on Syriam Flats, Rangoon whilst on a voyage from Rangoon to Calcutta with a cargo of rice.
5.2.1919: Register closed.

G21. GLENGARRY (1) 1883-1904 Iron
O.N. 87643 3,034g 1,956n 360.2 x 43.3 x 24.5 feet.
C.2-cyl. by London and Glasgow Engineering and Iron Shipbuilding Co. Ltd., Glasgow (48" and 88" x 57"); 530 NHP, 2,700 IHP.
2-5.1892: T. 3-cyl. by Wallsend Slipway and Engineering Co. Ltd., Newcastle-upon-Tyne (24¹/₂", 38" and 68" x 57"); 330 NHP/2,000 IHP.
9.2.1883: Launched by London and Glasgow Engineering and Iron Shipbuilding Co. Ltd., Glasgow (Yard No. 231) for McGregor, Gow and Co., Glasgow.
20.4.1883: Registered at Glasgow
5.1883: Completed at a cost of £64,519.
2-5.1892: Converted to triple expansion.
1.1904: Sold to Nippon Shosen K.K., Tokyo, Japan for £12,250 and renamed KOTO MARU.
26.2.1904: Register closed.
9.1905: Wrecked.

G22. GLENELG 1883-1884 Iron
O.N. 87683 3,034g 1,956n 360.2 x 43.3 x 24.5 feet.
C.2-cyl. by London and Glasgow Engineering and Iron Shipbuilding Co. Ltd., Glasgow (48" and 88" x 57"); 530 NHP.
6.6.1883: Launched by London and Glasgow Engineering and Iron Shipbuilding Co. Ltd., Glasgow (Yard No. 232) for McGregor, Gow and Co., Glasgow.
25.7.1883: Registered at Glasgow.
28.7.1883: Ran trials and completed that month.
29.7.1884: Wrecked off Ile de Keller, Ushant whilst on a voyage from London to Penang with general cargo. All the crew were saved.
9.8.1884: Register closed.

G23. GLENGYLE (2) 1886-1904
O.N. 93320. 3,455g 2,244n 370.0 x 45.1 x 26.6 feet.
T.3-cyl. by London and Glasgow Engineering and Iron Shipbuilding Co. Ltd., Glasgow (34", 53" and 87" x 54"); 550 NHP.
31.8.1886: Launched by London and Glasgow Engineering and Iron Shipbuilding Co. Ltd., Glasgow (Yard No. 252) for McGregor, Gow and Co., Glasgow.
21.10.1886: Registered at Glasgow.
22.10.1886: Ran trials and completed that month at a cost of £63,510.
3.1904: Sold to Hiroumi Nisaburo, Segoshi, Japan for £20,000 and renamed MIYOSHINO MARU.
3.6.1904: Register closed.
1920: Owners became Hiroumi Shoji K.K.
1930: Laid up and later scrapped.

Glengyle was the first steel-hulled, triple-expansion-engined ship in the fleet. She is seen here as a Boer War transport.
[Ambrose Greenway collection]

Glenesk photographed at Amsterdam on 3rd May 1899 by W.M. Holtzapffel. *[Gerrit J de Boer collection]*

G24. GLENSHIEL (1) 1887-1904

O.N. 93355 3,455g 2,204n 370.0 x 45.1 x 26.6 feet.
T.3-cyl. by London and Glasgow Engineering and Iron Shipbuilding Co. Ltd., Glasgow (34", 53" and 87" x 54"); 550 NHP.
11.1.1887: Launched by London and Glasgow Engineering and Iron Shipbuilding Co. Ltd., Glasgow (Yard No. 253) for McGregor, Gow and Co., Glasgow.
4.3.1887: Registered at Glasgow.
9.3.1887: Ran trials and completed that month at a cost of £63,638.
5.1904: Sold to K. Matsugata, Kobe, Japan for £19,400 and renamed KOTOHIRA MARU.
8.8.1904: Register closed.
1917: Sold to Gingiro Katsuda, Kobe and registered at Tarumi.
27.7.1917: Wrecked on Amtichika Island whilst on a voyage from Kobe to San Francisco with general cargo.

G25. GLENARTNEY (2) 1889-1904

O.N. 97588 3,026g 1,944n 339.5 x 41.0 x 18.5 feet.
T.3-cyl. by Thomas Richardson and Sons, Hartlepool (28", 44" and 72" x 48"); 400 NHP, 2,400 IHP; 11½ knots.
28.10.1889: Launched by James Laing, Sunderland (Yard No 492) for McGregor, Gow and Co., Glasgow.
12.1889: Completed at a cost of £47,218.
18.12.1889: Registered at Glasgow.
7.1904: Sold to Mitsui Bussan Kaisha Ltd., Kuchinotsu, Japan for £23,000 and renamed TAIKOSAN MARU.
12.7.1904: Register closed.
1909: Sold to K. Hashimoto, Nishinomaya, Japan.
1917: Sold to Inui Gomei Kaisha (S. Inui, manager), Takesago, Japan.
1920: Broken up in Japan.

G26. GLENESK 1891-1912

O.N. 98632 3,524g 2,275n 340.5 x 43.0 x 26.5 feet.
T.3-cyl. by Robert Stephenson and Co. Ltd., Newcastle-upon-Tyne (28", 44" and 72" x 48"); 400 NHP, 2,100 IHP; 11 knots.

25.3.1891: Launched by Robert Stephenson and Co. Ltd., Newcastle-upon-Tyne (Yard No. 21) for McGregor, Gow and Co., Glasgow.
25.5.1891: Registered at Glasgow.
6.1891: Completed at a cost of £49,000.
18.1.1911: Owners became Glen Line (McGregor, Gow and Co.) Ltd.
12.1912: Sold to Inui Gomei Kaisha (Inui Shin Bei, managers), Dairen, Manchuria for £16,000 and renamed KENKON MARU NO.11.
5.7.1913: Register closed.
6.2.1916: Abandoned in a sinking condition in mid-Atlantic whilst on a voyage from Marseilles and Carthagena to Baltimore.

G27. GLENFARG 1894-1914

O.N. 104522 3,647g 2,350n 360.0 x 44.0 x 27.9 feet.
T.3-cyl. by London and Glasgow Engineering and Iron Shipbuilding Co. Ltd. (29", 47" and 76" x 48"); 450 NHP, 3,000 IHP; 11½ knots.
10.5.1894: Launched by London and Glasgow Engineering and Iron Shipbuilding Co. Ltd., Glasgow (Yard No. 279) for McGregor, Gow and Co., Glasgow.
15.6.1894: Registered at Glasgow.
21.6.1894: Ran trials and completed that month at a cost of £48,778.
18.1.1911: Owners became Glen Line (McGregor, Gow and Co.) Ltd.
14.8.1914: Struck a rock and foundered near Shirose Lighthouse, Gola Islands, Japan whilst on a voyage from Kuchinotsu to Shanghai with a cargo of railway sleepers. All saved.
8.10.1914: Register closed.

Glenfarg. [Ian J. Farquhar collection]

Glenlochy in the River Thames, 14th March 1914. *[F. W. Hawks/J. and M. Clarkson collection]*

G28. GLENLOCHY (1) 1896-1919
O.N. 105990 4,654g 2,997n 400.0 x 49.2
x 29.6 feet.
T.3-cyl. by London and Glasgow
Engineering and Iron Shipbuilding Co.
Ltd. (29", 47" and 77" x 48"); 575 NHP,
2,270 IHP; 11$\frac{1}{4}$ knots.
15.2.1896: Launched by London and
Glasgow Engineering and Iron
Shipbuilding Co. Ltd., Glasgow (Yard No.
286) for McGregor, Gow and Co.,
Glasgow.
6.4.1896: Registered at Glasgow.
8.4.1896: Ran trials and completed that
month at a cost of £57,915.
18.1.1911: Owners became Glen Line
(McGregor, Gow and Co.) Ltd.
13.6.1917: Owners became Glen Line Ltd.
4.6.1918: Damaged by fire. Two crew
killed.
6.1919: Sold to D. Anghelatos, Argostoli,
Greece for £170,000 and renamed
OLYMPIA.

4.7.1919: Register closed.
16.6.1921: Wrecked on Farmigas Rocks,
Azores whilst on a voyage from Norfolk,
Virginia to Haifa with a cargo of coal.
Loss found to be caused by barratry and
insurance not paid by underwriters.

G29. GLENTURRET 1896-1918
O.N. 106031 4,696g 3,026n 400.0 x 49.2
x 29.6 feet.
T.3-cyl. by London and Glasgow
Engineering and Iron Shipbuilding Co.
Ltd. (29", 47" and 77" x 54"); 575 NHP,
3,500 IHP; 12 knots.
11.8.1896: Launched by London and
Glasgow Engineering and Iron
Shipbuilding Co. Ltd., Glasgow (Yard No.
287) for McGregor, Gow and Co.,
Glasgow.

10.9.1896: Registered at Glasgow.
12.9.1896: Ran trials and completed that
month at a cost of £57,915.
18.1.1911: Owners became Glen Line
(McGregor, Gow and Co.) Ltd.
28.10.1914: Captured by the German
cruiser EMDEN off Penang but released
due to proximity of an Allied warship.
13.6.1917: Owners became Glen Line Ltd.
6.7.1917: Damaged by gunfire from the
German submarine U 155 east of the
Azores.
26.7.1918: Stranded at Cordemais, River
Loire and became a total loss whilst on a
voyage from Buenos Aires to Nantes with
a cargo of grain.
5.10.1921: Forward part refloated and
beached at Mindin.
25.11.1921: After part refloated and
beached at Mindin. Wreck demolished in
situ.
2.1.1924: Register closed.

Glenturret. A sister to the *Glenlochy* above, her hull livery has changed at some point. *[J. and M. Clarkson collection]*

Glenroy. [Barnard & Straker/J. and M. Clarkson collection]

G30. GLENROY (2) 1901-1915

O.N. 113932 4,901g 3,141n 400.9 x 49.2 x 29.2 feet.
T.3-cyl. by London and Glasgow Engineering and Iron Shipbuilding Co. Ltd. (29", 47" and 76" x 48"); 450 NHP, 3,100 IHP; 12 knots.
6.12.1900: Launched by London and Glasgow Engineering and Iron Shipbuilding Co. Ltd., Glasgow (Yard No. 308) for McGregor, Gow and Co., Glasgow.
31.1.1901: Registered at Glasgow.
5.2.1901: Ran trials and completed that month.
18.1.1911: Owners became Glen Line (McGregor, Gow and Co.) Ltd.
7.4.1915: Wrecked on Falloden Shoal near Singapore whilst on a voyage from Portland, Oregon and Vladivostock to London with general cargo and soya beans.
7.6.1915: Register closed.

G31. GLENLOGAN (1) 1901-1916

O.N. 105861 5,838g 3.809n 420.0 x 54.1 x 29.4 feet.
T.3-cyl. by Workman, Clark and Co. Ltd., Belfast (27", 44¹/₂" and 74" x 54"); 650 NHP, 3,250 IHP; 14¹/₂ knots.
27.5.1896: Launched by Workman, Clark and Co. Ltd., Belfast (Yard No. 125) for the Denton Grange Steamship Co. Ltd. (Houlder Brothers and Co. Ltd., managers), London as DENTON GRANGE.
2.8.1896: Ran trials and completed that month.
29.8.1896: Registered at London.
1.6.1899: Owners became Houlder Line Ltd., London.
12.1899: Stranded at Las Palmas whilst on Government charter to South Africa.
1.1900: Abandoned to the Underwriters.
6.1900: Refloated by the East Coast Salvage Co.
8.1900: Arrived at Wallsend in tow of tugs BLAZER and OCEANA.
20.9.1900: Acquired at auction by McGregor, Gow and Co. Ltd., London for £46,000.

4.1901: Repaired and renamed GLENLOGAN.
19.4.1901: Registered at Glasgow.
18.1.1911: Owners became Glen Line (McGregor, Gow and Co.) Ltd.
31.10.1916: Torpedoed and sunk by the German submarine U 21 in the

Mediterranean 10 miles south east of Stromboli Island whilst on a voyage from Yokohama to London and Hull with general cargo.
16.11.1916: Register closed.

Denton Grange. [Raul Maya/J. and M. Clarkson collection]

Glenlogan, ex Denton Grange. [J. and M. Clarkson collection]

G32. GLENSTRAE (1) 1905-1917

O.N. 120503 4,718g 3.054n 400.0 x 49.3 x 38.2 feet.

T.3-cyl. by Wallsend Slipway and Engineering Co., Newcastle-on-Tyne (28", 46" and 75" x 48"); 456 NHP, 2,600 IHP; 11¼ knots.

21.1.1905: Launched by Hawthorn, Leslie and Co. Ltd., Newcastle-on-Tyne (Yard No 400) for Glen Line Ltd., London.

28.2.1905: Registered at London.

3.1905: Completed.

18.1.1911: Owners became Glen Line (McGregor, Gow and Co.) Ltd.

2.1915: Chartered to Cunard Line for six months.

22.11.1916: Owners became Glen Line Ltd.

28.7.1917: Torpedoed and sunk by the German submarine UC 62 in the Atlantic 66 miles south west by a quarter south from Bishop Rock in position 48.40 north by 06.55 west whilst on a voyage from Dakar to Dunkirk and London with general cargo. One man was lost.

14.8.1917: Register closed.

Glenstrae on 2nd September 1912. *[F.W. Hawks/J. and M. Clarkson collection]*

G33. GLENEARN (2) 1905-1910

O.N. 120643 4,461g 2,855n 381.6 x 47.5 x 28.2 feet.

T.3-cyl. by Wallsend Slipway and Engineering Co., Newcastle-on-Tyne (23½", 40" and 69" x 48"); 420 NHP, 2,400 IHP; 12¼ knots.

Laid down as NETHERBY HALL for Ellerman Lines Ltd. (Hall Line Ltd., managers), Liverpool.

10.1905: Launched by Swan, Hunter and Wigham Richardson Ltd., Newcastle-upon-Tyne (Yard No. 751) for McGregor, Gow and Co., London as GLENEARN.

9.12.1905: Ran trials and completed that month.

11.12.1905: Registered at London.

15.7.1910: Sold to Ellerman Lines Ltd.

2.12.1910: Renamed NETHERBY HALL.

10.1.1917: Captured and sunk with bombs by the German auxiliary cruiser MÖWE 300 miles east by north of Pernambuco.

19.4.1917: Register closed.

Netherby Hall, formerly the *Glenearn*. *[Peter Newall collection]*

G34. GLENAVON (3) 1906-1910

O.N. 118149 4,262g 2,728n 374.7 x 46.6 x 27.7 feet.

T.3-cyl. by Wallsend Slipway and Engineering Co., Newcastle-on-Tyne (23½", 40" and 69" x 48"); 420 NHP, 2,400 IHP; 12¼ knots.

25.10.1904: Launched by Swan, Hunter and Wigham Richardson Ltd., Newcastle-upon-Tyne (Yard No.723) for Ellerman Lines Ltd. (Hall Line Ltd., managers), Liverpool as BRANKSOME HALL.

26.11.1904: Registered at Liverpool.

30.11.1904: Ran trials and completed.

6.7.1906: Acquired by McGregor, Gow and Co, London.

12.7.1906: Renamed GLENAVON.

15.7.1910: Sold to Ellerman Lines Ltd.

11.1.1911: Renamed BRANKSOME HALL.

2.11.1917: Damaged by a torpedo from the German submarine UC 65 in the English Channel, 3½ miles south west of Bolt Head whilst on a voyage from

Glenavon. [Ambrose Greenway collection]

Falmouth to St. Helena with a cargo of military stores. Beached on Salcombe bar. Refloated and repaired.

18.7.1918: Torpedoed and sunk by the German submarine UB 105 in the Mediterranean 68 miles north west by

west from Marsa Susa whilst on a voyage from Newport, Monmouthshire to Port Said with a cargo of coal.

15.10.1918: Register closed.

G35. GLENEARN (3) 1914

O.N. 135307 4,828g 3,032n 390.0 x 50.5 x 28.1 feet.
T.3-cyl. by John Dickinson and Sons Ltd., Sunderland (26", 43" and 71" x 48"); 401 NHP, 1,960 IHP; 11 knots.
Laid down for Cambrian Steam Navigation Co. Ltd. (J. Mathias and Sons, managers), London as SALOPIAN.
Purchased on the stocks for £60,500 by Glen Line (McGregor, Gow and Co.) Ltd., London.
28.10.1913: Launched by Bartram and Sons Ltd., Sunderland (Yard No.230) as GLENEARN.
3.1.1914: Registered at London.
6.1.1914: Ran trials and completed that month.
4.8.1914: Seized by the German government at Hamburg. Compensation paid to Glen by the British government.
1917: Renamed first GLATZ and then SPERRBRECHER II
12.1918: Returned to British ownership and reverted to GLENEARN.
9.4.1919: Formally sold to the Liverpool and London War Risks Insurance Association.
10.5.1919: Sold to Sir Robert J. Thomas, London at auction for £120,000.
17.12.1919: Sold to William Thomas Shipping Co. Ltd. (Robert J. Thomas and Co., managers), London
31.3.1923: Renamed CAMBRIAN PRINCESS.
30.3.1931: Sold by order of High Court of Justice, Chancery Division to "Corrado" Societa Anonima di Navigazione, Genoa, Italy for £13,000 and renamed DANTE.
15.4.1931: Register closed.
6.1940: Interned in Argentina.

Cambrian Princess, completed as the *Glenearn* in 1914, but seized at Hamburg on the outbreak of war. *[A. Duncan/I. W. Rooke collection]*

25.8.1941: Seized by the Argentine government. Assigned to Flota Mercante del Estado, Buenos Aires and renamed RIO SEGUNDO.
1946: Returned to owners and reverted to DANTE.
1952: Sold to Societa Per Azioni di Navigazione Concordes, Genoa.
22.7.1952: Arrived at Spezia for demolition.
10.11.1952: Demolition commenced.

G36. GLENGYLE (3) 1914-1916

O.N. 136711 9,395g 5,900n 500.2 x 62.3 x 34.7 feet.
Two T.3-cyl. by Wallsend Slipway and Engineering Co. Ltd., Newcastle-on-Tyne

(24", 40½" and 68" x 48") driving twin screws; 988 NHP, 5,600 IHP; 12 knots.
9.7.1914: Launched by Hawthorn, Leslie and Co. Ltd., Newcastle-on-Tyne (Yard No. 465) for Glen Line (McGregor, Gow and Co.) Ltd., London.
10.1914: Completed.
6.10.1914: Registered at London.
1.1.1916: Torpedoed and sunk by the German submarine U 34 in the Mediterranean 240 miles east by south from Malta whilst on a voyage from Bombay to Genoa with a cargo of cotton and linseed. Ten members of the crew were lost.
31.1.1916: Register closed.

Glengyle of 1914 at Seattle on her maiden voyage. *[Peter Newall collection]*

G37. GLENIFFER (2) 1915-1947

O.N. 139052 9,429g 6,021n 500.1 x 62.3 x 34.6 feet.
Two T.3-cyl. by Wallsend Slipway and Engineering Co.Ltd., Newcastle-on-Tyne (24", 40½" and 68" x 48") driving twin screws; 988 NHP, 5,600 IHP; 12 knots.
7.1.1915: Launched by Hawthorn, Leslie and Co. Ltd., Newcastle-on-Tyne (Yard No. 466) for Glen Line (McGregor, Gow and Co.) Ltd., London.
6.1915: Completed at a cost of £182,000.
3.6.1915: Registered at London.
20.6.1917: Owners became Glen Line Ltd.
1947: Sold to British Iron and Steel Corporation (Salvage) Ltd. for £20,000 and allocated to T.W. Ward Ltd. for demolition.
25.9.1947: Arrived at Barrow-in-Furness for demolition.
15.5.1948: Register closed.

G38. GLENARTNEY (3) 1916-1918

O.N. 137812 7,263g 4,599n 435.9 x 55.3 x 35.2 feet.
Two 6-cyl. 4SCSA oil engines by Harland and Wolff Ltd., Irvine (670 mm x 1,000 mm) driving twin screws; 655NHP, 3,350 IHP; 11½ knots.
14.4.1915: Launched by Harland and Wolff Ltd., Irvine (Yard No. 467I) for Elder, Dempster and Co. Ltd., Liverpool as MONTEZUMA.
5.1915: Acquired by Glen Line (McGregor, Gow and Co.) Ltd., London for £171,000 and renamed GLENARTNEY.
5.1916: Completed.
8.5.1916: Registered at Glasgow.
13.6.1917: Owners became Glen Line Ltd.
5.2.1918: Torpedoed and sunk by the German submarine UC 54 in the Mediterranean 30 miles north east of Cape Bon whilst on a voyage from Singapore and Alexandria to London with general cargo with the loss of two crew.
22.2.1918: Register closed.

G39. GLENGYLE (4) 1916-1923

O.N. 137487 6,225g 3,964n 399.1 x 52.2 x 33.9 feet.
Two 6-cyl. 4SCSA oil engines by Harland and Wolff Ltd., Glasgow (630 mm x 850 mm) driving twin screws; 534 NHP, 2,950 IHP; 11 knots.
19.1.1915: Launched by Harland and Wolff Ltd., Glasgow (Yard No 466G) for Frederick Leyland and Co. Ltd., Liverpool as BOSTONIAN.
16.11.1915: Registered at Liverpool.
7.12.1915: Ran trials and completed that month.
23.3.1916: Sold to Glen Line (McGregor, Gow and Co.) Ltd., London for £150,000.
3.4.1916: Registered at London.
7.4.1916: Renamed GLENGYLE.
10.6.1917: Escaped from gunfire attack by the German submarine U 34 off Valencia with slight damage.
20.6.1917: Owners became Glen Line Ltd.
18.7.1923: Sold to Pacific Steam Navigation Company, Liverpool.
17.8.1923: Renamed LAUTARO.
2.5.1947: Sold to the Jenny Steamship Co. Ltd. (George J. Livanos, manager), London.

Gleniffer. [J. and M. Clarkson collection]

Gleniffer at the time of the Sino-Japanese War. *[Peter Newall collection]*

Glengyle, the former *Bostonian. [J. and M. Clarkson collection]*

Lautaro, on 21st February 1935. *[F. W. Hawks/J. and M. Clarkson collection]*

11.7.1947: Renamed RIVER SWIFT.
28.7.1948: Damaged by fire and explosion at Rio de Janeiro whilst on a voyage from Immingham to Buenos Aires with a cargo of coal.

29.8.1948: Beached and fire extinguished but written off as beyond economic repair.
5.2.1949: Register closed.
1950: Broken up locally.

G40. GLENOGLE (2) 1916-1917

O.N. 139136 7,682g 4,857n 469.8 x 58.2 x 32.3 feet.
Q.4-cyl. by Wallsend Slipway and Engineering Co. Ltd., Newcastle-on-Tyne (29", 42", 60" and 86" x 57"); 842 NHP, 4,100 IHP; 12 knots.
21.3.1916: Launched by Hawthorn, Leslie and Co. Ltd., Newcastle-on-Tyne (Yard No. 470) for Glen Line (McGregor, Gow and Co.) Ltd., London.
8.1916: Completed.
19.7.1916: Registered at London.
27.3.1917: Torpedoed and sunk by the German submarine U 24 in the Atlantic 207 miles south west from Fastnet Rock in position 48.20 north by 12.00 west whilst on a voyage from Tees and London to Yokohama with general cargo.
19.4.1917: Register closed.

G41. GLENAMOY 1916-1936

O.N. 137826 7,269g 4,656n 436.0 x 55.3 x 35.2 feet.
Two 6-cyl. 4 SCSA oil engines by Harland and Wolff Ltd., Irvine (670 mm x 1,000 mm) driving twin screws; 655 NHP, 3,350 BHP; 11½ knots.
2.5.1916: Launched by Harland and Wolff Ltd., Irvine (Yard No. 468I) for Glen Line (McGregor, Gow and Co.) Ltd., London.
9.1916: Completed at a cost of £185,000.
13.10.1916: Registered at Glasgow.
22.10.1916: Owner renamed Glen Line Ltd.
13.6.1917: Owners became Glen Line Ltd.
1.2.1918: Torpedoed and damaged by the German submarine U 33 in the eastern Mediterranean 240 miles from Alexandria.
11.7.1936: Sold to the White Shipping Co. Ltd. and Springwell Shipping Co. Ltd., London for £15,400 in order to be traded in under the Government's 'Scrap and Build' scheme, and subsequently sold to Metal Industries Ltd. for £11,500.
11.7.1936: Arrived at Rosyth for demolition.
18.11.1936: Work began.
7.1.1937: Register closed.

G42. GLENAVY 1917-1923

O.N. 137855 5,075g 3,208n 385.1 x 52.2 x 30.3 feet.
Two 6-cyl. 4SCSA oil engines by Harland and Wolff Ltd., Glasgow (24 13/16" x 32 7/16"); 369 NHP, 2,950 IHP; driving twin screws; 11° knots.
17.5.1917: Launched by Harland and Wolff Ltd., Glasgow (Yard No. 465G) for Glen Line Ltd., London.
21.8.1917: Registered at Glasgow.
9.1917: Completed at a cost of £212,000.
13.6.1923: Sold to Pacific Steam Navigation Company, Liverpool.
23.6.1923: Renamed LAGARTO.
12.1947: Arrived at Liverpool with engine trouble and subsequently laid up at Birkenhead.
24.9.1948: Sailed from Liverpool to be broken up at Troon by the West of Scotland Shipbreaking Co. Ltd.
29.3.1949: Register closed.

Glenamoy. [J. and M. Clarkson collection]

Glenavy with dazzle paint. Note the long yards. [Peter Newall collection]

Glenavy. [Peter Newall collection]

Glenavy in the Mersey as *Lagarto.* [B. & A. Feilden/J. and M. Clarkson collection]

G43. GLENAPP (1) 1918-1920
O.N. 141887 7,374g 4,623n 450.5 x 55.8 x 36.6 feet.
Two 8-cyl. 4SCSA oil engines by Harland and Wolff Ltd., Glasgow (750 mm x 1,100mm) driving twin screws, 114 NHP, 6,000 EIHP; 13½ knots.
16.3.1918: Launched by Barclay Curle and Co. Ltd., Glasgow (Yard No.519) for Glen Line Ltd., Glasgow having been laid down for the Imperial Russian Government.
9.1918: Completed.
9.9.1918: Registered at Glasgow.
5.8.1920: Sold to British and African Steam Navigation Co. Ltd. (Elder, Dempster and Co. Ltd., managers), Liverpool for rebuilding as passenger liner.

12.10.1920: Registered at Liverpool.
28.10.1921: Renamed ABA.
11.1921: Entered service. 7,937g 4,596n; 225 first class, and 140 second and third class passengers.
8.1922: Towed disabled Portuguese destroyer GUADIANA to Las Palmas.
5.12.1929: Steering gear disabled in storm off Ireland. Towed into Queenstown by salvage tug ZWARTE ZEE.
4.6.1931: Grounded off Customs Wharf, Lagos, but later refloated.
23.5.1933: Owners became Elder, Dempster Lines Ltd, Liverpool.
9.1939: Requisitioned by the Admiralty for conversion into a hospital ship.
17.5.1941: Bombed and damaged by German aircraft 50 miles south of Crete.

15.3.1944: Bombed and damaged by German aircraft at Naples, with the loss of three lives.
7.1.1947: Returned to owners.
28.4.1947: Sold to Bawtry Steamship Co. Ltd. (George J. Livanos, manager), London for £55,000.
8.9.1947: Renamed MATRONA.
31.10.1947: Capsized in Bidston Dock, Birkenhead due to removal of ballast.
8.6.1948: Righted but declared beyond repair and sold for scrap.
4.10.1948: Arrived at Barrow-in-Furness for demolition by T.W. Ward Ltd.
24.1.1952: Register closed.

Glenapp. [Peter Newall collection]

Aba, the rebuilt *Glenapp.* [B. & A. Feilden/J. and M. Clarkson collection]

Top: *Matrona* photographed on her side in Bidston Dock, Birkenhead on 31st October 1947. *[John McRoberts/ J. and M. Clarkson collection]*

Middle: Upright and afloat again in Bidston Dock, June 1948. *[C. Parsons/J. and M. Clarkson collection]*

Right: In the early stages of demolition at Barrow-in-Furness. *[World Ship Society Photo Library]*

G44. GLENADE 1919-1923

O.N. 141913 6,802g 4,144n 406.2 x 54.2 x 23.6 feet.

Two 6-cyl. 4SCSA oil engines by Harland and Wolff Ltd., Glasgow (670 mm x 1,000 mm) driving twin screws; 655 NHP, 3,200 IHP; 11¼ knots.

15.4.1919: Launched by Harland and Wolff Ltd., Glasgow (Yard No. 511G) for Glen Line Ltd., Glasgow.

7.1919: Completed at a cost of £381,179.

11.7.1919: Registered at Glasgow.

3.7.1923: Sold to the Pacific Steam Navigation Company, Liverpool and renamed LORETO.

14.11.1951: Sold to Motor Lines Ltd. (Clunies Shipping Co., managers), Greenock and renamed BARBETA.

24.11.1951: Re-registered at Greenock.

11.1952: Sold to British Iron and Steel Corporation (Salvage) Ltd.

21.11.1952: Arrived at Briton Ferry for breaking up by T.W. Ward Ltd.

16.7.1953: Register closed.

Above: *Glenade* on her maiden voyage in the Thames on 16th August 1919. *[F. W. Hawks/J. and M. Clarkson collection]*

Middle: *Loreto. [B. & A. Feilden/J. and M. Clarkson collection]*

Bottom: In New Zealand waters as the *Barbeta. [Ian J. Farquhar collection]*

G45. GLENARIFFE 1919-1923

O.N. 141927 6,795g 4,126n 406.0 x 54.2 x 23.6 feet.

Two 6-cyl. 4SCSA oil engines by Harland and Wolff Ltd., Glasgow (670 mm x 1,000 mm) driving twin screws; 655 NHP, 3,200 IHP; 11½ knots.

10.7.1919: Launched by Harland and Wolff Ltd., Glasgow (Yard No. 512G) for Glen Line Ltd., Glasgow.
10.1919: Completed at a cost of £377,472.
18.10.1919: Registered at Glasgow.
2.8.1923: Sold to Pacific Steam Navigation Company, Liverpool.
25.9.1923: Renamed LORIGA.
28.5.1951: Sold to Audax Steamship Co. Ltd. (C.Y. Tung, manager), Hong Kong.
1.6.1951: Renamed OCEAN VENUS.
22.2.1953: Arrived at Osaka to be broken up.
30.3.1953: Demolition began.
30.3.1953: Register closed.

G46. GLENSPEY 1919-1920

O.N. 142726 6,498g 4,040n 412.4 x 55.8 x 34.4 feet.

T.3-cyl. by Harland and Wolff Ltd., Belfast (27", 44" and 73" x 48"); 518 NHP, Wolff 3,200 IHP; 11½ knots.

2.11.1918: Launched by Harland and Wolff Ltd., Belfast (Yard No. 544) for the Shipping Controller, London (Clyde Shipping Co. Ltd., Glasgow, managers), as WAR MUSIC.
28.11.1918: Registered at London.
12.1918: Completed.
30.8.1919: Sold to Glen Line Ltd., London for £265,500.
4.9.1919: Renamed GLENSPEY.
15.12.1920: Sold to King Line Ltd. (Philipps, Philipps and Co. Ltd., managers), London for £243,630.
20.8.1921: Renamed KING BLEDDYN.
1923: Management transferred to Dodd, Thompson and Co.
3.1937: Sold to Halcyon-Lijn N.V., Rotterdam, Holland and renamed STAD MAASLUIS.
15.3.1937: Register closed.
1950: Sold to Francescu Pittaluga fu Giacomo, Genoa, Italy and renamed FRANCESCU.
6.4.1954: Stranded off Bats in the Schelde estuary whilst on a voyage from Bona to Antwerp with a cargo of iron ore. Broke in two and became a total loss.
1955: Wreck demolished.

Top: *Loriga* [B. and A. Feilden/J. and M. Clarkson collection]
Middle: The newly launched *War Music* at Belfast on 2nd November 1918. Note the outlines of the dazzle painting on her hull. *[Ulster Folk Transport Museum, H&W 415]*
Bottom: *War Music* on trials on 5th December 1918. *[Ulster Folk Transport Museum, H&W 447]*

G47. GLENSANDA 1919-1928

O.N. 142684 6,625g 4,068n 412.2 x 55.8 x 34.2 feet.

T.3-cyl. by Swan, Hunter and Wigham Richardson Ltd., Newcastle-upon-Tyne (27", 44" and 73" x 48"); 518 NHP, 3,200 IHP; 11½ knots.

10.1918: Completed by Armstrong Whitworth and Co. Ltd., Newcastle-upon-Tyne (Yard No. 952) for the Shipping Controller, London (Lowden, Connell and Co., Liverpool, managers) as WAR COURAGE.

17.10.1918: Registered at London.

3.9.1919: Acquired by Glen Line Ltd., London for £250,991.

12.9.1919: Renamed GLENSANDA.

21.6.1928: Sold to Essex Line Ltd. (Meldrum and Swinson Ltd., managers), London for £35,000.

27.6.1928: Renamed ESSEX LANCE.

12.3.1941: Bombed and damaged by German aircraft near Dover.

16.9.1942: Torpedoed and damaged by the German submarine U 165 near Matane in the Gulf of St. Lawrence whilst on a voyage from Sydney, Cape Breton to Quebec City in ballast in Convoy SQ.36.

16.10.1943: Torpedoed and sunk by the German submarine U 426 in the North Atlantic in position 57.53 north by 28.00 west whilst on a voyage from Swansea and Milford Haven to Halifax with a cargo of 4,000 tons of anthracite while straggling from Convoy ONS.20. All 44 crew and 8 gunners were saved.

7.2.1944: Register closed.

G48. GLENSHANE 1919-1932

O.N. 142765 6,498g 4,012n 412.4 x 55.8 x 34.4 feet.

Glensanda, the former *War Courage*. [Ambrose Greenway collection]

T.3-cyl. by Harland and Wolff Ltd., Belfast (27", 44" and 73" x 48"); 518 NHP, 3,200 IHP; 11½ knots.

5.12.1918: Launched by Harland and Woff Ltd., Belfast (Yard No.545) for the Shipping Controller, London (Clyde Shipping Co. Ltd., Glasgow, managers), as WAR DREAM.

1.1919: Completed.

6.1.1919: Registered at London.

8.9.1919: Acquired by Glen Line Ltd., London for £253,251 and renamed GLENSHANE.

1932: Sold to H. Makita, Japan.

17.5.1933: Register closed.

1933: Sold to Kyokko Kaiun K.K. (Frank M. Jonas, manager), Hong Kong and renamed SUNSHINE.

1934: Sale fell through, name reverted temporarily to GLENSHANE. Provisional Registration Certificate provided at Kobe on 30.6.1934.

19.9.1934: Registered at Shanghai in the name of Frank M. Jonas, Kobe, Japan and renamed MILTONIA.

2.11.1935: Resold to Ding Yao Dung (Tanaka Shoji K.K., managers), Chefoo and renamed CHANG LUNG. Final sale price £10,500.

14.11.1935: Register closed.

1938: Sold to Syoryu Kisen K.K. (Tanaka Shoji K.K., managers), Dairen, Manchuria and renamed SYORYU MARU.

4.5.1944: Torpedoed and sunk by the submarine USS PARCHE in the Pacific in position 20.48 north by 118.03 east.

Glenshane at Boston, U.S.A. on 26th May 1920. [Robert Hildebrand/E. Johnson collection/supplied by Wm. A. Schell]

Above: *War Climax* on trials. *[Ian Rae collection]*   Below: *Glenstrae* as *Banbury Castle*. *[J. and M. Clarkson collection]*

G49. GLENSTRAE (2) 1919-1920

O.N. 142647 6,429g 4,002n 412.4 x 55.8 x 34.4 feet.
T.3-cyl. by Swan, Hunter and Wigham Richardson Ltd., Newcastle-upon-Tyne (27", 44" and 73" x 48"); 517 NHP, 3,200 IHP; 11½ knots.
8.8.1918: Launched by Swan, Hunter and Wigham Richardson Ltd., Newcastle-upon-Tyne (Yard No. 1089) for the Shipping Controller, London (Lowden, Connell and Co., Liverpool, managers) as WAR CLIMAX.
17.9.1918: Registered at London.
10.1918: Completed.
17.9.1919: Acquired by Glen Line Ltd., London for £265,500.
29.9.1919: Renamed GLENSTRAE.
15.12.1920: Sold to the Union-Castle Mail Steamship Co. Ltd., London for £241,279.
22.7.1921: Renamed BANBURY CASTLE.
17.9.1931: Register closed.
1931: Sold to G. Vergottis, Argostoli, Greece and renamed ROKOS.
1935: Sold to S.G. Razis, Argostoli.
1935: Sold to Ionian Steamship Co. Ltd. (Vergottis Ltd., managers), Argostoli.
26.5.1941: Bombed and damaged by German aircraft while at anchor in Suda Bay, Crete. Grounded and subsequently became a total loss.

G50. GLENLUCE 1920-1936

O.N. 141941 6,755g 4,120n 405.9 x 54.2 x 23.6 feet.
Two 6-cyl. 4SCSA oil engines by Harland and Wolff Ltd., Glasgow (670mm x 1,000mm) driving twin screws; 655 NHP, 3,200 IHP; 11½ knots.
25.9.1919: Launched by Harland and Wolff Ltd., Glasgow (Yard No. 514G) for Glen Line Ltd., Glasgow.
1.1920: Completed at a cost of £359,110.
8.1.1920: Registered at Glasgow.
10.7.1924: Chartered to Pacific Steam Navigation Company, Liverpool for one year.
1934: Laid up.

5.8.1935: Chartered to 'Italia', Genoa, Italy.
18.5.1936: Sold to P. Wigham Richardson and Co. Ltd., London for £20,000.
9.10.1936: Renamed IONOPOLIS.
1937: Sold to Skibs A/S Vigrid (Bruun and von der Lippe, managers), Tonsberg, Norway and renamed VIGEO.
26.4.1937: Register closed.
1938: Sold to Rederi A/B Jamaica and Stockholm (Sven Salen, manager), Stockholm, Sweden and renamed KORSHAMN.
17.3.1941: Torpedoed and sunk by the German submarine U 99 in the North Atlantic in position 61.09 north by 12.40 west whilst on a voyage from New York to Liverpool with 7,979 tons of general cargo sailing in Convoy HX112. There were 11 survivors but 26 men were lost.

G51. GLENTARA 1920-1929

O.N. 144193 6,754g 4,123n 406.0 x 54.2 x 23.5 feet.
Two 6-cyl. 4SCSA oil engines by Harland and Wolff Ltd., Glasgow (670 mm x 1,000mm) driving twin screws; 655 NHP, 3,200 IHP, 2,400 BHP; 11½ knots.
25.12.1919: Launched by Harland and

Wolff Ltd., Glasgow (Yard No. 513G) for Glen Line Ltd., Glasgow.
31.3.1920: Registered at Glasgow.
4.1920: Completed at a cost of £367,682.
3.1.1929: Sold to Elder Dempster and Co. Ltd., Liverpool for £120,000 and renamed MILVERTON.
16.1.1929: Registered at Liverpool.
1930: Laid up in River Tyne.
23.5.1933: Owners became Elder Dempster Lines Ltd.
24.5.1934: Sold to W.R. Carpenter and Co. Ltd., Sydney, New South Wales for £12,750
3.8.1934: Renamed SALAMAUA.
7.9.1936: Liverpool register closed.
17.10.1936: Registered at Suva, Fiji Islands.
3.6.1938: Sold to W.R. Carpenter Oversea Shipping Ltd., Rabaul, New Guinea.
6.10.1941: Bombed and damaged by German aircraft when at anchor in Straits of Jubal, Suez.
12.5.1948: Sold to Pacific Shipowners Ltd., Suva, Fiji Islands
14.10.1948: Renamed LAUTOKA.
8.1953: Sold for demolition in Japan.
1.9.1953: Register closed
12.9.1953: Demolition began by Amakaso Sangyo K.K. at Osaka.

Top: *Glenluce. [Ships in Focus]*

Middle: *Glentara. [Ships in Focus]*

Right: Elder, Dempster's *Milverton*, ex *Glentara* at Cape Town. *[F. W. Hawks]*

Glenogle: a builder's photograph dated 19th August 1920. *[Ulster Folk Transport Museum, Ref. 905]*

Glenogle in peacetime colours. *[Ships in Focus]*

G52. GLENOGLE (3) 1920-1949
O.N. 144217 9,513g 5,880n 485.8 x 62.3 x 35.8 feet.
Two 8-cyl. 4SCSA oil engines by Harland and Wolff Ltd., Glasgow (740 mm x 1,150 mm) driving twin screws; 1,144 NHP; 12½ knots.
15.4.1920: Launched by Harland and Wolff Ltd., Glasgow (Yard No. 502G) for Glen Line Ltd., London.
8.1920: Completed at a cost of £622,252.
1929: Fitted with superchargers; 14 knots.
13.4.1949: Sold to Ocean Steam Ship Co. Ltd. (Alfred Holt and Co., managers), Liverpool for £8,739 and renamed DEUCALION.
3.1956: Sold to British Iron and Steel Corporation (Salvage) Ltd.
11.3.1956: Arrived at Briton Ferry to be broken up by T.W. Ward Ltd.

Glenogle photographed by the United States Coast Guard on 12th December 1941. *[E. Johnson collection/Wm.A. Schell]*

Glenapp. [Ships in Focus]

Glenapp as the Dardanus after her sale to Ocean Steam Ship Co. Ltd. in 1949. [J. and M. Clarkson collection]

G53. GLENFARNE/GLENAPP (2) 1920-1949

O.N. 144230 9,503g 5,877n 485.6 x 62.3 x 35.8 feet.
Two 8-cyl. 4SCSA oil engines by Harland and Wolff Ltd., Glasgow (740 mm x 1,150 mm) driving twin screws; 1,144 NHP; 12½ knots.

14.7.1920: Launched by Harland and Wolff Ltd., Glasgow (Yard No. 504G) as GLENAPP for Glen Line Ltd., London having originally been laid down as GLENFARNE.
12.1920: Completed at a cost of £631,765.
1929: Fitted with superchargers; 14 knots.
18.1.1949: Sold to Ocean Steam Ship Co.

Ltd., Liverpool for £8,841 and renamed DARDANUS.
1956: Laid up in Holy Loch pending disposal.
18.7.1957: Sold to British Iron and Steel Corporation (Salvage) Ltd.
19.7.1957: Arrived at Inverkeithing to be broken up by T.W. Ward Ltd.

Glengarry. [Ships in Focus]

Glenstrae, formerly *Glengarry*, a unique renaming in the Glen Line fleet. *[Tom Rayner/J. and M. Clarkson collection]*

G54. GLENGARRY (2)/GLENSTRAE (3) 1922-1949
O.N. 146283 9,460g 5,843n 485.6 x 62.3 x 35.2 feet.
Two 8-cyl. 4SCSA oil engines by Harland and Wolff Ltd., Glasgow (740 mm x 1,150 mm) driving twin screws; 1,144 NHP, 4,500 IHP, 6,000 BHP, 12½ knots.
30.9.1920: Launched by Harland and Wolff Ltd., Glasgow (Yard No. 503G) for Glen Line Ltd., London.
Work delayed by shortage of materials.
2.1922: Completed at a cost of £622,532.
17.2.1922: Registered at Glasgow.
11.1922: Grounded in the Whangpo River. Refloated after cargo discharged into lighters.
1925: Collided with tug HEATHERCOCK at Leith.
1929: Fitted with superchargers, speed now 14 knots.
6.9.1939: Renamed GLENSTRAE.

7.9.1940: Damaged by bomb attack in London Docks.
28.1.1949: Registered at Liverpool.
10.2.1949: Sold to Ocean Steam Ship Co. Ltd., Liverpool for £19,491 and renamed DOLIUS.
7.1952: Hit dock wall at Gladstone Dock and cracked starboard thrust block. Sold to British Iron and Steel Corporation (Salvage) Ltd.
20.8.1952: Arrived at Briton Ferry to be broken up by T.W. Ward Ltd.
22.1.1953: Register closed.

G55. GLENBEG (1) 1922-1949
O.N. 146292 9,461g 5,846n 485.6 x 62.3 x 35.8 feet.
Two 8-cyl. 4SCSA oil engines by Harland and Wolff Ltd., Glasgow (740 mm x 1,150 mm) driving twin screws; 1,144 NHP, 6,000 IHP, 4,500 BHP; 12½ knots.
25.12.1920: Launched by Harland and

Wolff Ltd., Glasgow (Yard No. 505G) for Glen Line Ltd., London.
Work delayed by shortage of materials.
4.1922: Completed at a cost of £617,234.
15.4.1922: Registered at Glasgow.
1923: Grounded on coast of Jutland whilst on a voyage from Vladivostock to Copenhagen.
1929: Fitted with superchargers, speed now 14 knots.
2.7.1949: Registered at Liverpool.
3.8.1949: Sold to Ocean Steam Ship Co. Ltd. (Alfred Holt and Co., managers), Liverpool for £18,722 and renamed DYMAS.
9.4.1954: Sold to British Iron and Steel Corporation (Salvage) Ltd.
8.4.1954: Arrived at Dalmuir to be broken up by W.H. Arnott Young and Co. Ltd.
3.8.1954: Hulk towed to Old Kilpatrick for final demolition.
11.9.1954: Register closed.

Glenbeg. [Martin Lindenborn/J. and M. Clarkson collection]

G56. GLENSHIEL (2) 1924-1942
O.N. 145439 9,415g 5,803n 485.7 x 62.2 x 35.5 feet.
Two 8-cyl. 4SCSA oil engines by Harland and Wolff Ltd., Belfast (740 mm x 1,150 mm) driving twin screws; 1,144 NHP, 6,000 IHP; 12½ knots.
24.1.1924: Launched by Harland and Wolff Ltd., Belfast (Yard No. 594) for Glen Line Ltd., London.
She had been laid down as GLENCREE.
15.5.1924: Registered at Belfast.
22.5.1924: Completed at a cost of £434,532.
3.4.1942: Torpedoed and sunk by the Japanese submarine I-7 300 miles east of the Maldives in position 01.00 south by 78.11 east whilst on a voyage from Bombay and Karachi to Fremantle with general cargo. HMS FORTUNE saved all 79 crew, 9 gunners and 12 passengers.
7.7.1942: Register closed.

Above: Glenshiel having part of an engine lifted onboard during fitting out at Belfast on 19th February 1924. [Ulster Folk Transport Museum, Ref.1814] Below: Glenshiel in service. [Ships in Focus]

Carnarvonshire. [Nautical Photo Agency/J. and M. Clarkson collection]

G57. CARNARVONSHIRE (4) 1933-1936

O.N. 132049 9,406g 5,955n 500.3 x 62.4 x 34.6 feet.

Two T.3-cyl. by Workman, Clark and Co. Ltd., Belfast (24", 40½" and 68" x 48") driving twin screws; 978 NHP, 5,000 IHP; 12½ knots.

13.12.1913: Launched by Workman, Clark and Co. Ltd., Belfast (Yard No. 325) for Royal Mail Steam Packet Company, London.

5.3.1914: Registered at Belfast.

7.3.1914: Completed at a cost of £170,095.

1920: Placed on Glen-Shire service to the Far East.

12.10.1932: Owner became Royal Mail Lines Ltd., London.

8.4.1933: Sold to Glen Line Ltd., London together with PEMBROKESHIRE and Shire Line conference rights for a total price of £15,000.

1.10.1935: Sold to The Red R Steamship Co. Ltd. and Whalton Shipping Co. Ltd. (Stephens, Sutton Ltd., managers), Newcastle-upon-Tyne for £20,000 in order to be traded in under the Government's 'Scrap and Build' scheme.

14.10.1935: Sold to Pedder and Mylchrist Ltd, London

10.1935: Sold to Italian breakers for £17,500, but contract cancelled and re-sold to Amakusa Sangyo Kisen K.K., Osaka for £20,000.

26.2.1936: Arrived at Osaka.

29.10.1936: Register closed.

G58. PEMBROKESHIRE (6) 1933-1936

O.N. 136349 7,821g. 4,968n. 470.2 x 58.3 x 32.2 feet.

Q.4-cyl. by Workman, Clark and Co. Ltd., Belfast (27½", 39½", 57" and 82" x 54"); 735 NHP, 3,750 IHP; 12 knots.

7.12.1914: Launched by Workman, Clark and Co. Ltd., Belfast (Yard No.337) for

Royal Mail Steam Packet Co., London.

13.4.1915: Registered at Belfast.

13.4.1915: Completed at a cost of £155,689.

1920: Placed on Glen-Shire service to the Far East.

12.10.1932: Owner became Royal Mail Lines Ltd.

8.4.1933: Sold to Glen Line Ltd., London together with CARNARVONSHIRE and Shire Line conference rights for a total price of £15,000.

24.1.1936: Sold to Queen Line Ltd. (Thomas Dunlop and Sons, managers), Glasgow for £19,750 in order to be traded in under the Government's 'Scrap and Build' scheme.

1936: Sold to Danzig breakers for £14,700.

4.4.1936: Arrived at Danzig.

23.4.1936: Register closed.

Pembrokeshire off Erith on 4th May 1935. [World Ship Photo Library]

G59. GLENEARN (4) 1933-1935

O.N. 162370 5,348g 3,225n 421.3 x 56.0 x 25.5 feet.

8-cyl. 4SCSA Burmeister & Wain-type oil engine by J.G. Kincaid and Co. Ltd., Greenock (740 mm x 1,500 mm); 652 NHP, 4,240 IHP, 3,180 BHP; 12 knots.

29.7.1930: Launched by Lithgows Ltd., Port Glasgow (Yard No. 844) as TOLTEN and placed under the management of Lowden, Connell and Co. Ltd., Liverpool, the sale to the originally contracted owner Compañia Sud Americana de Vapores, Valparaiso, Chile having fallen through.

10.1930: Completed.

19.11.1932: Registered at Liverpool in the name of Lithgows Ltd., Port Glasgow.

29.6.1933: Sale of vessel to Glen Line Ltd., London agreed for £120,000 payable in September1934. Entered immediate Glen service under monthly charter.

15.7.1933: Renamed GLENEARN.

1934: Sale cancelled following company re-structuring, charter extended.

26.11.1935: Formally re-sold to Lithgows Ltd., and then sold to Lowden, Connell and Co. Ltd., Liverpool.

11.12.1935: Name reverted to TOLTEN.

9.3.1938: Sold to Trinder, Anderson and Co., London.

14.5.1942: Sold to the South American Saint Line Ltd. (B. and S. Shipping Co. Ltd., managers), Newport.

16.5.1942: Re-registered at Newport.

14.11.1945: Renamed ST. MERRIEL.

1.1950: Sold to O/Y Oceanfart A/B (Birger Krogius, manager), Helsingfors, Finland and renamed HELIOS.

3.2.1950: Register closed.

1959: Sold to the Santa Irini Shipping Co. Ltd., Monrovia, Liberia (Emmanuel A. Karavias) (Nomikos (London) Ltd., London, managers) and renamed TASSOS under the Lebanese flag.

14.4.1967: Arrived at Hong Kong for scrapping by Leung Yau Company, who had bought her for £62,500.

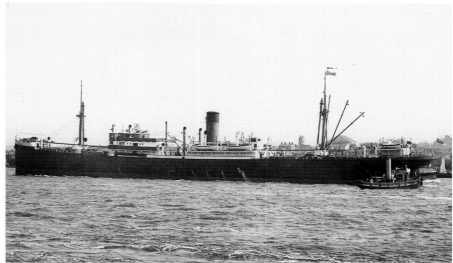

Top: *Tolten. [Ian J. Farquhar collecton]* Middle: *Glenearn* off Gravesend on 2nd June 1934. *[F. W. Hawks/Peter Newall collection]* Bottom: The Lebanese flag *Tassos,* ex *Glenearn,* in June 1964. *[Roy Fenton collection]*

G60. FLINTSHIRE (4) 1935-1939

O.N. 147220 7,726g 4,856n 459.5 x 58.4 x 32.6 feet.
One Brown Curtis steam turbine by Workman, Clark and Co. Ltd., Belfast; 1,150 NHP, 6,600 IHP, 6,000 SHP; 14 1/2 knots.
18.4.1923: Launched by Workman, Clark and Co. Ltd., Belfast (Yard No. 460) for Ocean Steamship Co. Ltd. (Alfred Holt and Co., managers), Liverpool as DARDANUS.
The keel of DARDANUS had been laid 21.1.1921, but work was suspended in February 1921, restarting on 1.5.1922.
13.6.1923: Ran trials and completed that month.
7.6.1923: Registered at Liverpool.
30.7.1935: Acquired by Glen Line Ltd., London for £72,641.
8.8.1935: Renamed FLINTSHIRE.
20.2.1939: Sold to Ocean Steam Ship Co. Ltd. (Alfred Holt and Co., managers), Liverpool for £59,820.
3.3.1939: Renamed DARDANUS.
5.4.1942: Bombed and damaged by Japanese carrier aircraft off Vizagapatnam, India whilst on a voyage from Calcutta and Sandheads for Colombo and UK in ballast. Taken in tow by the steamer GANDARA (5,281/1919; Britsh India Steam Navigation Co. Ltd).
6.4.1942: Further damaged by bombs and then sunk by gunfire and torpedo by Japanese surface ships in position 15.55 north by 82.05 east. The entire crew of 74 and four gunners survived.
21.9.1942: Register closed.

G61. GLENFINLAS (2) 1935-1947 and 1950-1952

O.N. 137536 7,572g 4,811n 455.3 x 56.3 x 32.5 feet.
T.3-cyl. by North Eastern Marine Engineering Co. Ltd., Newcastle-upon-Tyne (31", 51 1/2" and 86" x 60"); 573 NHP, 4,750 IHP; 14 knots.
14.9.1916: Launched by Hawthorn, Leslie and Co. Ltd., Newcastle-upon-Tyne (Yard No.471) for China Mutual Steam Navigation Co. Ltd. (Alfred Holt and Co., managers), Liverpool as ELPENOR.
1.1917: Completed.
3.2.1917: Registered at Liverpool.
27.8.1935: Acquired by Glen Line Ltd., London for £22,485.
9.10.1935: Renamed GLENFINLAS.
16.4.1941: Damaged by German aircraft bombs and machine gun fire in the North Sea off Harwich. Nine lives were lost.
12.11.1942: Damaged by German aircraft bombs in Bougie Harbour during the OPERATION TORCH landings.
13.11.1942: Allowed to sink in shallow water to prevent explosion of aviation fuel in cargo.
7.1943: Raised and taken into Oran. Further damaged by explosion (with the loss of two lives) and collision.
10.1943: Returned to Sunderland for permanent repairs.
21.1.1947: Sold to China Mutual Steam Navigation Co. Ltd. (Alfred Holt and Co., managers), Liverpool for £11,750.
12.4.1947: Renamed ELPENOR.
4.8.1950: Re-sold again to Glen Line Ltd. for £9,366.
12.8.1950: Renamed GLENFINLAS.
6.1952: Sold to British Iron and Steel Corporation (Salvage) Ltd. for £97,000 for breaking up.
10.6.1952: Arrived at Blyth for demolition by Hughes, Bolckow Ltd.
5.11.1952: Register closed.

G62. GLENAFFARIC (1) 1935-1947 and 1950-1951

O.N. 143674 7,782g 4,906n 459.2 x 56.3 x 32.5 feet.
T.3-cyl. by Caledon Ship Building and Engineering Co. Ltd., Dundee (31", 51 1/2" and 86" x 60"); 571 NHP, 4,512 BHP, 4,800 IHP; 14 knots.
20.4.1920: Launched by Caledon Ship Building and Engineering Co. Ltd., Dundee (Yard No.252) for Ocean Steam Ship Co. Ltd. (Alfred Holt and Co., managers), Liverpool as MACHAON.
1920: Completed.
25.9.1920: Registered at Liverpool.
8.11.1935: Acquired by Glen Line Ltd for £45,217.
2.12.1935: Renamed GLENAFFARIC.
4.10.1942: Missed by a submarine torpedo 240 miles south of Karachi.
15.8.1947: Re-sold to Ocean Steam Ship Co. Ltd. (Alfred Holt and Co., managers), Liverpool for £20,989.
15.9.1947: Renamed MACHAON.
22.6.1950: Acquired by Glen Line Ltd., London for £17,291.
30.6.1950: Renamed GLENAFFARIC.
1.1951: Sold to British Iron and Steel Corporation (Salvage) Ltd. for £55,000 for breaking up.
14.1.1951: Arrived at Briton Ferry for demolition by T.W. Ward Ltd.
7.12.1951: Register closed.

Top: *Flintshire*, River Thames on 4th September 1937. *[F. W. Hawks/J. and M. Clarkson collection]* Middle: *Glenfinlas*, *[P. A. Vicary/Ian J. Farquhar collection]* Bottom: *Machaon* later renamed *Glenaffaric*. *[B. & A. Feilden/J. and M. Clarkson collection]*

Above: *Glenaffaric* in the Mersey. *[Frank Barr/British Transport Heritage]*

G63. RADNORSHIRE (5) 1936-1939
O.N. 147222 7,726g 4,809n 458.3 x 58.2 x 32.6 feet.
Two 8-cyl. 4SCSA oil engines by Akt. Burmeister & Wain, Copenhagen (29" x 45¼") driving twin screws; 680 NHP, 6,000 IHP, 4,500 BHP; 13¾ knots.
2.2.1923: Launched by Caledon Ship Building and Engineering Co. Ltd., Dundee (Yard No.278) for Ocean Steamship Co. Ltd. (Alfred Holt and Co., managers), Liverpool as TANTALUS.
6.1923: Completed.
13.6.1923: Registered at Liverpool.
22.2.1936: Acquired by Glen Line Ltd. for £68,940.
7.4.1936: Renamed RADNORSHIRE.
16.1.1939: Sold to Ocean Steam Ship Co. Ltd. (Alfred Holt and Co., managers), Liverpool for £62,013.
26.1.1939: Name reverted to TANTALUS.
5.12.1941: At Hong Kong undergoing engine repair when Japanese attack began. Towed to Manila.
26.12.1941: Bombed and set on fire by Japanese aircraft while at anchor off Manila. Abandoned and sank. The 39 crew and 6 gunners became prisoners-of-war whilst the 23 Chinese crew were landed at Manila.
4.11.1942: Register closed.

Above: *Glenaffaric* in grey. *[Peter Newall collection]*

Below: *Radnorshire. [Ships in Focus]*

113

G64. GLENEARN (5) 1938-1970

O.N. 166254 8,986g 5,394n 483.1 x 66.4 x 31.3 feet.

Two 6-cyl. 2SCDA oil engines by Akt. Burmeister & Wain Maskin-og-Skibsbyggeri, Copenhagen (620 mm x 1,400 mm) driving twin screws; 2,469 NHP, 19,700 IHP, 12,000 BHP.

29.6.1938: Launched by Caledon Ship Building and Engineering Co. Ltd., Dundee (Yard No. 368) for Glen Line Ltd., London but registered at Liverpool.

11.1938: Completed (trials 6.12.1938) at a cost of £440,500.

15.10.1939: Requisitioned by the Admiralty as a Fleet Supply Ship.

22.10.1939: Arrived Palmers Hebburn Co. Ltd., Newcastle-upon-Tyne for conversion.

25.4.1940: Commissioned but placed temporarily on commercial service.

2.7.1940: Recalled for conversion to Landing Ship (Infantry) (Large) at Liverpool.

13.12.1940: Commissioned.

22.4.1941: Bombed and damaged by German aircraft off Greece.

26.4.1941: Further damaged by near misses south of Nauplia. Machinery unseated. Returned to Egypt.

12.1941: Arrived at Colombo for repairs.

1942: Refitted and further modified in the UK.

4.1945: Damaged by a fuel explosion at Sydney, New South Wales.

7.1946: Handed back to owners. Reconverted by Smith's Dock Co. Ltd.

6.12.1947: Handed over for return to commercial service.

11.12.1970: Arrived at Kaohsiung for breaking up by Tung Cheng Steel and Iron Works.

10.1.1971: Demolition began.

28.2.1971: Demolition completed.

Left: *Glenearn*, under government requisition and Harrison Line management, loading asphalt in Trinidad in 1940. *[G. Holmes collection]* Above: Seen from *HMAS Hobart* whilst aground in Suez Bay on 14th July 1941. *[NMM. D.2241/b]*

Above: Aground in Suez Bay on 14th July 1941, again from *HMAS Hobart*, with Cunard White Star's burning *Georgic* on her starboard side. *[NMM. D.2241/C]* Below: After further modification towards the end of the war. *[Ian J. Farquhar]*

114

Left: *HMS Glenearn* on 5th December 1942. *[Peter Newall collection]*

Middle: *Glenearn* in peacetime, accompanied by the tug *Uno* owned by the Adelaide Steamship Co.Ltd.. *[Peter Newall collection]*

Bottom: *Glenearn* displaying her port of registry - Liverpool, a result of Holt's takeover. *[Roy Fenton collection]*

Above: Seen from *HMS Dido* in May 1941, *HMS Glenroy* (Landing Ship Infantry Large) is moored in Alexandria Harbour after the evacuation of the army from Greece. Note the unusual funnel marking, also there are no landing craft or boats on board, only liferafts. The Greek cruiser *Averoff* is behind her. *[NMM N.34644]*

Right: *HMS Glenroy* on 29th February 1944 showing her 1942 modifications. *[Peter Newall collection]*

Bottom: In May 1946, shortly before return to her owners and refit at Falmouth. *[Wright & Logan/Roy Fenton collection]*

G65. GLENROY (3) 1938-1966
O.N. 166256 8,997g 5,390n 483.0 x 66.4
x 31.3 feet.
Two 6-cyl. 2SCDA oil engines by Akt.
Burmeister & Wain Maskin-og-
Skibsbyggeri, Copenhagen (620 mm x
1,400 mm) driving twin screws; 2,469
NHP, 19,700 IHP, 12,000 BHP.
15.8.1938: Launched by Scotts' Ship
Building and Engineering Co. Ltd.,
Greenock (Yard No. 571) for Glen Line
Ltd., London, but registered at Liverpool.
28.12.1938: Ran trials and completed that
month at a cost of £442,750.
10.1939: Requisitioned by the Admiralty
as a Fleet Supply Ship.
29.10.1939: Conversion work begun.
30.4.1940: Commissioned but placed
temporarily on commercial service.
10.6.1940: Recalled for conversion to
Landing Ship (Infantry) (Large) at
Liverpool.
12.9.1940: Damaged during air raid.
24.11.1940: Commissioned.
22.4.1941: Damaged by grounding at
Alexandria.
30.5.1941: Bombed and damaged off
Crete. Repaired at Alexandria.
23.11.1941: Damaged by aircraft torpedo
off Tobruk and beached at Mersa Matruh.
26.11.1941: Refloated and returned to
Alexandria for repairs.
11.1942: Repairs completed and then
returned to UK for refit and further
modification.
21.2.1943: Re-commissioned.
17.6.1944: Damaged by mine off Utah
Beach, Normandy.
1.1945: Repairs completed.
21.6.1946: Returned to owners.
Reconverted at Silly, Cox and Co.,
Falmouth.
27.5.1948: Handed back for return to
commercial service.
9.1966: Sold to Ataka & Co. Ltd., Japan
for demolition at Onomichi, but
subsequently resold.
2.11.1966: Demolition began by
Tarumoto Sangyo K.K. at Kure.

Above: *Glenroy* in the Thames during 1956. *[Ships in Focus]*
Middle: At Aden. *[Ambrose Greenway collection]*
Bottom: In the Straits of Malacca. *[Peter Foxley/Ian J. Farquhar collection]*

G66. DENBIGHSHIRE (4) 1939-1967
O.N. 166276 8,983g 5,393n 483.1 x 66.4 x 30.8 feet.
Two 6-cyl. 2SCDA oil engines by Akt. Burmeister & Wain Maskin-og-Skibsbyggeri, Copenhagen (620 mm x 1,400 mm) driving twin screws; 2,469 NHP, 19,700 IHP, 12,000 BHP.
29.10.1938: Launched by N.V. Nederlandsche Scheepsbouw Maatschappij, Amsterdam (Yard No.269) for Glen Line Ltd., Liverpool.
7.7.1939: Ran trials and completed that month at a cost of £428,600.
12.1967: Sold to China Mutual Steam Navigation Co. Ltd. (Alfred Holt and Co., managers), Liverpool and renamed SARPEDON.
5.1969: Sold for scrap.
11.8.1969: Arrived at Kaohsiung for breaking up by Tui Cheng Co. Ltd.
10.1969: Demolition began.

Opposite, top: A grey and defensively armed *Denbighshire*. [NMM P22150]
Middle: At Singapore in 1960. [Ambrose Greenway collection]
Bottom: *Denbighshire* well battened down and making good speed. [Ian J. Farquhar collection]

This page, top: *Denbighshire*. [F. R. Sherlock/Roy Fenton collection]
Middle: Swinging in the Thames in March 1959. [Ships in Focus]
Bottom: When *Denbighshire* went to China Mutual Steam Navigation Co.Ltd. she was renamed *Sarpedon*, a name held for only eighteen months before being sold for demolition. [J. and M. Clarkson.]

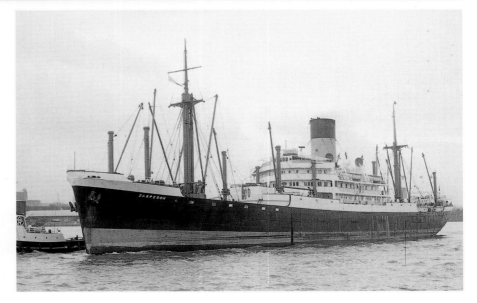

G67. BRECONSHIRE (4) 1939-1942
O.N. 172758 8,982g 5,384n 483.0 x 66.4 x 31.2 feet.
Two 6-cyl. 2SCDA oil engines by Akt. Burmeister & Wain Maskin-og-Skibsbyggeri, Copenhagen (620 mm x 1,400 mm) driving twin screws; 2,469 NHP, 14,700 IHP, 12,000 BHP; 18 knots.
2.2.1939: Launched by Taikoo Dockyard and Engineering Co. Ltd., Hong Kong (Yard No.276) for Glen Line Ltd., Liverpool.

21.7.1939: Ran trials and completed that month at a cost of £365,900.
26.7.1939: Registered at Hong Kong.
22.8.1939: Registered at Liverpool.
1939: Requisitioned by the Admiralty as a Fleet Supply Ship.
1941: Sold to the Admiralty.
7.11.1941: Register closed.
23.3.1942: Bombed and damaged by German aircraft off Malta.

26.3.1942: Further damaged by bombs and set on fire off Marsaxlokk.
27.3.1942: Sank off Marsaxlokk.
8.1950: Raised and sold to Leopoldo Rodriguez, Malta.
1.9.1950: Towed upside-down to Messina where she was beached.
1952: Sold to Navigazione Libera Triestina, towed to Taranto and righted.
1954: Towed to Trieste and broken up.

Above: *Breconshire* fitting out at Hong Kong on 16th April 1939. *[Ian J. Farquhar collection]*
Below: *Breconshire* on trials off the Hong Kong coast. *[W. A. Laxon collection]*

Above: The supply ship *Breconshire* enters the Grand Harbour, Malta in January 1942. Her foremast has been removed, probably to improve the arcs of fire of her anti-aircraft guns. *[Kevin J. O'Donoghue collection]*
Below: A series of pictures taken on board *Breconshire* during a gale on her final run into Malta in March 1942.

The anti-aircraft guns which have constantly been in action are re-ammunitioned. *[IWM. AX 111 A]*

The enemy approaches, a destroyer lays a smoke screen and the forward guns are manned. *[IWM. AX.110A]*

The crew fight one of the fires. *[IWM. AX.114]*

Nearly in port and *Breconshire* has been struck by a bomb. The cruiser *HMS Penelope* passes a line to try to tow her into harbour. *[IWM. AX.112A]*

Above: The fire gets out of control and *Breconshire* settles in the shallow water. *[IWM AX 115A]*

Royal Navy salvage craft surround *Breconshire* as she is refloated before being towed to Italy for demolition. *[IWM. A.31714]*

G68. GLENORCHY (3) 1939-1942

O.N. 172760 8,982g 5,383n 483.0 x 66.4 x 31.2 feet.
Two 6-cyl. 2SCDA oil engines by Akt. Burmeister & Wain Maskin-og-Skibsbyggeri, Copenhagen (620 mm x 1,400 mm) driving twin screws; 2,469 NHP, 12,000 BHP, 14,700 IHP; 18 knots.
5.1939: Launched by Taikoo Dockyard and Engineering Co. Ltd., Hong Kong (Yard No. 277) for Glen Line Ltd., London.
21.11.1939: Registered at Hong Kong.

28.12.1939: Ran trials and completed that month at a cost of £366,500.
27.3.1940: Re-registered at Liverpool.
13.8.1942: Torpedoed and sunk by the Italian motor torpedo boat Ms31 in the Sicilian Narrows five miles north west of Kelibia Island whilst on a voyage from the Clyde and Gibraltar to Malta in naval service during Operation Pedestal. The master and six crew were lost, and the remaining 67 crew and 7 gunners were taken as prisoners of war or interned.
4.11.1942: Register closed.

Being completed early in the war and only having a life of two and a half years, few pictures exist of *Glenorchy*.

Above: *Glenorchy* in a South African port. *[Ian Shiffman collection]*

Bottom: Bombs falling astern of *Glenorchy* on 12th August 1942, the day before she was lost. The photograph was taken from *HMS Manchester*. *[IWM A11171]*

G69. GLENGYLE (5) 1940-1970

O.N. 166293 9,919g 6,054n 483.1 x 66.4
x 31.3 feet.
Two 6-cyl. 2SCDA oil engines by Akt.
Burmeister & Wain Maskin-og-
Skibsbyggeri, Copenhagen (620 mm x
1,400 mm) driving twin screws; 2,469
NHP, 19,700 IHP, 12,000 BHP.
18.7.1939: Launched by Caledon
Shipbuilding and Engineering Co. Ltd.,
Dundee (Yard No. 372) for Glen Line
Ltd., Liverpool.
10.1939: Requisitioned prior to
completion by the Admiralty as a Fleet
Supply Ship.
7.4.1940: Conversion completed but taken
back in hand almost immediately for
conversion at Glasgow to Landing Ship
(Infantry) (Large) at a cost of £446,500.
10.9.1940: Commissioned.
6.1944: Returned to the UK for refit and
further conversion.
17.7.1946: Returned to owners.
Reconverted by Vickers, Armstrong,
Newcastle-upon-Tyne.
3.3.1948: Handed over for return to
commercial service.
10.1970: Sold to Ocean Steam Ship Co.
Ltd. (Alfred Holt and Co., managers),
Liverpool and renamed DEUCALION.
9.8.1971: Demolition began at Kaohsiung
by Tung Cheng Steel and Iron Works.

Top: *Glengyle. [University of Dundee GD324/6/3/64/12]*
Middle: The modified *Glengyle* arrives at Malta on 8th January 1942. She could accommodate almost 700 troops. *[Kevin J. O'Donoghue collection]*
Bottom; *Glengyle* in the Clyde on 16th November 1942. *[IWM FL8888]*

Top: *Glengyle* in the Straits of
Malacca. *[Peter Foxley/J. and M.
Clarkson collection]*
Left: *Glengyle* battened down in the
Thames. *[Ships in Focus]*
Bottom left: One of the few known
photographs of *Deucalion*,
ex *Glengyle*, a name she sailed under
for less than one year. *[J. and M.
Clarkson collection]*
Below: *Glengyle* in Gallions Reach
17th April 1957. *[R. A. Snook/Roy
Fenton collection]*

Glenartney on trials.   *[University of Dundee   GD324/6/3/65/14]*

Glenartney alongside Holt's Wharf, Hong Kong after the Second World War. *[Peter Newall collection]*

G70. GLENARTNEY (4) 1940-1967
O.N. 166297 9,795g 5,944n 483.1 x 66.4
x 31.3 feet.
Two 6-cyl. 2SCDA oil engines by Akt.
Burmeister & Wain Maskin-og-
Skibsbyggeri, Copenhagen (620 mm x
1,400 mm) driving twin screws; 2,469
NHP, 19,700 IHP, 12,000 BHP.
27.12.1939: Launched by Caledon
Shipbuilding and Engineering Co. Ltd.,
Dundee (Yard No. 373) for Glen Line
Ltd., Liverpool.
30.9.1940: Completed at a cost of
£465,800.
1967: Sold to Seibu Kogyu K.K., Japan
for £140,000.
1.4.1967: Demolition began at Onomichi.

Top: *Glenartney* in peacetime colours.
[Ships in Focus]

Middle and bottom: Glen Line cargoes
often included heavy machinery. The
middle picture shows a number of
boilers lined up awaiting shipment on
the *Glenartney*. In the lower photo the
chassis of locomotive 2343 is being
lifted onboard. As the photographer
was based in Antwerp we must
assume these were being loaded
there. *[J. and M. Clarkson collection]*

G71. GLENGARRY (3) 1946-1970 and 1971

O.N. 181037 9,144g 5,392n 507.0 x 66.4 x 30.4 feet.

Two 6-cyl. 2SCDA oil engines by Akt. Burmeister & Wain Maskin-og-Skibsbyggeri, Copenhagen (620 mm x 1,400 mm) driving twin screws; 12,000 BHP.

6.11.1939: Launched by Akt. Burmeister & Wain Maskin-og-Skibsbyggeri, Copenhagen (Yard No. 643) for Glen Line Ltd.

4.1940: Seized by Germany while fitting out.

10.1940: Completed for Hamburg-Amerika Linie, Hamburg as MEERSBERG.

11.1940: U-boat target ship.

6.1941: To Rotterdam for conversion to surface raider 'Schiff 5'.

1943: Moved to Hamburg with work incomplete.

10.2.1944: Renamed HANSA and commissioned as artillery cadet training ship.

5.1945: Recaptured in Kiel Roads, allocated to the Ministry of War Transport and renamed EMPIRE HUMBER and selected for conversion to Combined Operations Headquarters Ship.

6.6.1946: Returned to Glen Line Ltd. and reverted to GLENGARRY.

4.1947: Re-entered commercial service after conversion. Total cost after write-off of reconversion costs was £421,229.

8.1970: Sold to Ocean Steam Ship Co. Ltd. (Blue Funnel Line Ltd., managers), Liverpool and renamed DARDANUS.

1.1971: Returned to Glen Line Ltd. and reverted to GLENGARRY at Kaohsiung for voyage to Japan to be broken up.

10.2.1971: Delivered to breakers at Sakaide.

1.3.1971: Demolition commenced by Miyayi Salvage Corporation, Taduju.

What appears to be an impressive view of *Glengarry* when newly built but may have been retouched. Note the buff funnel. The vessel was completed as *Meersberg* and therefore never went to sea as *Glengarry* until 1947. *[J. and M. Clarkson collection]*

Above: *Glengarry* as *Meersberg*. *[Prof. Theodor Siersdorfer collection]*
Below: *Glengarry* in 1953. *[Ships in Focus]*

Above: *Glengarry* at Singapore in 1959. *[Ambrose Greenway collection]*

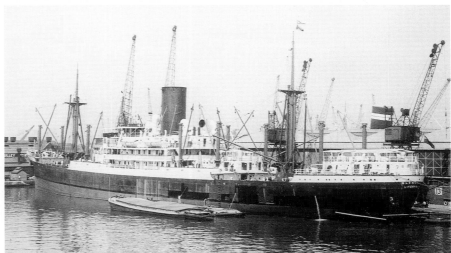

Right: *Glengarry* in the Port of London Docks. *[J. and M. Clarkson collection]*

Below: *Glengarry*, renamed *Dardanus* in August 1970, discharging in Branch No.1, Gladstone Dock, Liverpool on 3rd October 1971. Six months later she was in the breaker's hands. *[Paul H. Boot]*

G72. BRECONSHIRE (5) 1946-1967

O.N. 181025 9,061g 5,399n 512.0 x 66.4 x 30.5 feet.

Two 6-cyl. 2SCDA oil engines by J.G. Kincaid and Co. Ltd., Greenock (620 mm x 1,400 mm) driving twin screws; 8,000 BHP, 16 knots.

30.5.1942: Launched by Caledon Shipbuilding and Engineering Co. Ltd., Dundee (Yard No. 388) as the escort aircraft carrier HMS ACTIVITY having been laid down as TELEMACHUS for Ocean Steam Ship Co. Ltd. (Alfred Holt and Co., managers), Liverpool and requisitioned during construction by the Ministry of War Transport and allocated the name EMPIRE ACTIVITY.

10.1942: Completed.

1946: Returned to Alfred Holt and Co., Liverpool for £207,000.

26.4.1946: Sent to Palmer's Hebburn Co. Ltd., Newcastle-upon-Tyne for reconversion to a cargo vessel at an additional cost of £657,685.

4.6.1946: Owners became Ocean Steam Ship Co. Ltd. (Alfred Holt and Co., managers), Liverpool

14.7.1946: Acquired by Glen Line Ltd., Liverpool and renamed BRECONSHIRE.

12.9.1947: Delivered for commercial service.

26.4.1967: Arrived at Mihara for demolition by Ataka and Co. Ltd.

5.1967: Work began at Etajima Island, near Kure.

Top: *Breconshire* as *HMS Activity* in a photograph issued in 1944. *[IWM A.21850]*

Right: *Breconshire* on 14th June 1951 taken by Flying Officer Finch. *[J. and M. Clarkson collection]*

Top: *Breconshire* [*F.R. Sherlock/Roy Fenton collection*]

Middle: *Breconshire* at Singapore in 1959. [*Ambrose Greenway collection*]

Bottom: *Breconshire* in her latter years pushing along in the Straits of Malacca. [*Peter Foxley/J. and M. Clarkson collection*]

G73. GLENORCHY (4) 1948-1970

O.N. 168821 9,324g 5,473n 512.8 x 66.4 x 30.6 feet.

Two 6-cyl. 2SCDA oil engines by J.G. Kincaid and Co. Ltd., Greenock (620 mm x 1,400 mm) driving twin screws; 12,000 BHP, 17½ knots.

25.6.1941: Launched by Caledon Shipbuilding and Engineering Co. Ltd., Dundee (Yard No. 387) for Ocean Steam Ship Co. Ltd. (Alfred Holt and Co., managers), Liverpool as PRIAM, having been requisitioned by the Admiralty during construction for conversion into an escort aircraft carrier but returned to owners due to advanced state of completion.

1941: Completed.

20.10.1948: Acquired by Glen Line Ltd., London for £446,484 and renamed GLENORCHY.

1970: Returned to Ocean Steam Ship Co. Ltd. (Alfred Holt and Co., managers), Liverpool and renamed PHEMIUS.

1971: Sold to Tung Cheng Steel and Iron Works, Kaohsiung for demolition at $64 per light ton.

27.4.1971: Arrived at Kaohsiung.

20.6.1971: Demolition commenced.

2.8.1971: Demolition complete.

Top: *Glenorchy*, on 5th March 1961. *[Captain C.L. Reynolds/Roy Fenton collection]*

Middle: Undergoing alterations to her funnel and being repainted, probably during a change of ownership. *[J. and M. Clarkson collection]*

Bottom: Late in her career as *Phemius*. *[Wm. A. Schell]*

G74. RADNORSHIRE (6) 1949-1962
O.N. 182399 7,632g 4,449n 487.0 x 62.3 x 28.2 feet.
8-cyl. 2SCDA oil engine by J.G. Kincaid and Co. Ltd., Greenock (550 mm x 1,200 mm); 6,800 BHP.
16.9.1947: Launched by Caledon Shipbuilding and Engineering Co. Ltd., Dundee (Yard No. 430) for Ocean Steam Ship Co. Ltd. (Alfred Holt and Co., managers), Liverpool as ACHILLES.
12.1947: Completed.
9.5.1949: Acquired by Glen Line Ltd., London for £606,630 and renamed RADNORSHIRE.

4.12.1962: Re-sold to Ocean Steam Ship Co. Ltd. (Alfred Holt and Co., managers), Liverpool for £196,118 and renamed ASPHALION.
1.1966: Owners became Nederlandsche Stoomvaart Maatschappij 'Ocean', Amsterdam, Holland and renamed POLYPHEMUS.
11.1972: Returned to Ocean Steam Ship Co. Ltd. (Blue Funnel Line Ltd., managers), Liverpool and reverted to ASPHALION.
15.1.1973: Owners became Ocean Transport and Trading Ltd.

10.1975: Sold to Gulf (Shipowners) Ltd. (Gulf Shipping Lines Ltd. (Abbas K. and Murtaza K. Gokal)), London (Gulfeast Ship Management Ltd., Hong Kong, managers) and renamed GULF ANCHOR under the British flag.
28.4.1979: Arrived at Kaohsiung for demolition by Nan Feng Steel Enterprise Co. Ltd.

GLENAFFARIC 1950-1951 See G62.

GLENFINLAS 1950-1951 See G61.

Two views of *Radnorshire*, the lower picture dated 16th September 1961. *[Above: World Ship Photo Library, lower: Captain C.L. Reynolds/Roy Fenton collection]*

133

G75. FLINTSHIRE (5) 1950-1957

O.N. 169744 7,297g 4,350n 441.7 x 57.1 x 27.8 feet.

T.3-cyl. by General Machinery Corporation, Hamilton, Ohio ($24^{1}/_{2}$", 37" and 70" x 48"); 2,500 IHP.

16.11.1943: Launched by Bethlehem-Fairfield Shipyards Inc., Baltimore, Maryland (Yard No. 2274) for the United States War Shipping Administration, Washington as JAMES CARROLL

11.1943: Completed as SAMGARA on Lend-Lease bare-boat charter to the Ministry of War Transport, London (Alfred Holt and Co., Liverpool, managers).

1947: Sold to Ocean Steam Ship Co. Ltd. (Alfred Holt and Co., managers), Liverpool and renamed TITAN.

6.9.1950: Acquired by Glen Line Ltd., London for £93,622 and renamed FLINTSHIRE.

21.11.1957: Re-sold to Ocean Steam Ship Co. Ltd. for £34,429 and reverted to TITAN.

30.1.1962: Sold to Tidewater Commercial Co. Inc., Baltimore, Maryland, USA (Alberto Ravano fu Pietro, Genoa, Italy) for £92,500 and renamed TITANUS under the Liberian flag.

20.10.1969: Arrived at Mihara for demolition by Seibu Kogyo K.K.

12.1969: Demolition commenced.

Top: *James Carroll* soon after her launch. *[John Hill collection]*

Middle: *Samgara. [John Hill collection]*

Bottom: *Flintshire* in 1951. *[Ships in Focus]*

G76. PEMBROKESHIRE (7) 1950-1957

O.N. 169681 7,292g 4,318n 441.6 x 57.0 x 27.8 feet.

T.3-cyl. by General Machinery Corporation, Hamilton, Ohio (24½", 37" and 70" x 48"); 2,500 IHP.

5.11.1943: Launched by Bethlehem-Fairfield Shipyards Inc., Baltimore, Maryland (Yard No. 2265) for the United States War Shipping Administration as AUGUSTINE HERMAN.

11.1943: Completed as SAMSETTE on Lend-Lease bare-boat charter to the Ministry of War Transport, London (Alfred Holt and Co., Liverpool, managers).

4.1947: Sold to China Mutual Steam Navigation Co. Ltd. (Alfred Holt and Co., managers), Liverpool and renamed EURYPYLUS.

4.11.1950: Acquired by Glen Line Ltd., London for £93,622 and renamed PEMBROKESHIRE.

19.9.1957: Re-sold to China Mutual Steam Navigation Co. Ltd. for £36,792 and reverted to EURYPYLUS.

10.6.1960: Sold to Federal Shipping Co. Ltd., Hong Kong (Gibson Shipping Co. Ltd., Macao) and renamed KOTA BAHRU.

1966: Owners became Cresta Shipping Co. Inc., Panama (Gibson Shipping Co. Ltd., Macao) and renamed CRESTA.

12.1967: Sold to Tung Cheng Steel and Iron Works, Kaohsiung for demolition.

13.1.1968: Arrived at Kaohsiung.

10.1968: Work began.

Samsette. [John Hill collection]

Eurypylus in the Mersey on 19th February 1949. *[John McRoberts/J. and M. Clarkson collection]*

Pembrokeshire. [Ian J. Farquhar collection]

G77. GLENBEG (2) 1950-1958
O.N. 180554 7,234g 4,345n 441.8 x 57.1 x 27.8 feet.
T.3-cyl. by General Machinery Corporation, Hamilton, Ohio (24½", 37" and 70" x 48"); 2,500 IHP.
14.3.1944: Launched by Bethlehem-Fairfield Shipyards Inc., Baltimore, Maryland (Yard No. 2339) on Lend-Lease bare-boat charter from the United States War Shipping Administration to the Ministry of War Transport, London (Alfred Holt and Co., Liverpool, managers) as SAMJACK
4.1944: Completed.
1947: Sold to Ocean Steam Ship Co. Ltd. (Alfred Holt and Co., managers), Liverpool and renamed TYDEUS.
14.12.1950: Acquired by Glen Line Ltd., London for £93,622 and renamed GLENBEG.

9.4.1958: Sold to Forman Shipping and Trading Inc., Panama (Augusto Moretti & C. S.r.L, Milan, Italy) for £149,000 and renamed ROAN.
1960: Sold to West African Carriers Corporation, Monrovia (Overland Trust Bank, Lugano, Switzerland) and renamed JUCAR.
1967: Sold to Nichimen Co. Ltd., Nagoya for demolition for $115,000.
2.5.1967: Arrived at Nagoya but re-sold to Koshin Sangyo K.K.
1.6.1967: Arrived at Mihara for demolition.

G78. GLENIFFER (3) 1951-1952
O.N. 135467 7,552g 4,814n 455.3 x 56.3 x 32.5 feet.
T.3-cyl. by North East Marine Engineering Co. Ltd., Newcastle-upon-

Tyne (31", 51½" and 86" x 60"); 835 NHP, 4,750 IHP;14 knots.
8.4.1913: Launched by Hawthorn, Leslie and Co. Ltd., Newcastle-upon-Tyne (Yard No. 458) for China Mutual Steam Navigation Co. Ltd. (Alfred Holt and Co., managers), Liverpool as LYCAON.
30.5.1913: Registered at Liverpool.
31.5.1913: Ran trials and completed.
2.2.1951: Acquired by Glen Line Ltd., London for £5,552.
13.2.1951: Renamed GLENIFFER.
6.1952: Sold to British Iron and Steel Corporation (Salvage) Ltd. for £95,000 and allocated to Metal Industries Ltd.
11.7.1952: Arrived at Faslane for demolition.
8.1952: Demolition commenced.
22.1.1953: Register closed.

Above: *Glenbeg. [Ships in Focus]*
Below: *Gleniffer. [B. and A. Feilden/J. and M. Clarkson collection]*

G79. GLENSHIEL (3) 1952-1957

O.N. 169690 7,308g 4,379n 441.7 x 57.0 x 27.8 feet.

T.3-cyl. by General Machinery Corporation, Hamilton, Ohio (24½", 37" and 70" x 48"); 2,500 IHP.

9.10.1943: Launched by Bethlehem-Fairfield Shipyards Inc., Baltimore, Maryland (Yard No. 2250) for the United States War Shipping Administration, Washington as SIMON B. ELLIOTT.

10.1943: Completed as SAMNESSE on Lend-Lease bare-boat charter to the Ministry of War Transport, London (Alfred Holt and Co., Liverpool, managers).

1947: Sold to China Mutual Steam Navigation Co. Ltd. (Alfred Holt and Co., managers), Liverpool and renamed EUMAEUS.

19.3.1952: Acquired by Glen Line Ltd., London for £76,179 and renamed GLENSHIEL.

10.7.1957: Re-sold to China Mutual Steam Navigation Co. Ltd., Liverpool for £34,836 and renamed EURYADES.

20.3.1961: Sold to Bounty Shipping Co. Ltd., Hong Kong (Marine Navigation Co. Ltd., London, managers) for £120,000 and renamed MARINE BOUNTY.

25.2.1966: Grounded at Hsie-Shan, China whilst on a voyage from Chingwangtao to Singapore with a cargo of coal. Refloated but driven aground again and broke in two.

Samnesse.   [John Hill collection]

Glenshiel.   [F.R. Sherlock/World Ship Photo Library]

Glenshiel.   [Ian J. Farquhar collection]

G80. GLENLOGAN (2) 1952-1957
O.N. 168749 7,314g 4,405n 441.7 x 57.0 x 27.8 feet.
T.3-cyl. by Worthington Pump and Machinery Corp., Harrison, NJ. (24¹/₂", 37" and 70" x 48"); 2,500 IHP.
9.8.1943: Launched by Bethlehem-Fairfield Shipyards Inc., Baltimore, Maryland (Yard No. 2214) for the United States War Shipping Administration, Washington as MATTHEW BRUSH.
8.1943: Completed as SAMOA on Lend-Lease bare-boat charter to the Ministry of War Transport, London (Alfred Holt and Co., Liverpool, managers).

1947: Sold to China Mutual Steam Navigation Co. Ltd. (Alfred Holt and Co., managers), Liverpool for £135,197 and renamed EURYMEDON.
3.10.1952: Acquired by Glen Line Ltd. for £76,186 and renamed GLENLOGAN.
23.5.1957: Re-sold to China Mutual Steam Navigation Co. Ltd. for £37,519 and reverted to EURYMEDON.
1958: Sold to Etolika Compania Naviera S.A., Panama (A. Lusi Ltd., London) and renamed ANGELOS under the Costa Rican and later the Greek flag.
1964: Sold to Michael A. Araktingi, Beirut, Lebanon and renamed MIMOSA.

1966: Sold to Alplata Shipping Corporation, Monrovia, Liberia (Sociedad Anonima Flemar, Montevideo, Uruguay) and renamed ALPLATA.
1967: Sold to Maria de Lourdes Shipping Co. Ltd., Famagusta, Cyprus (Shipping and Produce Co. Ltd., London) and renamed ANKA.
25.6.1971: Arrived at Bilbao for demolition by Ferrobirques SA.
11.10.1971: Work began by Alfonso Garcia, at Bilbao.

Matthew Brush at her launch. She was completed as *Samoa* and managed by Holts. *[John Hill collection]*

Glenlogan. [J. and M. Clarkson collection]

G81. GLENIFFER (4) 1954-1958
O.N. 169715 7,291g 4,312n 441.8 x 57.0 x 27.8 feet.
T.3-cyl. by Ellicot Machinery Corporation, Baltimore, Maryland (24½", 37" and 70" x 48"); 2,500 IHP.
25.8.1943: Launched by Bethlehem-Fairfield Shipyards Inc., Baltimore, Maryland (Yard No. 2217) for the United States War Shipping Administration, Washington as PETER COOPER.

9.1943: Completed as SAMARKAND on Lend-Lease bare-boat charter to the Ministry of War Transport, London (Alfred Holt and Co., Liverpool, managers).
1947: Sold to Ocean Steam Ship Co. Ltd. (Alfred Holt and Co., managers), Liverpool and renamed TALTHYBIUS.
22.3.1954: Acquired by Glen Line Ltd. for £56,808 and renamed GLENIFFER.

15.4.1958: Sold to Colombine Shipping Co., Monrovia, Liberia (James R. Twiss Ltd., London) for £170,000 and renamed DOVE.
1965: Sold to Patriarch Steamship Co., Monrovia, Liberia (Andrew Gabriel, New York) and renamed PATRAIC SKY under the Liberian flag.
30.3.1971: Arrived at Split for demolition by Brodospas.
13.4.1971: Demolition commenced

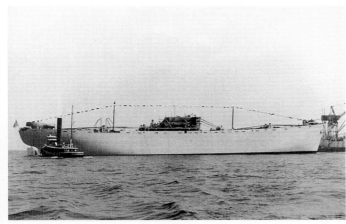

The *Gleniffer* is seen at six stages of her career, firstly when launched at Baltimore as *Peter Cooper*, a name carried for only a few days. *[John Hill collection]*

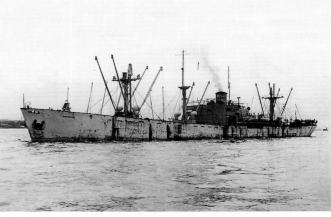

Under charter to the Ministry of War Transport and managed by Holts as *Samarkand*. *[Ian J. Farquhar collection]*

Samarkand was bought by Holts in 1947 and renamed *Talthybius*. *[B. and A. Feilden/J. and M. Clarkson]*

She ran as *Gleniffer* between 1954 and 1958. *[J. and M. Clarkson]*

Her first name under flag-of-convenience ownership was *Dove*. *[John Hill collection]*

Her final name was *Patraic Sky*. *[John Hill collection]*

G82. GLENLOCHY (2) 1957-1958
O.N. 162340 7,797g 4,803n 459.6 x 59.3 x 29.2 feet.
Two 8-cyl. 4SCSA oil engines by Akt. Burmeister & Wain Maskin-og-Skibsbyggeri, Copenhagen (740 mm x 1,500 mm) driving twin screws; 2,469 NHP.
19.12.1930: Launched by Scotts' Ship Building and Engineering Co. Ltd., Greenock (Yard No. 361) for Ocean Steam Ship Co. Ltd. (Alfred Holt and Co., managers), Liverpool as AJAX.
17.4.1931: Ran trials and completed that month.
1.9.1957: Acquired by Glen Line Ltd., London for £ 28,650 and renamed GLENLOCHY. Modernized at further cost of £43,100.

12.11.1958: Re-sold to Ocean Steam Ship Co. Ltd. for £66,254 and renamed SARPEDON.
7.8.1962: Arrived in tow at Curacao with fire on board. Fire extinguished and vessel sold for scrap.
31.12.1962: Demolition commenced at Hong Kong by Shin Wing Hong.

Glenlochy. [J. and M. Clarkson collection]

G83. CARDIGANSHIRE (6) 1957-1972
O.N. 183793. 7,707g. 4,491n. 487.0 x 62.3 x 28.2 feet.
8-cyl. 2SCSA oil engine by J.G. Kincaid and Co. Ltd., Greenock (750 mm x 1,500 mm); 7,600 BHP, 16 knots.
2.5.1950: Launched by Caledon Shipbuilding and Engineering Co. Ltd., Dundee (Yard No.473) for Ocean Steam Ship Co. Ltd. (Alfred Holt and Co., managers), Liverpool as BELLEROPHON.
10.1950: Completed.

23.9.1957: Acquired by Glen Line Ltd., London for £202,936, renamed CARDIGANSHIRE and registered Liverpool. Refrigerated at a cost of £141,795.
1972: Owners became China Mutual Steam Navigation Co. Ltd. (Blue Funnel Line Ltd., managers), Liverpool and renamed BELLEROPHON.
15.1.1973: Owners became Ocean Transport and Trading Co. Ltd.
10.1973: Owners became Elder Dempster Lines Ltd., Liverpool.

1976: Owners became China Mutual Steam Navigation Co. Ltd.
6.1976: Sold to Orri Navigation Lines, Piraeus, Greece (M. Orri, Jeddah, Saudi Arabia) and renamed OBHOR under the Saudi Arabian flag.
1976: Owners became Saudi Europe Lines Ltd. (M. Orri), Jeddah, Saudi Arabia.
23.9.1978: Arrived at Karachi after sale to shipbreakers.
11.1978: Demolition began at Modern Commercial Corporation, Gadani Beach.

Cardiganshire. [Captain C.L. Reynolds/Roy Fenton collection]

G84. MONMOUTHSHIRE (3) 1957-1963
O.N. 168864 7,868g 4,421n 489.0 x 61.4 x 28.4 feet.
8-cyl. 2SCDA oil engine by J.G. Kincaid and Co. Ltd., Greenock (550 mm x 1,200 mm); 8,000 BHP, 15½ knots.
18.5.1943: Launched by Caledon Shipbuilding and Engineering Co. Ltd., Dundee (Yard No. 398) for Ocean Steam Ship Co. Ltd. (Alfred Holt and Co., managers), Liverpool as TELEMACHUS.
10.1943: Completed.
17.10.1957: Acquired by Glen Line Ltd., London for £98,169 and renamed MONMOUTHSHIRE.
21.10.1963: Re-sold to Ocean Steam Ship Co. Ltd. (Alfred Holt and Co., managers), Liverpool for £62,254 and renamed GLAUCUS.
1964: Chartered to China Navigation Co. Ltd., Hong Kong and renamed NAN CHANG.
1968: Returned to Ocean Steam Ship Co. Ltd.
1.4.1968: Arrived at Hong Kong for demolition by Leung Yau.

Monmouthshire in August 1958. *[J. and M. Clarkson collection]*

G85. GLENFRUIN (2) 1957-1962
O.N. 182419 7,648g 4,459n 487.0 x 62.3 x 28.3 feet.
8-cyl. 2SCDA oil engine by J.G. Kincaid and Co. Ltd., Greenock (550 mm x 1,200 mm); 6,800 BHP, 15½ knots.
20.10.1947: Launched by Scotts' Ship Building and Engineering Co. Ltd., Greenock (Yard No. 637) for China Mutual Steam Navigation Co. Ltd. (Alfred Holt and Co., managers), Liverpool as ASTYANAX.
4.1948: Completed.
8.11.1957: Acquired by Glen Line Ltd., London for £186,477 and renamed GLENFRUIN.
24.9.1962: Re-sold to China Mutual Steam Navigation Co. Ltd. for £124,321 and reverted to ASTYANAX.
1967: Managers became Blue Funnel Line Ltd.
18.12.1972: Arrived at Kaohsiung for breaking up by Cheung Yuan Steel Co.
4.1.1973: Demolition commenced.

Glenfruin. [J. and M. Clarkson collection]

G86. GLENFINLAS (3) 1957-1962
O.N. 181071 7,639g 4,459n 487.0 x 62.3
x 28.3 feet.
8-cyl. 2SCDA oil engine by Harland and
Wolff Ltd., Belfast (550 mm x 1,200 mm);
6,800 BHP; 15½ knots.
27.8.1946: Launched by Harland and
Wolff Ltd., Belfast (Yard No.1310) for
Ocean Steam Ship Co. Ltd. (Alfred Holt
and Co., managers), Liverpool as
CALCHAS.
1.1947: Completed.
19.12.1957: Acquired by Glen Line Ltd.,
London for £171,254 and renamed
GLENFINLAS.
29.10.1962: Re-sold to Ocean Steam Ship
Co. Ltd. (Alfred Holt and Co., managers),
Liverpool for £114,506 and reverted to
CALCHAS.
1967: Managers became Blue Funnel Line
Ltd.
22.12.1971: Owners became Elder
Dempster Lines Ltd., Liverpool.
1972: Owners became China Mutual
Steam Ship Navigation Co. Ltd. (Blue Funnel
Line Ltd., managers), Liverpool.
22.7.1973: Badly damaged by fire while
loading at Port Keelung. Towed out of
harbour and beached.
12.8.1973: Refloated but declared a
constructive total loss.
23.10.1973: Arrived in tow at Kaohsiung
for demolition by Keun Hwa Iron and
Steel Works and Enterprise Co. Ltd.
23.11.1973: Demolition commenced.

Glenfinlas in October 1958. *[Ships in Focus]*

G87. GLENSHIEL (4) 1958-1963
O.N. 181024 10,195g 6,022n 497.3 x
64.3 x 29.7 feet.
8-cyl. 2SCSA oil engine by J. G. Kincaid
and Co. Ltd., Greenock (550 mm x 1,200
mm); 6,800 BHP; 14½ knots.
4.12.1945: Launched by Caledon
Shipbuilding and Engineering Co. Ltd.,
Dundee (Yard No.410) for Ocean Steam
Ship Co. Ltd. (Alfred Holt and Co.,
managers), Liverpool as STENTOR,
having been laid down for the Ministry of
War Transport, London.
6.1946: Completed.
12.11.1958: Acquired by Glen Line Ltd.,
London for £239,273 and renamed
GLENSHIEL.
16.1.1963: Sold to China Mutual Steam
Navigation Co. Ltd. (Alfred Holt and Co.,
managers), Liverpool for £166,405 and
renamed STENTOR.
9.1963: Owners became Ocean Steam
Ship Co. Ltd. (Alfred Holt and Co.,
managers), Liverpool.
1969: Managers became Blue Funnel Line
Ltd.
1975: Owners became China Mutual
Steam Ship Navigation Co. Ltd. (Blue Funnel
Line Ltd., managers), Liverpool and
placed on Elder Dempster's West African
trades.
5.3.1975: Sold to Nan Kwang Steel and
Iron Works, Kaohsiung for demolition and
renamed TENTO for delivery voyage.
6.4.1975: Arrived at Kaohsiung.
22.5.1975: Demolition commenced.

Glenshiel. *[G. E. P. Brownell/World Ship Photo Library]*

Glenshiel. *[World Ship Photo Library]*

G88. GLENOGLE (4) 1962-1978
O.N. 304350 11,918g 7,002n 543.8 x
74.7 x 30.1 feet.
9-cyl. 2SCSA oil engine by Sulzer
Brothers Ltd., Winterthur (900 mm x
1,550 mm); 18,000 BHP; 20 knots.
3.5.1962: Launched by Fairfield
Shipbuilding and Engineering Co. Ltd.,
Glasgow (Yard No.812) for Glen Line
Ltd., London.
28.9.1962: Completed at a cost of
£2,229,500.
30.9.1977: Sold to Hemisphere Shipping
Co. Ltd., Hong Kong (Ocean Tramping
Co. Ltd., Hong Kong, managers)
(Government of the People's Republic of
China, Peking) and renamed HARVEST.
1.1978: Owners became China Ocean
Shipping Co., Shanghai (later became
Shanghai Ocean Shipping Co. and
renamed YANG CHENG.
1992: Owners became Lianyungyang
Ocean Shipping Co.
17.5.2002: Deleted from Lloyd's Register
as continued existence in doubt.

Top: *Glenogle* in the Mersey on 23rd January 1976. *[Paul H. Boot/Ships in Focus]*
Middle: In the Straits of Malacca. *[Peter Foxley/J. and M. Clarkson collection]*
Bottom: At Singapore as *Yang Cheng*. *[Wm.A. Schell]*

G89. GLENLYON (2) 1962-1975 and 1975-1978
O.N. 304336 11,918g 7,002n 543.8 x 74.7 x 30.1 feet.
9-cyl. 2 SCSA oil engine by Sulzer Bros. Ltd., Winterthur (900 mm x 1,550 mm); 18,000 BHP; 20 knots.
17.3.1962: Launched by Nederlandsche Dok & Scheepsbouw Maatschappij VOF, Amsterdam (Yard No. 510) for Glen Line Ltd., London.
19.10.1962: Completed at a cost of £2,156,750.
31.1.1975: Owners became Elder Dempster Lines Ltd., Liverpool.
5.1975: Returned to Glen Line Ltd.
10.1975: Transferred to China Mutual Steam Navigation Co.Ltd. (Blue Funnel Line Ltd, managers), Liverpool.
10.1976: Owners became the Ben Line Steamers Ltd. (William Thomson and Co., managers), Leith, for one round voyage within the BenOcean pool.
1.1977: Reverted to Glen Line Ltd.
1.1978: Laid up at Tilbury.
6.1978: Sold to Tarbord Shipping Co. Ltd., Hong Kong (Univan Ship Management, Singapore, managers) and renamed EMERALD EXPRESS under the Singapore flag.
5.3.1979: Sold to Sie Yung Steel Mill Co. Ltd., Kaohsiung.
30.3.1979: Demolition commenced.

Top: *Glenlyon. [Peter Foxley/J. and M. Clarkson collection]*
Middle: *Glenlyon* clearly showing her port of registry. *[Peter Newall collection]*
Bottom: *Glenlyon* in August 1977 in Elder, Dempster colours. *[J. and M. Clarkson collection]*

Above: Flintshire. [W. A. Laxon collection]
Middle: In Oceaan ownership with Amsterdam as her port of registry. *[Peter Newall collection]*

G90. FLINTSHIRE (6) 1962-1974
O.N. 304392 11,918g 7,002n 543.8 x
74.7 x 30.1 feet.
9-cyl. 2SCSA oil engine by Sulzer
Brothers Ltd., Winterthur (900 mm x
1,550 mm); 18,000 BHP; 20 knots.
18.6.1962: Launched by N.V. C. van der
Giessen Scheepswerven, Krimpen (Yard
No. 809) for Glen Line Ltd., London.
12.12.1962: Ran trials
21.12.1962: Completed at a cost of
£2,251,550.
1974: Owners became Nederlandsche
Stoomvaart Maatschappji 'Oceaan' NV,
Amsterdam. Holland.
1977: Chartered to Nigerian National
Line.
1978: Chartered to Djakarta-Lloyd and
then laid up at Singapore.
6.1978: Sold to Bastion Maritime Inc.,
Monrovia, Liberia (Univan Ship
Management, Singapore, managers) and
renamed ORIENT EXPRESS under the
Singapore flag.
1979: Sold to Sie Yung Steel Mill Co.
Ltd., Kaohsiung.
11.3.1979: Arrived at Kaohsiung.
23.5.1979: Demolition commenced.

Flintshire under the Singapore flag as *Orient Express.* *[Ambrose Greenway collection]*

**G91. GLENFALLOCH (2) 1963-1975
and 1976-1977**
O.N. 304437 11,918g 6,966n 543.8 x
74.7 x 30.1 feet.
9-cyl. 2SCSA oil engine by Sulzer
Brothers Ltd., Winterthur (900 mm x
1,550 mm); 18,000 BHP; 20 knots.
3.7.1962: Launched by Fairfield
Shipbuilding and Engineering Co. Ltd.,
Glasgow (Yard No. 813) for Glen Line
Ltd., London.
26.11.1963: Completed at a cost of
£2,223,600.
24.8.1975: Owners became Elder
Dempster Lines Ltd., Liverpool.
9.1976: Reverted to Glen Line Ltd.
10.1976: Owners became the Ben Line
Steamers Ltd. (William Thomson and Co.,
managers), Leith, for one round voyage
within the BenOcean pool.
1.1977: Reverted to Glen Line Ltd.
8.11.1977: Sold to China Ocean Shipping
Co., Peking for $2.65 million, renamed
QING HE CHENG and registered at
Shanghai.
1979: Owners became Shanghai Ocean
Shipping Co.
17.5.2002: Deleted from Lloyd's Register
as continued existence in doubt.

Top: *Glenfalloch.* *[J. and M. Clarkson
collection]*

Middle: With her funnel in Ben Line
colours in 1977. *[Peter Foxley/J. and
M. Clarkson collection]*

Bottom: At Singapore with her
Chinese name *Qing He Cheng.*
[Wm. A. Schell]

G92. GLENALMOND (1) 1966-1973

O.N. 309709 12,229g 6,570n 522.0 x
77.5 x 44.0 feet.
9-cyl. 2SCSA oil engine by Mitsubishi
Heavy Industries Ltd., Nagasaki (900 mm
x 1,550 mm); 18,900 BHP; 21 knots.
22.2.1966: Launched by Mitsubishi Heavy
Industries Ltd., Nagasaki (Yard No. 1613)
for Glen Line Ltd., London.
9.1966: Completed.
1973: Owners became Ocean Transport
and Trading Ltd. (Blue Funnel Line Ltd.,
managers), Liverpool and renamed
PATROCLUS. Subsequently owners
became China Mutual Steam Navigation
Co. Ltd. (same managers).
1974: Owners became Nederlandsche
Stoomvaart Maatschappji 'Oceaan' NV,
Amsterdam, Holland.
1978: Reverted to China Mutual Steam
Navigation Co. Ltd.
2.1982: Sold to Rajab and Co., Jeddah,
Saudi Arabia and renamed RAJAB I.
18.7.1984: Damaged by fire whilst on a
voyage from Bangkok to Dubai with
general cargo.
22.7.1984: Fire extinguished after having
arrived at Port Rashid, Dubai.
1984: Sold for demolition to Molasses
Trading and Export Co., Gadani Beach
and renamed SAHAR for delivery voyage.
26.11.1984: Arrived at Gadani Beach and
demolition commenced.

*Top: Glenalmond. [Roy Fenton
collection]*
*Middle: Glenalmond after being
renamed Patroclus.*
[Jean M. Otten/G. Holmes collection]
*Bottom: Patroclus in Barber Blue Sea
Line colours. [M.R. Dippy/G. Holmes
collection]*

Above: A general view of John Brown's East Yard with the almost complete *Glenfinlas* in the foreground. Yard no. 736 - *Queen Elizabeth 2* - is on the slipway in the background. *[John Brown & Co. (Clydebank) Ltd./J. and M. Clarkson collection]*
Below: *Glenfinlas* on trials in the Clyde on 29th December 1966. *[Glasgow University Archives UCS1/116/201/188]*

G93. GLENFINLAS (4) 1967-1972
O.N. 309819 12,094g 6,558n 521.0 x 77.5 x 44.0 feet.
9-cyl. 2SCSA oil engine by Akt. Burmeister & Wain Maskin-og-Skibsbyggeri, Copenhagen (840 mm x 1,800 mm); 22,500 BHP.
3.8.1966: Launched by John Brown and Co. (Clydebank) Ltd., Clydebank (Yard No. 731) for Glen Line Ltd., London.
1.1967: Completed.
1972: Owners became Ocean Steam Ship Co. Ltd. (Blue Funnel Line Ltd., managers), Liverpool and renamed PHEMIUS.
15.1.1973: Owners became Ocean Transport and Trading Ltd.
1975: Owners became China Mutual Steam Navigation Co. Ltd.
1978: Sold to China Navigation Co. Ltd., Hong Kong and renamed KWEICHOW.
1982: Sold to Saudi Venture Corporation Ltd. (Saudi International Shipping S.A. (M. Orri), managers), Jeddah, Saudi Arabia and renamed SAUDI KAWTHER.
1984: Sold to Chinese shipbreakers.

G94. PEMBROKESHIRE (8) 1967-1972

O.N. 309888 12,299g 6,673n 522.0 x 77.5 x 44.0 feet.

9-cyl. 2SCSA oil engine by Mitsubishi Heavy Industries Ltd., Nagasaki (900 mm x 1,550 mm); 18,900 BHP; 21 knots.

5.7.1966: Launched by Mitsubishi Heavy Industries Ltd., Nagasaki (Yard No. 1614) for Glen Line Ltd., London.

3.1967: Completed.

1972: Owners became Ocean Steam Ship Co. Ltd. (Blue Funnel Line Ltd., managers), Liverpool. Subsequently owners became China Mutual Steam Navigation Co. Ltd. (same managers) and renamed PHRONTIS.

1973: Owners became Ocean Transport and Trading Ltd., Liverpool.

1975: Owners became China Mutual Steam Navigation Co. Ltd.

1982: Sold to Gulf Shipping Lines Ltd. (Abbas K and Murtaza K. Gokal)), London (Gulfeast Ship Management Ltd., Hong Kong, managers) and renamed GULF OSPREY under the British flag.

1983: Sold to Islamic Republic of Iran Shipping Lines, Tehran, Iran and renamed IRAN EJTEHAD.

1995: Sold for scrap and renamed DOLPHIN VIII for delivery voyage.

29.4.1995: Arrived at Gadani Beach for demolition.

Top: *Pembrokeshire.* [Ships in Focus]

Middle: *Phrontis.* [Peter Foxley/J. and M. Clarkson collection]

Bottom: *Pembrokeshire as Iran Ejtehad.* [Peter Foxley/J. and M. Clarkson collection]

G95. RADNORSHIRE (7) 1967
O.N. 334684 12,094g 6,471n 521.0 x
77.5 x 44.0 feet.
9-cyl. 2SCSA oil engine by Akt.
Burmeister & Wain Maskin-og-
Skibsbyggeri, Copenhagen (840 mm x
1,800 mm); 22,500 BHP.
13.3.1967: Launched by Vickers Ltd.,
Newcastle-upon-Tyne (Yard No. 188) for
Glen Line Ltd., London.
11.1967: Completed and owners became
China Mutual Steam Navigation Co. Ltd.
(Alfred Holt and Co., managers),
Liverpool.
1967: Managers became Blue Funnel Line
Ltd.
1972: Owners became Ocean Steam Ship
Co. Ltd. (same managers) and renamed
PERSEUS.
15.1.1973: Owners became Ocean
Transport and Trading Ltd.
1973: Reverted to China Mutual Steam
Navigation Co. Ltd.
1978: Sold to China Navigation Co. Ltd.,
Hong Kong and renamed KWANGSI.
1982: Transferred to Panama registry and
renamed ASIA DRAGON.
1982: Sold to Saudi Falcon Navigation
Co. Ltd. (Saudi International Shipping Co.
S.A. (M. Orri), managers), Jeddah, Saudi
Arabia and renamed SAUDI ZAM ZAM.
1984: Sold to Chinese shipbreakers.

Top: *Radnorshire.* [Ships in Focus]

Middle: *Perseus.* [Peter Foxley/J. and
M. Clarkson collection]

Bottom: *Radnorshire* as *Saudi
Zamzam* - a name she held for little
more than two years.
[Paul H. Boot/G. Holmes collection]

G96. GLENAFFRIC (2) 1968-1970
O.N. 185443 7,802g 4,368n 464.9 x 64.3 x 31.1 feet.
Three steam turbines reduction geared to single shaft by Metropolitan Vickers Electric Co. Ltd., Manchester; 8,250 BHP.
26.3.1952: Launched by Caledon Shipbuilding and Engineering Co. Ltd., Dundee (Yard No. 485) for Ocean Steam Ship Co. Ltd. (Alfred Holt and Co., managers), Liverpool as NESTOR.
10.1952: Completed.

1967: Managers became Blue Funnel Line Ltd.
12.1968: Owners became Glen Line Ltd., London and renamed GLENAFFRIC.
7.1970: Owners became Ocean Steam Ship Co. Ltd. (Blue Funnel Line Ltd., managers), Liverpool and renamed ORESTES.
6.1971: Owners became Glen Line Ltd.
1971: Sold to N.D. Papalios, Piraeus, Greece and renamed AEGIS DIGNITY.
1971: Owners became Kimon Companhia Naviera S.A., Panama (Aegis Shipping

Co. Ltd. (N.D. Papalios), Piraeus, Greece) under the Greek flag.
1972: Owners became Adelais Maritime Co. Ltd., Famagusta, Cyprus (Aegis Shipping Co. Ltd. (N.D. Papalios), Piraeus, Greece).
6.12.1973: Arrived at Whampoa for demolition by China National Metal and Mineral Import and Export Corporation.

Glenaffric in June 1969. When used previously, the name had been spelt *Glenaffaric.[J. and M. Clarkson]*

G97. GLENROY (4) 1970-1972
O.N. 187111 7,968g 4,558n 491.5 x 62.3 x 28.4 feet.
6-cyl. 2SCSA oil engine by Harland and Wolff Ltd., Belfast (750 mm x 1,500 mm); 8,000 BHP.
24.1.1955: Launched by Vickers Armstrong Ltd., Newcastle-upon-Tyne (Yard No. 147) for Ocean Steam Ship Co. Ltd. (Alfred Holt and Co., managers), Liverpool as DEMODOCUS.
8.1955: Completed.
1967: Managers became Blue Funnel Line Ltd.
7.1970: Owners became Glen Line Ltd., London and renamed GLENROY.
4.1972: Reverted to Ocean Steam Ship Co. Ltd. and DEMODOCUS.
1973: Owners became Ocean Transport and Trading Ltd.
1973: Sold to Nan Yang Shipping Co., Macao (Ocean Tramping Co. Ltd., Hong Kong, managers) (Government of the People's Republic of China, Peking) and renamed HUNGSIA under the Somali flag.

1977: Owners became Dawn Maritime Corporation S.A., Panama (Ocean Tramping Co. Ltd., Hong Kong, managers) (Government of the People's Republic of China, Peking)
1979: Owners became the Government of the Peoples' Republic of China (Bureau of

Maritime Transport Administration, Kwang Chow Branch, managers), China and renamed HONG QI 137.
1981: Owners became the managers Guangzhou Branch.
2.1982: Condemned and demolished.

Glenroy, the former *Demodocus* [Peter Foxley/Roy Fenton collection]

G98. GLENBEG (3) 1970-1972

O.N. 187141 7,980g 4,567n 491.5 x 62.3 x 28.4 feet.

6-cyl. 2SCSA oil engine by J.G. Kincaid and Co. Ltd., Greenock (750 mm x 1,500 mm); 8,000 BHP.

12.4.1956: Launched by Caledon Shipbuilding and Engineering Co. Ltd., Dundee (Yard No. 501) for China Mutual Steam Navigation Co. Ltd. (Alfred Holt and Co., managers), Liverpool as DIOMED.

9.1956: Completed.

1967: Managers became Blue Funnel Line Ltd.

7.1970: Acquired by Glen Line Ltd., London and renamed GLENBEG.

5.1972: Reverted to China Mutual Steam Navigation Co. Ltd., Liverpool and DIOMED.

1973: Sold to Nan Yang Shipping Co., Macao (Ocean Tramping Co. Ltd., Hong Kong, managers) (Government of the People's Republic of China, Peking) and renamed KAISING under the Somali flag.

1977: Owners became Golden City Maritime Corporation S.A., Panama (Ocean Tramping Co. Ltd., Hong Kong, managers) (Government of the People's Republic of China, Peking).

1982: Sold to China Dismantled Vessels Trading Corporation, Kaohsiung.

12.1982: Demolition commenced.

G99. GLENFRUIN (3) 1970-1972

O.N. 187121 7,960g 4,539n 491.5 x 62.3 x 28.4 feet.

6-cyl. 2SCSA oil engine by Harland and Wolff Ltd., Belfast (750 mm x 1,500 mm); 8,000 BHP.

4.8.1955: Launched by Harland and Wolff Ltd., Belfast (Yard No. 1497) for Ocean Steam Ship Co. Ltd. (Alfred Holt and Co., managers), Liverpool as DOLIUS.

1.1956: Completed.

1967: Managers became Blue Funnel Line Ltd.

8.1970: Acquired by Glen Line Ltd., London and renamed GLENFRUIN.

4.1972: Reverted to Ocean Steam Ship Co. Ltd. and to DOLIUS.

1972: Sold to Nan Yang Shipping Co., Macao (Ocean Tramping Co. Ltd., Hong Kong, managers) (Government of the People's Republic of China, Peking) and renamed HUNG MIEN under the Somali flag.

1973: Owners became the Ocean Tramping Co. Ltd., Hong Kong (Government of the People's Republic of China, Peking), under the Somali flag.

1976: Owners became United Freighter Corporation (Panama) S.A, Panama (Ocean Tramping Co. Ltd., Hong Kong, managers) (Government of the People's Republic of China, Peking).

1977: Owners became the Government of the Peoples Republic of China (Bureau of Maritime Transport Administration, Kwang Chow Branch, managers), China and renamed HONG QI 119.

1983: Transferred to the managers' Shanghai Branch and renamed ZHAN DOU 51.

11.1991: Deleted from Lloyd's Register as continued existence in doubt.

Glenbeg as *Diomed* during her long Blue Funnel career. *[J. and M. Clarkson]*

Glenbeg. [Peter Foxley/J. and M. Clarkson collection]

Glenfruin. [R. Weeks]

G100. GLENLOCHY (3) 1970-1972
O.N. 187165 7,974g 4,550n 491.5 x 62.3 x 28.4 feet.
6-cyl. 2SCSA oil engine by J.G. Kincaid and Co. Ltd., Greenock (750 mm x 1,500 mm); 8,000 BHP.
4.10.1956: Launched by Vickers-Armstrong (Shipbuilders) Ltd., Newcastle-upon-Tyne (Yard No. 152) for China Mutual Steam Navigation Co. Ltd. (Alfred Holt and Co., managers), Liverpool as ANTENOR.
7.1957: Completed.
1967: Managers became Blue Funnel Line Ltd.

12.1970: Acquired by Glen Line Ltd., London and renamed GLENLOCHY.
6.1972: Reverted to China Mutual Steam Navigation Co. Ltd. and renamed DYMAS.
1973: Sold to Nan Yang Shipping Co., Macao (Ocean Tramping Co. Ltd., Hong Kong, managers) (Government of the People's Republic of China, Peking), and renamed KAIYUN under the Somali flag.
1976: Owners became Highseas Navigation Corp. S.A., Panama (Ocean Tramping Co. Ltd., Hong Kong, managers) (Government of the People's Republic of China, Peking).

1983: Sold to the China National Metals and Minerals Import and Export Corporation, China.
24.5.1983: Arrived at Huangpu for demolition.

GLENGARRY (3) 1971 see G71.

GLENLYON (2) 1975-1978 see G89.

GLENFALLOCH (2) 1976 and 1977-1978 see G91.

Above: *Antenor.* [W. D. Harris - Fotoship/J. and M. Clarkson collection]
Below: *Glenlochy.* [Peter Foxley/Roy Fenton collection]

153

Ocean Group ships briefly transferred to Glen Line Ltd. without renaming

G101. MALLAM 1967
O.N. 181110 4,810g 2,636n 408.5 x 57.2 x 20.7 feet.
4-cyl. 2SCSA Doxford-type oil engine by Scott's Shipbuilding and Engineering Co. Ltd., Greenock (560 x 2,160mm); 3,100 BHP.
19.8.1947: Launched by Scott's Shipbuilding and Engineering Co. Ltd., Greenock (Yard No. 642) for Elder, Dempster Ltd., Liverpool as SHONGA.
11.1947: Completed.
1965: Owners became Guinea Gulf Line Ltd. (Elder Dempster Lines Ltd., managers), Liverpool and renamed MALLAM.
1967: Owners became Glen Line Ltd.
25.11.1967: Sold to Pacific International Lines Ltd. (Y.C. Cheng), Singapore for $100,000, and renamed KOTA MAJU.
1972: Owners became Pacific International Lines (Private) Ltd.
14.10.1977: Arrived at Karachi for demolition.

ORESTES 1971 see G96.

G102. TELAMON 1971
O.N. 301354 8,922g 5,273n 449.1 x 61.6 x 38.3 feet.
Three steam turbines by the Parsons Marine Steam Turbine Company, Wallsend, reduction geared to a single screw shaft; 6,800 SHP.
3.6.1950: Launched by J.L. Thompson and Son, Sunderland (Yard No. 668) for Silver Line Ltd. (S. and J. Thompson, managers), London as SILVERLAUREL.
12.1950: Completed for Nederlandsche Stoomvaart Maatschappij Oceaan, Amsterdam, Holland as TEUCER.
1960: Owners became the China Mutual Steam Navigation Co. Ltd. (Alfred Holt and Co., managers), Liverpool and renamed TELAMON.
1967: Managers became Blue Funnel Line Ltd.
6.1971: Owners became Glen Line Ltd.
1971: Sold to Apsyrtos Shipping Co. Ltd., Famagusta, Cyprus (Aegis Shipping Co. Ltd. (N.D. Papalios), Piraeus, Greece) and renamed AEGIS EPIC.
31.5.1972: Delivered to the China National Metal and Mineral Import and Export Corporation for demolition at Shanghai.

G103. NELEUS 1971-1972
O.N. 185457 7,802g 4,366n 464.9 x 64.3 x 31.1 feet.
Three steam turbines by Metropolitan Vickers Electric Co. Ltd., Manchester reduction geared to single screw shaft; 8,250 SHP.
8.7.1952: Launched by the Caledon Shipbuilding and Engineering Co. Ltd., Dundee (Yard No. 486) for the China Mutual Steam Navigation Co. Ltd., (Alfred Holt and Co., managers), Liverpool.
2.1953: Completed.
1967: Managers became Blue Funnel Line Ltd.
6.1971: Owners became Glen Line Ltd.
14.9.1972: Sold to Akamas Shipping Co. Ltd., Famagusta, Cyprus (Aegis Shipping

Shonga owned by Glen Line as *Mallam*. [J. and M. Clarkson collection]

Telamon seen on 6th March 1971 shortly before transfer from Blue Funnel to Glen Line. [Malcolm Cranfield]

Neleus. [Peter Foxley/J. and M. Clarkson collection]

Co. Ltd. (N.D. Papalios), Piraeus, Greece) for £12,500 and renamed AEGIS FABLE.
1973: Sold to Alicacnassos Shipping Co. Ltd., Famagusta, Cyprus (Aegis Shipping Co. Ltd. (N.D. Papalios), Piraeus, Greece)

and renamed AEGIS TRUST.
29.3.1974: Delivered to the China National Metal and Mineral Import and Export Corporation, for demolition at Shanghai.

G104. TELEMACHUS 1971
O.N. 301352 8,924g 4,272n 449.1 x 61.7 x 38.3 feet.
Three steam turbines by the Parsons Marine Steam Turbine Company, Wallsend reduction geared to a single screw shaft; 6,800 SHP.
18.4.1950: Launched by J.L. Thompson and Son, Sunderland (Yard No. 666), for Silver Line Ltd. (S. and J. Thompson, managers), London as SILVERELM.
10.1950: Completed for the Nederlandsche Stoomvaart Maatschappij Oceaan, Amsterdam, Holland as TEIRESIAS.
1960: Owners became the Ocean Steam Ship Co. Ltd. (Alfred Holt and Co., managers), Liverpool and renamed TELEMACHUS.
1967: Managers became Blue Funnel Line Ltd.
6.1971: Owners became Glen Line Ltd.
1971: Sold to Anax Shipping Co. Ltd., Famagusta, Cyprus (Aegis Shipping Co. Ltd. (N.D. Papalios), Piraeus, Greece), and renamed AEGIS COURAGE.
22.1.1974: Delivered to the China National Metal and Mineral Import and Export Corporation, for demolition at Shanghai.

Telemachus. [J. and M. Clarkson]

G105. TALTHYBIUS 1971
O.N. 301360 7,713g 4,567n 439.1 x 62.1 x 34.5 feet.
Two steam turbines by the General Electric Corporation, Lynn, Massachusetts, reduction geared to screw shaft; 6,600 SHP.
24.11.1944: Launched by Permanente Metals (Shipyard No.1), Richmond (Yard No. 546) for the United States War Shipping Administration, Washington subsequently United States Maritime Commission as SALINA VICTORY.
12.1944: Completed.
1946: Sold to Nederlandsche Stoomvaart Maatschappij Oceaan, Amsterdam, Holland and renamed POLYDORUS.
1960: Owners became the Ocean Steam Ship Co. Ltd. (Alfred Holt and Co., managers), Liverpool and renamed TALTHYBIUS.
1967: Managers became Blue Funnel Line Ltd.
1971: Owners became Elder Dempster Lines Ltd.
11.1971: Owners became Glen Line Ltd. at Durban for voyage to Taiwan.
4.12.1971: Arrived at Kaohsiung for demolition by Nan Feng Steel Enterprises Company Ltd.
10.1.1972: Work completed.

Talthybius in the Bristol Channel. [W. D. Harris - Fotoship/J. and M. Clarkson collection]

G106. PATROCLUS 1972

O.N. 183758 10,109g 5,923n 489.4 x
68.3 x 35.2 feet.
Three steam turbines by Vickers-
Armstrongs Ltd., Barrow-in-Furness
reduction geared to a single screw shaft;
15,000 SHP.
8.7.1949: Launched by Vickers-
Armstrongs Ltd., Newcastle-upon-Tyne
(Yard No. 110) for the China Mutual
Steam Navigation Co. Ltd. (Alfred Holt

and Co., managers), Liverpool.
2.1950: Completed.
1967: Managers became Blue Funnel Line
Ltd.
6.1972: Owners became Glen Line Ltd.
10.1972: Reverted to the China Mutual
Steam Navigation Co. Ltd. and renamed
PHILOCTETES for her voyage to the
shipbreakers.
21.11.1972: Left Swansea.
12.2.1973: Delivered to Chin Tai Steel

Enterprises Company Ltd., Kaohsiung for
demolition.

According to one published source,
PATROCLUS was renamed
GLENALMOND (2) whilst under Glen
Line ownership from June to October
1972. This is erroneous; the first
GLENALMOND was still in service under
this name until early 1973.

Patroclus, in the River Mersey during 1969. *[J. and M. Clarkson]*

G107. ALCINOUS 1974

O.N. 181085 8,292g 4,910n 462.9 x 62.3 x
31.7 feet.
8-cyl. 2SCDA oil engine by J.G. Kincaid and
Co. Ltd., Greenock (550 mm x 1,200 mm);
6,800 BHP.
25.9.1946: Launched by the Caledon
Shipbuilding and Engineering Co.
Ltd., Dundee (Yard No. 23) for the
Ocean Steam Ship Co. Ltd. (Alfred
Holt and Co., managers), Liverpool
as ANCHISES.
4.1947: Completed.
6.1949: Bombed by Chinese
Nationalist aircraft at Whangpoa,
resulting in the engine room
becoming flooded causing the vessel
to settle by the stern in shallow water.
Subsequently towed up river for
discharge and once again was
bombed, without damage. Following
discharge, towed to Kobe, Japan, for
repairs.
1967: Managers became Blue Funnel
Line Ltd.
1.1973: Owners became
Nederlandsche Stoomvaart
Maatschappij Oceaan, Amsterdam,
Holland and renamed ALCINOUS.
3.1973: Owners became the China
Mutual Steam Navigation Co. Ltd.

8.1974: Owners became Glen Line Ltd.
11.1974: Owners became the China
Mutual Steam Navigation Co. Ltd.
5.9.1975: Delivered to Chi Shun Hua

Steel Co. Ltd., Kaohsiung for demolition.
27.12.1975: Hang Hua Enterprises Co.
Ltd. commenced work.

Alcinous on 6th June 1975. *[J. and M. Clarkson]*

156

Managed vessels

M1. WAR MELODY 1918-1919

O.N. 142702 6,498g 4,040n 412.4 x 55.8 x 34.4 feet.

T.3-cyl. by Harland and Wolff Ltd., Belfast (27", 44" and 73" x 48"); 518 NHP, 3,200 IHP; 11½ knots.

19.10.1918: Launched by Harland and Wolff Ltd., Belfast (Yard No.543) for the Shipping Controller (Glen Line Ltd., managers), London.

11.1918: Completed (trial trip 7.11.1918).

1918: Registered at London.

14.8.1919: Sold to Dollar Steam Ship Line (Robert Dollar Co., managers), San Francisco and renamed GRACE DOLLAR.

16.5.1921: Registered at Vancouver in the ownership of Dollar Steamship Lines Ltd., Vancouver.

7.8.1922: Sold to Charles Edward Hartnell-Beavis, Hong Kong.

30.9.1922: Registered at Hong Kong.

27.12.1922: Resold to Dollar Steamship

Lines Ltd., Hong Kong.

1.1924: Sold to Tatsuuma Kisen K.K., Dairen and renamed HAKUTATSU MARU.

7.2.1924: Register closed.

1937: Sold to Ryuun Kisen K.K., Dairen and renamed RYUUN MARU.

1942: Sold to Nissan Kisen K.K., Tokyo and renamed NIKKYU MARU.

4.7.1943: Torpedoed and sunk by the American submarine USS JACK south of Shimizu in position 34.31 north by 138.35 east.

War Melody on 18th October 1918, shortly after her launch. The outlines of her dazzle paint have been marked on the hull. *[Ulster Folk Tranport Museum, ref H&W.405]*

War Melody in the River Mersey. *[B. and A. Feilden/J. and M. Clarkson collection]*

M2. PANGANI 1919-1921

O,N, 143430 5,735g 3,598n 420.0 x 56.3 x 27.9 feet.

Q.4-cyl. by Blohm and Voss, Hamburg (610 mm, 880 mm, 1,280 mm and 1,850 mm x 1,372 mm); 608 NHP, 3,300 IHP; 12 knots.

15.7.1915: Launched by Blohm & Voss, Hamburg (Yard No. 232) for Deutsche Ost-Afrika Linie, Hamburg. Laid up in an incomplete state.
13.7.1919: Completed.
8.9.1919: Surrendered to Great Britain.
13.9.1919: Allocated to the Shipping Controller (Glen Line Ltd., managers), London.
20.9.1919: Registered at London.
23.5.1921: Sold to David Steamship Co. Ltd. (W.S. Mitchell, manager), London and renamed CASSIO.
27.6.1921: Re-registered at London.
1.1922: Sold to Vereenigde Nederlandsche Scheepvaart Maatschappij NV, The Hague, Holland and renamed NIJKERK.
12.1.1922: Register closed.
1931: Management passed to Maatschappij Holland-Afrika Lijn NV.
18.2.1950: Arrived at Hendrik Ido Ambacht for demolition by Frank Rijsdijks Industrieele Onderneming.

M3. WAR DIANA 1919

O.N. 141934 7,943g 4,970n 449.5 x 58.2 x 37.1 feet.

Two T.3-cyl. by Barclay, Curle and Co. Ltd., Glasgow (26½", 44" and 73" x 48"); 752 NHP, 7,000 IHP; 14 knots.

26.6.1919: Launched by Barclay, Curle and Co. Ltd., Glasgow (Yard No. 573) for the Shipping Controller (Glen Line Ltd., managers), London.
Sold while fitting out to Peninsular and Oriental Steam Navigation Co. Ltd., London and renamed PESHAWUR.
12.1919: Completed (trials trip 18.12).
10.12.1919: Registered at Glasgow.
23.12.1943: Torpedoed and sunk by the Japanese submarine RO-111 north of Ceylon in position 11.11 north by 80.11 east whilst on a voyage from Swansea to Calcutta with general cargo and government stores. All saved.
9.2.1944: Register closed.

M4. FRITZ 1919-1920

O.N. 143592 3,083g 1,863n 332.0 x 44.8 x 23.1 feet.

Two 6-cyl. 2SCDA oil engines by Blohm and Voss, Hamburg (480 mm x 710 mm); 334 NHP, 2,300 IHP, 9½ knots.
8.1923: Two T.3-cyl. by Cooper and Greig Ltd., Dundee (16¼", 26½" and 44" x 34"); 219 NHP, 1,400 IHP; 9½ knots.
24.2.1914: Launched by Blohm und Voss, Hamburg (Yard No. 207) for Woermann Linie A.G., Hamburg.
15.5.1914: Completed.
13.11.1919: Surrendered to Great Britain.
13.12.1919: Allocated to the Shipping Controller (Glen Line Ltd., managers), London, and registered at London.
15.11.1920: Sold to Ellerman Lines Ltd. (Ellerman and Papayanni Lines Ltd., managers), Liverpool.
14.2.1921: Registered at Liverpool and renamed ASSYRIAN.
8.1923: Re-engined.

Pangani, later in her career as *Nijkerk*. *[Ian J. Farquhar]*

War Diana after her sale to British India as *Peshawur*. *[B. and A. Feilden/J. and M. Clarkson collection]*

The German *Fritz* built by Blohm & Voss for experiments with newly developed diesel engines. *[Prof. Theodor F. Siersdorfer]*

19.10.1940: Torpedoed and sunk by the German submarine U 101 in the North Atlantic in position 57.12 north by 10.43 west whilst on a voyage from New Orleans and Sydney, Cape Breton to Liverpool with general cargo, sailing as commodore ship in Convoy SC7. Seventeen lives were lost from a crew of 39, commodore and five staff, and three passengers.
24.10.1940: Register closed.

M5. FRIESLAND 1920-1921

O.N. 144656 10,800g 6,677n 520.7 x 64.2 x 38.1 feet.

Two T.3-cyl. by Bremer Vulkan Schiffbau & Maschinenfabrik, Vegesack (720 mm, 1,190 mm and 1,920 mm x 1,300 mm) driving twin screws; 740 NHP, 5,800 IHP.

1912: Ordered by Hamburg-Amerikanische Packetfahrt A.G., Hamburg from Bremer Vulkan Schiffbau & Maschinenfabrik, Vegesack (Yard No. 577) as the cargo vessel FRIESLAND.

1913: Order changed to one for the passenger vessel RHEINLAND, but keel not laid until 1916, by which time order had reverted to a cargo vessel.

13.10.1917: Launched as RHEINLAND, but renamed FRIESLAND while fitting out in 1919.

30.6.1920: Ran trials.

6.7.1920: Arrived at Leith and surrendered to the Allied Control Commission.

19.7.1920: Registered at London under the ownership of the Shipping Controller (Glen Line Ltd., managers), London.

22.4.1921: Sold to Federal Steam Navigation Co. Ltd., London and laid up at Falmouth.

4.4.1922: Registered anew at London.

9.5.1922: Recommissioned and renamed HERTFORD.

3-11.1923: Converted to oil fuel and refrigeration equipment installed at Falmouth.

7-11.1931: Laid up at Falmouth.

10.4.1940: Requisitioned for the Liner Division.

7.12.1940: Damaged by a mine laid by the German raider PINGUIN off the mouth of the Spencer Gulf in position 33.50 south by 135.25 east whilst on a voyage from Liverpool to Brisbane with general cargo.

9.12.1940: Arrived under tow at Spalding Cove, Port Lincoln.

1.4.1941: Arrived under tow at Adelaide.

22.8.1941: Arrived under tow at Sydney for final repairs.

Federal Steam Navigation's *Hertford*, managed by Glen Line for less than a year under her German name *Friesland*. [*J. and M. Clarkson collection*]

24.11.1941: Re-entered service.

29.3.1942: Torpedoed and sunk by the German submarine U 571 150 miles south east of New Bedford, Massachusetts, USA in position 40.50 north by 63.31 west whilst on a voyage from Colon to Halifax with refrigerated and general cargo, with the loss of four lives.

8.4.1942: Register closed.

M6. D.A.D.G. 76 1920-1921

O.N. 144603 6,038g. 3,576n 449.9 x 58.2 x 26.9 feet.

Q.4-cyl. by Blohm & Voss, Hamburg (770 mm, 1,020 mm, 1,460 mm and 2,090 mm x 1,400 mm); 4,200 IHP; 13½ knots.

29.9.1919: Launched by Blohm & Voss, Hamburg (Yard No. 386) with the temporary name D.A.D.G.76, having been laid down for Deutsche-Australische D.G., Hamburg.

22.2.1920: Completed.

18.6.1920: Surrendered to Great Britain and allocated to the Shipping Controller (Glen Line Ltd., managers), London.

23.7.1920: Registered at London.

11.6.1921: Sold to David Steamship Co. Ltd. (W. S. Mitchell, manager), London and renamed CESARIO.

29.6.1921: Re-registered at London.

10.1921: Sold to Vereenigde Nederlandsche Scheepvaart Maatschappij NV, The Hague, Holland and renamed MELISKERK.

18.10.1921: Register closed.

1931: Management passed to Maatschappij Holland-Afrika Lijn NV.

8.1.1943: Wrecked half a mile off Port St. John, Cape Province whilst on a voyage from Liverpool to Durban.

Meliskerk was managed by Glen Line for the Shipping Controller as *D.A.D.G.76*. [*Ian J. Farquhar*]

M7. VOGTLAND 1920-1921

O.N. 144589 10,892g 6,777n 524.5 x 65.7 x 37.3 feet.

Two T.3-cyl. by J.C. Tecklenborg A.G., Geestemunde (710 mm, 1,150 mm and 1,880 mm x 1,300 mm) driving twin screws; 784 NHP, 5,200 IHP.

9.12.1916: Launched by J.C. Tecklenborg A.G., Geestemunde (Yard No. 271) for Hamburg-Amerikanische Packetfahrt A.G., Hamburg. Laid up incomplete.

27.11.1919: Ran trials.

14.5.1920: Arrived at Leith and surrendered to the Allied Control Commission.

4.6.1920: Registered at London under the ownership of the Shipping Controller (Glen Line Ltd., managers), London.

22.4.1921: Sold to Federal Steam Navigation Co. Ltd., London and laid up at Falmouth.

6.9.1922: Registered anew at London.

12.9.1922: Recommissioned and renamed CAMBRIDGE.

9-11.1923: Laid up at Falmouth.

1925: Converted to oil fuel and refrigeration equipment installed at Falmouth.

7.11.1940: Struck a mine laid by the German auxiliary PASSAT six miles east of Wilson's Promontory whilst on a voyage from Melbourne to Sydney and sank the next day, with the loss of one life.

21.11.1940: Register closed.

M8. VILLE DE ROUEN 1941-1942

O.N. 168817 5,598g 3,443n 370.4 x 51.2 x 25.7 feet.

T.3-cyl. by J.G. Kincaid and Co., Greenock (25", 41" and 68" x 48"); 748 NHP, 2,200 IHP; 10 knots.

11.7.1919: Launched by North of Ireland Shipbuilding Co. Ltd., Londonderry (Yard No.73) for Compagnie Havraise Péninsulaire de Navigation à Vapeur, Havre, France.

10.1919: Completed.

1934: Sold to Nouvelle Compagnie Havraise Péninsulaire de Navigation, Havre.

22.7.1941: Captured by HMS DUNEDIN east of Natal. Taken over by the Ministry of War Transport (Glen Line Ltd., managers), London.

14.5.1942: Registered at Liverpool.

29.12.1942: Torpedoed and sunk by the German submarine U 662, having already been torpedoed and damaged on 28.12.1942 by the German submarine U 225 in the North Atlantic in position 43.25 north by 27.15 west whilst on a voyage from Glasgow to Ascension and Beira in Convoy ONS.154. All her crew of 64 and 7 gunners were saved.

27.1.1943: Register closed.

M9. FORT MCLEOD 1942-1944

O.N. 168320 7,127g 4,261n 424.6 x 57.2 x 34.9 feet.

T.3-cyl. by Dominion Engine Works Ltd., Montreal (24½", 39" and 70" x 48"); 229 NHP, 2,500 IHP; 11 knots.

14.4.1942: Launched by Yarrows Ltd., Esquimalt, British Columbia (Yard No. 67) for the United States War Shipping Administration.

30.6.1942: Completed and chartered to the Ministry of War Transport (Glen Line

The former German *Vogtland* was managed by Glen before her sale to Federal in 1921. *[Prof. Theodor F. Siersdorfer]*

Ville de Rouen, managed by Glen until her loss in 1942. *[A. Duncan/J. and M. Clarkson collection]*

Fort McLeod on 26th August 1942. *[United States Coast Guard/Ian J. Farquhar]*

Ltd., managers), London.

26.9.1942: Registered at London.

3.3.1944: Torpedoed and sunk by gunfire by the Japanese submarine I-162 east of the Maldives in position 02.01 north by 77.06 east whilst on a voyage from Cochin and Colombo to Durban with general cargo. All her crew of 49 and 9 gunners were saved.

26.6.1944: Register closed.

M10. OCEAN VERITY 1942-1946
O.N. 167858 7,174g 4,272n 425.1 x 57.0 x 34.8 feet.
T.3-cyl. by General Machinery Corp., Hamilton, Ontario (24½", 39" and 70" x 48"); 2,500 IHP.
14.5.1942: Launched by Permanente Metals Corporation, Shipyard No.1, Richmond, California, USA (Yard No.24) for the United States War Shipping Administration.
6.1942: Completed for the Ministry of War Transport (Glen Line Ltd., managers), London.
1946: Chartered to Clan Line Steamers Ltd. (Cayzer, Irving and Co. Ltd., managers), London.
1948: Sold to Clan Line Steamers Ltd. and renamed CLAN KEITH.
5.11.1961: Wrecked on Ecuils des Sorelles Rocks, near Cape Bon whilst on a voyage from Middlesbrough and Malta to Colombo with general cargo with heavy loss of life. Only five of her crew of 68 survived.

M11. OCEAN TRADER 1942-1947
O.N. 168834 7,178g 4,280n 425.1 x 57.0 x 34.8 feet.
T.3-cyl. by General Machinery Corporation, Hamilton, Ohio (24½", 39" and 70" x 48"); 505 NHP, 2,500 IHP, 12 knots
14.6.1942: Launched by Todd-Bath Iron Shipbuilding Corporation, Portland, Maine (Yard No. 13) for the Ministry of War Transport (Glen Line Ltd., managers), London.
28.8.1942: Registered at Liverpool.
1.5.1947: Owners became Ministry of Transport.
30.4.1947: Sold to Drake Shipping Co. Ltd. (Lykiardopulo and Co. Ltd., managers), London and renamed MERCHANT ROYAL.
5.5.1947: Re-registered at London.
10.1951: Owners became Compania Armadora Transoceanica S.A., Panama (Lykiardopulo and Co. Ltd., London, managers) and renamed OCEANA.
5.10.1951: Register closed.
1960: Sold to Compania Armadora Sabinal S.A., Panama (Lykiardopulo and Co. Ltd., London, managers) and renamed OKEANIS under the Greek flag.
1966: Sold to Salinamar S.A., Panama (Fratelli Cosulich S.p.A, Trieste, Italy) and renamed FIDES.
1968: Owners became Marasalina Shipping Co. Ltd., Famagusta, Cyprus (Fratelli Cosulich S.p.A, Trieste, Italy) and renamed DEFIS.
20.8.1969: Arrived at Osaka to be broken up by Amakasu Sangyo K.K. at Sakaide.

M12. EMPIRE CAPULET 1943-1944
O.N. 169050 7,044g 4,869n 430.9 x 56.2 x 35.2 feet.
T.3-cyl. by John Readhead and Sons Ltd., South Shields (24½", 39" and 70" x 48"); 558 NHP, 2,550 IHP; 11 knots.
20.1.1943: Launched by John Readhead and Sons Ltd., South Shields (Yard No. 532) for the Ministry of War Transport (Glen Line Ltd., managers), London.
3.1943: Completed.
1944: Management transferred to Cayzer, Irvine and Co. Ltd.

Clan Keith, managed by Glen Line from 1942 to 1946 as *Ocean Verity*. [B. and A. Feilden/J. and M. Clarkson]

Ocean Trader. [World Ship Photo Library]

Empire Capulet. [George Scott collection]

1945: Sold to British and South American Steam Navigation Co. Ltd. (Houston Line (London) Ltd., managers), London and renamed HESIONE.
1946: Owners became Clan Line Steamers Ltd.
1948: Reverted to British and South American Steam Navigation Co. Ltd.
1957: Owners became Houston Line Ltd. (Cayzer, Irvine and Co. Ltd., managers).
5.10.1960: Arrived at Hong Kong for demolition by Shun Hing Ironworks Ltd.
28.10.1960: Demolition commenced.

Empire Lancer was torpedoed and sunk whilst under Glen management. *[George Scott collection]*

M13. EMPIRE LANCER 1943-1944

O.N. 168990 7,037g 4,908n 432.7 x 56.2 x 34.2 feet.
T.3-cyl. by David Rowan and Co. Ltd., Glasgow (24$^{1}/_{2}$", 39" and 70" x 48"); 558 NHP, 2,550 IHP; 11 knots.
31.8.1942: Launched by Lithgows Ltd., Port Glasgow (Yard No.971) for the Ministry of War Transport (Alfred Holt and Co., Liverpool, managers), London.
29.10.1942: Registered at Greenock.
11.1942: Completed.
14.8.1943: Management transferred to Glen Line Ltd, London.
16.8.1944: Torpedoed and sunk by the German submarine U 862 in the Mozambique Channel whilst on a voyage from Durban to Majunga, Tamatave, Aden and the UK with cargo of copper, general and military stores. From her crew of 71 and 8 gunners, 37 crew and 3 gunners lost.
14.10.1944: Register closed.

M14. SAMBAY 1943-1947

O.N. 169670 7,219g 4,380n 422.8 x 57.0 x 34.8 feet.
T.3-cyl. by Iron Fireman Manufacturing Co., Portland (24$^{1}/_{2}$", 39" and 70" x 48"); 2,500 IHP.
29.7.1943: Launched by Oregon Shipbuilding Corporation, Portland, Oregon (Yard No.733) for the United States War Shipping Administration, Washington as ANTON M. HOLTER.
8.1943: Completed for bareboat charter to the Ministry of War Transport (Glen Line Ltd., managers), London as SAMBAY.
29.5.1947: Sold to the Charente Steamship Co. Ltd. (T. and J. Harrison, managers), Liverpool.
20.6.1947: Registered at Liverpool as SENATOR.
8.6.1964: Sold to Belvientos Compania Naviera S.A., Panama (Rethymnis and Kulukundis Ltd., London) for £82,500 and renamed AJAX under the Greek flag.
2.1968: Sold to Nau-Tay Industries Co. Ltd., Taiwan for demolition.
29.4.1968: Arrived at Kaohsiung.
1.5.1968: Delivered.

Sambay at Liverpool on 28th October 1946. *[Michael Crowdy/J. and M. Clarkson collection]*

M15. SAMWATER 1944-1947
O.N. 169923 7,219g 4,380n 422.8 x 57.0
x 34.8 feet.
T.3-cyl. by General Machinery
Corporation, Hamilton, Ohio, USA (24½",
39" and 70" x 48"); 276 NHP, 2,500 IHP;
12 knots
9.8.1943: Launched by Bethlehem
Fairfield Shipyard Inc., Baltimore,
Maryland, USA (Yard No. 2210) for the
United States War Shipping
Administration as DAVID DE VRIES.
8.1943: Completed.
1944: Chartered to the Ministry of War
Transport (Glen Line Ltd., managers),
London and renamed SAMWATER.
14.7.1944: Registered at London.
29.1.1947: Abandoned on fire 35 miles
west of Finisterre in position 42.41 north

by 10.13 west whilst on a voyage from
Sydney to Liverpool with general cargo.
4.2.1947: Foundered.
27.3.1947: Register closed.

M16. EMPIRE ADMIRAL 1945-1946
O.N. 169038 7,884g 4,521n 470.0 x 67.0
x 27.0 feet.
Two steam turbines reduction geared to a
single shaft by Richardson, Westgarth and
Co. Ltd., Hartlepool.
26.3.1945: Launched by Vickers,
Armstrong Ltd., Barrow-in-Furness (Yard
No. 859) for the Ministry of War Transport
(Glen Line Ltd., managers), London.
1946: Management transferred to
Dalhousie Steam and Motorship Co. Ltd.,
London. Sold to managers and renamed

PETER DAL.
7.1951: Sold to Ben Line Steamers Ltd.
(William Thomson and Co., Leith and
renamed BENLEDI.
8.1963: Sold to Andros Navigation Co.
Ltd., Nassau and renamed ANDROS
TOMENNO.
1964: Sold to Frank Shipping Co. Inc.,
Monrovia, Liberia (Gibson Shipping Co.
Inc., Macao).
1966: Sold to Unique Marine Corporation,
Monrovia, Liberia (Robert Y.T. Chen,
Hong Kong) and renamed UNIQUE
CARRIER.
27.2.1969: Arrived at Kaohsiung for
demolition.
5.1969: Demolition commenced.

The heavy lift ship *Empire Admiral. [John McRoberts/J. and M. Clarkson collection]*

ENGINES FOR EARLY GLEN LINE MOTORSHIPS

The engines for the first Glen Line motor ships, delivered in 1920 onwards, had the fuel blasted into the cylinders using high-pressure air. This was before the development of solid injection of the fuel as now used universally. Running constantly, the powerful air compressors needed consumed a lot of fuel themselves. In some cases (although not these Glen engines) the compressors were part of the main engine itself. It is interesting to note that the ships' speed was originally 12.5 knots but later all but one were retrofitted with superchargers increasing the power to give 14 knots. For some reason this was not done in *Glenshiel*.

The erecting shop at Harland and Wolff, Finnieston, Clyde, with four of the Glen Line engines in the background, the one on the left is being prepared for a test run. Crankshafts, thrust shaft, bedplates, columns and other components for other engines are in the foreground. *[Ulster Folk and Transport Museum H & W 750]*

The starboard engine for the twin-screw motor vessel *Glengarry* connected to a Heenan Froude dynamometer (a water brake) to determine the shaft horse power during a test run. Two high-pressure air bottles are mounted at the front of the engine to provide blast air for fuel injection. *[Ulster Folk and Transport Museum 920]*

Top: Three Harland and Wolff diesel generators for the *Glenogle* with both main engines on the testbed in the background. The port engine is connected to the dynamometer. *[Ulster Folk and Transport Museum H & W 749]*

Below left: The column assembly of one of the two eight-cylinder engines is delivered to the *Glenshiel* at the fitting out berth. Note that all the running gear has been removed to reduce the weight to within the capacity of the crane. *[Ulster Folk and Transport Museum 1819]*

Bottom right: The four-cylinder column assembly being lifted aboard the *Glenshiel* with the second part of the assembly ready for the next lift. The electric motor and gearbox assembly beside the motor truck is probably the turning gear for this engine. This would be needed to facilitate the early on-board assembly of the engine. *[Ulster Folk and Transport Museum 1820]*

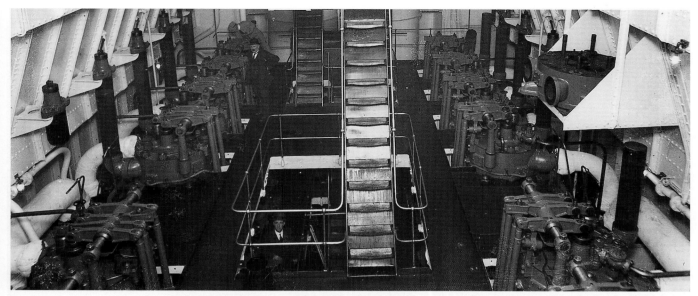

Three views on board the twin-screw *Glenogle*, all looking forward.

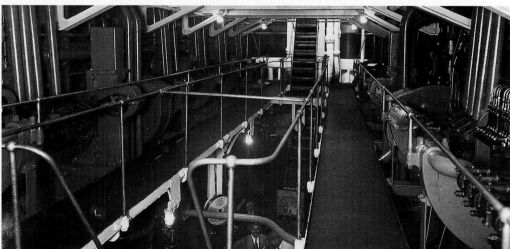

Top: The top platform showing the push rods and rockers on each cylinder head which operate the inlet and exhaust valves and the fuel valve. A spare cylinder head is shelved on the starboard casing.

Middle: The middle platform at camshaft level showing the lower ends of the valve-operating push rods.

Bottom: The manoeuvring platform with the starboard engine controls on the right hand side. The heavy overhead pipes carry starting air at a pressure of 350 pounds per square inch.
[Ulster Folk and Transport Museum 913 912 911]

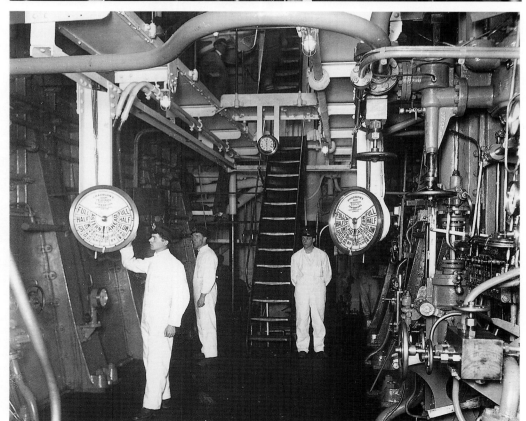

GLENBEG IN DRY DOCK

Top: In August 1970, the *Glenbeg* of 1956, formerly Blue Funnel's *Diomed*, appears dwarfed by the enormous dry dock in the Sembawang Shipyard at Singapore.

Middle: The crew leave a memento of the renaming of *Glenbeg* on the wall of the dry dock.

Bottom: The wheelhouse of *Glenbeg*. Within two years she had reverted to ownership by China Mutual Steam Navigation Co. Ltd. and the name *Diomed*. In 1973, along with the other Mark V 'A' class of Blue Funnel, she was sold to the People's Republic China and as *Kaising* lasted until 1982. *[All photos C. McCurdy]*

ENGINE ROOMS OF THE GLENLYONS

Top: The engine room top flat of *Glenlyon* (1974) with the second engineer taking cylinder head temperatures. The Sulzer RD90 engine was painted a tasteful blue.

Middle: The bottom engine room flat with one of the greasers. Although there was a telephone to the bridge, mounted in an acoustic booth, *Glenlyon* still carries a speaking tube, with whistle. The Chinese engine room staff have put a red ribbon round the clock to celebrate the Chinese New Year.

Bottom right: Not exactly the engine room but a part of the engineers' domain: looking down into the top of *Glenlyon's* funnel from the radar mast. The round exhaust is from the donkey boiler and behind the bulkhead is the main engine exhaust. The square trap in the foreground is an exit from the engine room and to the right the exhaust fan outlet.

Below: The manoeuvring controls in *Glenogle's* engine room. [All photos B. Cooil]

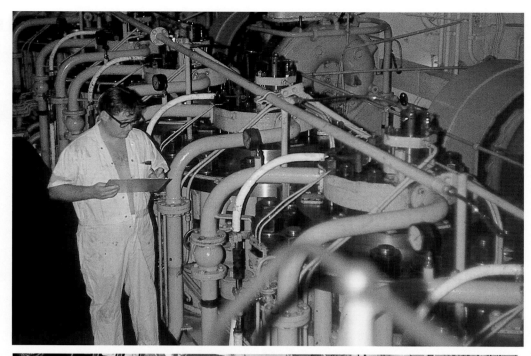

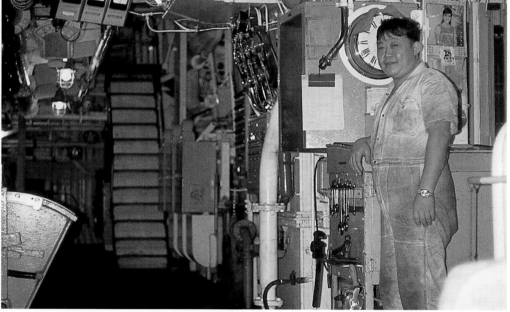

GLENLYON IN HEAVY WEATHER

The *Glenlyon* of 1962 experiences the full fury of the Atlantic off South West Africa. *[B. Cooil]*

INDEX

All ships mentioned are listed. Names in capitals are those carried whilst in Shire or Glen ownership or management. For these ships, the page numbers of fleet list entries are in bold type.

FLAGS AND FUNNELS OF SHIRE AND GLEN LINES

J.L. Loughran

 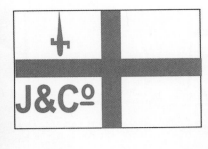

Jenkins and Co. 1861-1896
Jenkins and Co. Ltd. 1896-1906

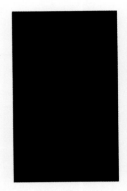 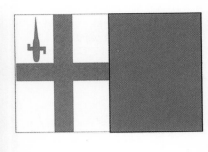

Jenkins-Brocklebank
1906-1907

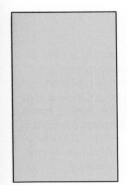 

Shire Line of Steamers Ltd.
1907-1911

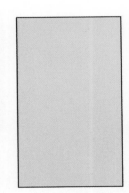 

Royal Mail Steam Packet Company
1911-1933

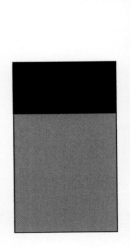 

Glen Line
1867-1974

GLEN LINE PORTRAITS

Denbighshire (3), a painting of the Chinese School. *[Courtesy of The British Mercantile Marine Memorial Collection]*

Merionethshire (3) in First World War camouflage grey. With the minute precision characteristic of Chinese ship portraiture, the vessel's name is inscribed across the front of her upper bridge. *[Courtesy of The British Mercantile Marine Memorial Collection]*

Cardiganshire (5), another Chinese School painting. *[Courtesy of The British Mercantile Marine Memorial Collection]*

Gleneagles, a Chinese School painting. *[Courtesy of The British Mercantile Marine Memorial Collection]*

Glencoe, depicted inward bound off Dover by R.H. Neville Cumming (1843-1920). *[Courtesy of The British Mercantile Marine Memorial Collection]*

Glenlogan signalling for a pilot off Naples. A Mediterranean School painting attributed to Luca Papaluca. *[Courtesy of The British Mercantile Marine Memorial Collection]*

GLEN LINE POST-WAR IN COLOUR

The new twin-screw, 18-knot motor ships that entered service from the end of 1938 marked the beginning of the rejuvenation of the company's fleet after a long period of decline. Designed by Harry Flett, this class of eight ships was the first of his masterful designs whose profiles would come to define Holt's post war fleet.

The Caledon-built *Glenearn* was the first to be delivered but gave barely a year's service before being requisitioned by the Admiralty. It was not until December 1947, after reconstruction lasting over twelve months, that she was able to take her place on the core Far Eastern service. The extensive damage sustained during the war did nothing to curtail her career, however, and she was one of the last of the group to be withdrawn, exactly 32 years after commissioning.

Top, opposite: *Glenearn* on the Thames in July 1957.
Left: Over a decade later, during the closure of the Suez Canal, sailing from Cape Town. Orient Lines' *Orcades* (28,164/48), partly visible to the right, would be another diverted visitor. *[Opposite top: Rupert Snook/F.W. Hawks collection; left: Ian Shiffman]*

Above: *Glenroy* entered service just a few weeks later than *Glenearn* and, like her, was requisitioned by the Admiralty soon after the outbreak of war and converted to a Landing Ship (Infantry). She participated in several major operations in which she sustained serious damage, including being mined during the Normandy landings in 1944. Well battered and bruised, her post-war conversion took nearly two years and she did not re-enter commercial service until May 1948. The first of the class to be withdrawn, she was handed over to Japanese breakers in 1966. On a fine Saturday afternoon in August 1960, *Glenroy* is at rest on her berth in the quiet of London's Royal Docks as she awaits the bustle of the coming week. *[Rupert Snook/F.W. Hawks collection]*

ON BOARD GLENEARN

Richard Woodman recorded these on-board scenes during a voyage to the Far East on board *Glenearn* in 1966.

This composite panoramic view of the foredeck has been produced from two photographs taken from the crosstrees on the foremast as *Glenearn* forges her way across the Indian Ocean. This elevated position highlights the exemplary condition of the ship and the perfectly clear exhaust from the funnel indicates that the engines of this 28-year-old ship are no less well maintained.

A crow's eye view of the forecastle with the foremast stay prominent.

Above left: Lifeboat drill under the canvas awnings. Note the well varnished gunwhales of the lifeboat.

Above: The view forward from the main mast. Of particular interest is the pronounced curve of the aft end of the superstructure as well as the extensive hardwood decking.

Left: A sam-pan alongside at Hong Kong

Delivered in September 1940, *Glenartney* was the last of the eight to be completed. Spared the rigours of naval service she was returned to the company in 1946. She was the only one of the class not to receive a full height funnel and retained her distinctive shortened version until withdrawn in 1967. *[F.W. Hawks collection]*

Seized by the Germans at Copenhagen in 1940 during the final stages of fitting out, *Glengarry* had a very different war to that of her sisters. Although recaptured at Kiel in May 1945, Glen Line did not take possession of her until June the following year. For almost a quarter of a century *Glengarry* then went quietly about her business with her career ending in a brief flurry of name and ownership changes prior to passing to breakers at Sakaide, Japan in February 1971.
Left: The slenderness of the funnel is emphasised in this evening view of her on the Thames in1968. *[Roy Kittle]*
Below: A later view at Cape Town. *[Ian Shiffman]*

In the immediate post-war reorganisation of the fleets, two Blue Funnel vessels were transferred to Glen as replacements for the new motor ships that had been lost. Very similar in design to these, *Glenorchy* had been built in 1940 as *Priam* and stayed with Glen until 1970 when she briefly returned to Blue Funnel as *Phemius* before disposal.
Above: In a fine period setting *Glenorchy* is discharging at the Tilbury Cargo Jetty on 8th June 1957 with an early East Asiatic Company motorship astern – records show the *Meonia* (5,218/1927) was due to have arrived the previous day. To the right *Orion* (23,371/1935) is berthed in Tilbury Dock.
Right: Over ten years later, departing from Cape Town.
[Top: Rupert Snook/F.W. Hawks collection; right: Ian Shiffman]

Built in 1943, *Telemachus* represented the next stage in the evolution of Holt's motor ship designs. She was the first of the single-screw types and was transferred to Glen in 1957 for six years as *Monmouthshire,* then briefly returning to Blue Funnel colours as *Glaucus.* In 1964 she was chartered to Swire's China Navigation Co., and renamed *Nanchang,* retaining this identity until scrapped in 1968. In her new guise *Nanchang* (left) ventured further afield and became a regular visitor to New Zealand. This view of her at Wellington was taken on 4th February 1967.
[L.Sawyer/V.H. Young collection]

Another transfer from Blue Funnel in 1957 to replace the Liberty steamers on the secondary services was the 1950-built 'Anchises' class *Bellerophon*. As *Cardiganshire*, she perpetuated another of the old Shire Line names. Glen immediately installed a modest refrigerated capacity at no little cost and retained her for the next fifteen years after which she reverted to her original identity. *[Ian Shiffman]*

Astyanax, one of the older, Mark I, 'Anchises' class, joined her younger sister a few weeks later becoming *Glenfruin* in November 1957. She stayed for just five years, however, and returned to Blue Funnel under her old name. Passing Tilbury Docks in April 1960, *Glenfruin* is appropriately escorted by a blue-funnelled Gamecock tug, probably *Atlantic Cock* (177/ 1935) *[Rupert Snook/ F. W. Hawks collection]*

A surprising transfer from Blue Funnel in 1968 was *Nestor,* one of three high-pressure, turbine-powered ships whose particularly demanding steam machinery fitted uneasily into an otherwise oil-engined fleet. As *Glenaffric* her stay was short and she was back with Ocean in little over eighteen months, now renamed *Orestes*.
For whatever reason Glen became the registered owners again in 1971 immediately prior to her sale.
Just four months into her brief time with Glen, *Glenaffric* makes her way slowly up the Thames. *[Roy Kittle]*

Top: 1970 saw what was to be the final transfer of Blue Funnel ships to Glen for their secondary 'B Service' and *Glenroy* was the first of four of the later 'A5' types to take up her new duties that year. Built as *Demodocus,* when Holt's were still favouring Vickers Armstrongs with their business, she reverted to her old name on return to Blue Funnel less than two years later. An already lengthy voyage to the Far East and back was greatly prolonged after the closure of the Suez Canal in 1967 with Cape Town and Durban being added to their extensive itinerary. The secondary service was by then becoming increasingly uneconomic and *Glenroy* is well off her marks as she eases her way out of Cape Town harbour, with Table Mountain providing the most dramatic of backdrops. *[Ian Shiffman]*

Middle: *Glenfruin,* leaving Cape Town. Built as *Dolius* she briefly regained her original name on returning to Blue Funnel in 1972 but was soon sold to the Chinese. *[Ian Shiffman]*

Bottom*: Antenor* was the last of the quartet to be transferred to Glen and stayed just eighteen months. During her short time as *Glenlochy* she heads for the open sea on her extended voyage around Africa. *[Ian Shiffman]*

Increasing competition - with faster more powerful vessels coming on to the Far Eastern service - led the company to order four fast cargo liners in 1958. These were the first new ships to be built to their own account since the *Glenearn* class over 20 years earlier. They were also to be the last of Flett's classic designs and he died in 1961 just as the first of these ships was beginning to take shape. *Glenlyon*, one of the two ordered from Dutch yards, was the first to be launched but narrowly missed being the first to be commissioned.

Above: *Glenlyon* makes an early morning arrival on the New Waterway in August 1974, passing Maassluis bound for Rotterdam. *[Dave Salisbury]*

Below: In home waters getting underway down Gallion's Reach after sailing from the Royal Docks on 15th July 1972. *[Roy Kittle]*

Fairfield succeeded in completing *Glenogle*, the first of their two ships, three weeks before *Glenlyon* and she embarked on her maiden voyage on 24th October 1962. The 20-knot service speed required of these ships was well within their ultimate capabilities and they could lay claim to be the fastest motor-engined cargo ships of their time. Sadly none of these ships achieved anything like their projected lifespan under the British flag and *Glenogle* was sold in

1978 to the Chinese who continued to run her for well over twenty years.
Above: On her only visit to the Mersey *Glenogle* angles up for the approach to Birkenhead's Alfred Locks, in January 1976.
Below: Passing Rozenburg inbound on the New Waterway in May 1975. *[Both: Paul Boot]*

Above: This sea-level view of *Glenfalloch* in the Singapore anchorage in March 1976 emphasises her well-flared bow lines. To achieve the required high service speed the hull design incorporated a bulbous bow, one of the earliest instances of its adoption in a cargo ship. In keeping with the elegant lines of these ships it was a far more modest and well-proportioned addition than the very obvious protuberances that later became the norm. *[F.W.Hawks collection]*

Below: A fine aerial portrait of *Glenfalloch* cutting through the water at speed. The effectiveness of the hull form is well evident from the minimal bow waves.   *[Ian Shiffman]*

Flintshire, the second of the Dutch built ships, came from C. van der Giessen whose yard at Krimpen on the Ijssel, upriver from Rotterdam and over twenty five miles from the sea, was an unlikely birthplace for ships of this size. In 1974 she was transferred to Holt's Dutch subsidiary NSMO as rationalisation and reduction of the conventional cargo services moved apace.

Top: Manoeuvring in the Royal Docks. Prominently stowed on the fore deck are containers of former arch rival Ben Line. *[Roy Kittle]*

Middle: Under the Dutch flag, *Flintshire* initially retained Glen colours albeit with the incongruous conjunction of her traditional Welsh name with an Amsterdam port of registry. *[David Salisbury]*

Right: Blue skies and Blue Funnel. Late in 1976 the red funnel gave way to the more appropriate pale blue and further changes were to come with charters to Nigerian National Line and Djakarta Lloyd. *Flintshire* is seen here at Singapore in May 1978 in Blue Funnel colours awaiting her fate and sporting an unusual grey boot-topping shortly before her sale. Her new Singapore owners seem to have cared little for this fine ship and despatched both her and the former *Glenlyon* to Taiwan breakers within months of acquiring them. *[Ian Shiffman]*

Top: The eight *Glenalmond/ Priam* class ships were a brave attempt to produce a design that would meet the challenges of the future. Their design had been a protracted affair and delivery came on the dawn of mass containerisation. Sadly, like the *Glenlyons*, they were destined to an early obsolescence. Whilst they lacked the elegance and poise of their predecessors, they were still fine ships and should have enjoyed long and successful careers. *Radnorshire,* one of the troubled Vickers-built ships, makes a splendid sight as she sails up Gallion's reach in the care of Alexander's tug *Sun III* (150/66) on 4th July 1969. *[Roy Kittle]*

Middle: *Glenfinlas,* together with the former *Radnorshire,* was sold by Blue Funnel to Swire's China Navigation Co. in 1978. Their functional colours did nothing to enhance the lines of these ships as is evidenced by *Kweichow* photographed at Wellington, New Zealand in October 1980. *[V.H. Young and L.A. Sawyer collection]*

Bottom: *Pembrokeshire* on the New Waterway in June 1969. Like her sisters she was absorbed into what was left of the Blue Funnel fleet in 1972 and became *Phrontis.* Sold to Gulf Shipping and later Iran Shipping Lines she outlasted her peers by some considerable measure, not being broken up until 1995. *[Roy Kittle]*